# Financial and Investment Analysis for Commercial Real Estate

Joseph L. Petrole, CCIM, MAI

Dearborn™
Real Estate Education

President: Roy Lipner
Vice President of Product Development & Publishing: Evan M. Butterfield
Managing Editor: Kate DeVivo
Editorial Project Manager: Amanda Rahn
Director of Production: Daniel Frey
Production Editor: Caitlin Ostrow
Creative Director: Lucy Jenkins
Production Artist: Virginia Byrne



Published by Dearborn™ Real Estate Education
30 South Wacker Drive
Chicago, Illinois 60606-7481
(312) 836-4400
www.dearbornRE.com



Printed in the United States of America
07 08 09 10 9 8 7 6 5 4 3 2 1

**Library of Congress Cataloging-in-Publication Data**

Petrole, Joseph L.

Financial & investment analysis for commercial real estate / Joseph L. Petrole.

p. cm.

Includes bibliographical references.

ISBN-13: 978-1-4195-2206-2

ISBN-10: 1-4195-2206-X

1. Commercial real estate—United States. 2. Real estate investment—United States. 3. Commercial real estate. 4. Real estate investment. I. Dearborn Real Estate Education (Firm) II. Title. III. Title: Financial and investment analysis for commercial real estate.

HD1393.58.U6.P482 2006

333.33068'1—dc22

20060290191

# DEDICATION

This book is dedicated to those persons who really made a difference in my life…

…to my entire family, who patiently demonstrated what is truly important, especially to my mother, Rosemary, for providing a fabulous start in life

…to my brother, Louis, for encouraging me to focus beyond my personal comfort zone

…to my cousin, Louis, for inspiring me to view the world from mountain tops

…to my grandfather, Louis, who prophetically told me, "Some day you *will* understand."

# CONTENTS

chapter 2

## VALUING COMMERCIAL REAL ESTATE VIA DIRECT CAPITALIZATION



chapter 3

## VALUING COMMERCIAL REAL ESTATE VIA YIELD CAPITALIZATION

## chapter 4 FINANCING COMMERCIAL REAL ESTATE AND MEASURING INVESTMENT PERFORMANCE

# NOTES TO THE READER



If you have any suggestions or comments, you may e-mail us at *jpetrole@petrogroup.net* or visit our Web site: *www.petrogroup.net*

# PREFACE

"Investors purchase commercial real estate primarily for what it provides them, namely the expected financial returns desired, and not necessarily what the property's physical and location attributes are. Market savvy investors want to know the expected returns, the risks associated with those expected returns, and the price they are willing to pay for those expected returns . . . before they buy it."

—Joseph Petrole

This reference material is custom designed for both those active in commercial real estate and those who need to know about the industry. This information-packed reference material will provide an insightful overview of the mind-set required for the successful analysis of commercial real estate that will *immediately* benefit you and your clients. The caliber of the information and the presentation is of the highest quality, drawing upon both extensive personal experience and some of the most prestigious references available anywhere at any price.

The educational chapters and the extensive reference materials provided at the back of this book are reader friendly, with numerous tables, charts, and exhibits along with a useable glossary of terms. The manual includes both technical definitions along with the business jargon that is the "language of real estate." Each chapter is designed to build upon the previous chapter and is organized to provide key terminology, an overview and learning objectives, chapter material, a summary, and review and application questions that will reinforce the reader's learning experience. Readers will obtain a clear understanding of both commercial real estate and sophisticated investment methodology employed by top institutional investors that they can put into practice immediately.

Following is a chapter preview highlighting how the reader will benefit from this material.

### Analyzing Income and Expenses for Commercial Real Estate

This chapter provides the analytical tools for understanding and developing a supportable current income and expense estimate, as well as projecting future income and expenses associated with an income-producing property. The individual components of income and expenses are presented and discussed in detail, providing the basis for a reconstructed operating statement. The reconstructed operating statement provides the core financial information that forms the basis of either a one-year forecast or a multiple-year forecast. The reconstructed operating statement is required for both direct and yield capitalization.

### Valuing Commercial Real Estate via Direct Capitilization

This chapter provides a comprehensive overview of the direct capitalization method of valuing income-producing property. "Direct cap" is a method used to convert an estimate of a single year's income expectancy into an indicator of value in one direct step, usually by dividing the income estimate by an appropriate income rate or multiplying by an appropriate factor. The reconstructed operating statement provides the core financial information that forms the basis of both a current year's value estimate or the following years' forecast of expected income and value.

### Valuing Commercial Real Estate via Yield Capitalization

This chapter provides a comprehensive overview of yield capitalization. Yield capitalization is a method used to convert expected future financial benefits into a present value by discounting each future benefit at an appropriate yield rate or developing an overall rate that reflects the investment's income pattern, value change, and yield rate. The reconstructed operating statement provides the core financial information that forms the basis of both a current year's estimated financial performance and projected financial performance.

### Financing Commercial Real Estate and Measuring Investment Performance

Property is typically acquired with some type of financing, with the property pledged as collateral for the loan. The financing component affects the property's value as well as the equity component. Financing is an acquisition vehicle that has much broader implications than simply allowing the investor to acquire the property. Financing is also used to "lever up" returns over and above those obtainable by using only cash, to build an asset base, and to "cash out" without triggering capital gains tax issues. Savvy investors "negotiate a property's purchase price for cash but measure its value and return based on leverage."

There are both benefits and burdens associated with investing in commercial real estate. When investing, what you don't know can and will hinder your ability to achieve your objectives. The financial performance of a real estate investment is quantifiable and can be measured economically. All real estate investment decisions should be based on quantifiable information, and that quantifiable information should be benchmarked against both industry standards and market norms. Investors should purchase property based on their personal investor sentiment and preferences. They should then measure investment performance against their expectations and objectives. Measuring an investment's performance also implies that the investor has actually identified clear *expectations* and *objectives*.

It is the author's intent that this material open new vistas of opportunity for you. If you can move closer to your goals, the author will have accomplished his objectives.

# ABOUT THE AUTHOR

Joseph L. Petrole, CCIM, MAI, is a seasoned real estate professional with over 25 years' experience in the industry. He is principal of PetroGroup Realty Advisors, Inc. PetroGroup was established in 1997 to serve the commercial real estate industry. PetroGroup's primary objective is to provide the highest-quality and results-oriented real estate services to investors and institutions in the areas of valuation advisory services (VAS), which includes litigation support services; market analysis and due diligence services; transaction services, which include property sale, acquisition, and investment advisory services; and capital market services, which include the identification and delivery of debt and equity to clients, capital structuring, and asset recapitalization. These three areas of service constitute the core of what the industry has come to define as real estate investment banking services.

Since 2003, Joseph has served as director of Beacon Realty Advisors, Inc., a real estate brokerage and mortgage brokerage services firm based in Coconut Grove, Florida, that specializes in real estate investments and capital markets services to investors, entrepreneurs, and institutions. Prior to joining Beacon as a director, Joseph was director of resources and a real estate investment banker with Aztec Group, one of Florida's most successful and respected privately held real estate investment banking firms. During his more than four-year tenure with Aztec, Joseph participated in a wide range of investment banking services, including the positioning and closing of investment-grade real estate transactions; analysis, underwriting, packaging, and marketing; and the identification, interpretation, and utilization of market information that directly influences transactions and capital market activities.

Joseph's career also included his role as a senior manager and senior vice president of Appraisal and Real Estate Economic Associates, Inc., one of Florida's most successful and respected privately held real estate valuation advisory services and consulting firms. During his more than 12 years at AREEA, Joseph participated in a wide range of valuation advisory services, including valuations, acquisition due diligence services, litigation support services, and appraisal review services. Joseph also has a formidable corporate financial and accounting background gained during four years as a senior financial analyst and cost accountant with Gang-Nail Systems, Inc., a wholly owned U.S. subsidiary of Redland Braas Corporation, a European-based multinational corporation providing vertically integrated real estate property design, engineering, truss fabrication, and building materials throughout the world.

Joseph has had the opportunity to participate in marketing, sale, financing, consulting, and valuation and has provided litigation support services to some of the most prominent investors, entrepreneurs, and institutions and highest-profile properties and developments in the United States and the Caribbean.

Joseph earned a BBA in finance and real estate from the University of Miami, where he also received the Dr. William G. Heuson award for his academic achievements. He has also earned the prestigious MAI designation from the Appraisal Institute and the prestigious CCIM designation from the CCIM Institute. Joseph is a practicing Florida licensed real estate broker, a practicing Florida certified appraiser, a practicing Florida licensed real estate instructor, and a graduate of the Dale Carnegie School for salesmanship.

# ACKNOWLEDGMENTS

The author gratefully acknowledges all of the sources of information employed in the development of this material. The sources are specifically referenced within the narrative sections of this text. Special acknowledgment goes to those who reviewed early drafts of this book, including Lee D. Ormiston, and Harold A. Ovsiowitz of the American Real Estate College.

c h a p t e r o n e

# ANALYZING INCOME AND EXPENSES FOR COMMERCIAL REAL ESTATE

1

## Key Terminology

Accrual Basis
Balance Sheet
Cash Basis
Cash Flow
Effective Gross Income
Fixed Expense
Net Operating Income
Operating Expenses
Potential Gross Income
Profit and Loss Statement
Replacement Reserves
Return of Capital
Return on Capital
Vacancy and Collection Loss
Variable Expenses

## Overview

This chapter focuses on the purpose for the analysis of income and expenses for investment real estate. The fundamentals of the analysis process are explained, and basic financial statements are introduced. The various line items that make up the "cash flow stack" are presented in great detail. The broad categories of revenues, expenses, and income are further broken down into their components.

As we explore the process of financial and investment analysis, we introduce numerous new terms, and the importance of applying practical mathematics to business decisions becomes apparent. Multistep calculations for determining revenues, expenses, and income are introduced, because the ability to monetarily measure the benefits and burdens of investing is fundamental to the decision-making process.

## Learning Objectives

After completing this chapter, you should be able to accomplish the following:

- Describe the difference between the return of capital, the return on capital, the rate of return on capital, and reversion
- Discuss why measuring operating income is important

- List the six tangible benefits of investing in real estate
- Explain the difference between a balance sheet and a profit and loss statement
- Describe the differences between the three types of income categories: potential gross income, effective gross income, and net operating income
- Differentiate between vacancy loss and collection loss
- Explain the difference between a fixed expense, a variable expense, and a replacement reserve
- Define an operating expense
- Describe the difference between cash basis and accrual basis
- Explain the purpose of and prepare a reconstructed profit and loss statement

## What Real Estate Investors Expect

Like all investors, real estate investors expect the recovery of all their invested capital as well as payment for the use of the capital.

**Return of capital** is the recovery of invested capital, usually through a property's income and reversion. The *income* component of the return of capital consists of the income stream generated by the investment. The *reversion* component of the return of capital is a lump-sum amount that an investor receives or anticipates to receive at the conclusion of an investment. The reversion component of the return of capital consists of the proceeds from the sale of the investment at the conclusion of the investor's holding period.

**Return on capital** is an additional amount received as compensation for the use of an investor's capital until it is returned. The actual or anticipated return on capital plus the return of capital equal the investor's rate of return on invested capital. The *rate of return on capital* is equivalent to the interest rate earned on the investment. As it applies to real estate investments, this interest rate is known as a yield rate. A *yield rate* is the overall rate of return earned or anticipated to be earned on capital invested in a real estate endeavor.

## Relevance to Commercial Real Estate

In any real estate investment, the investor's expected return of capital and return on capital are measurable and are based upon the investment's revenue, expense, and income estimate. Developing a supportable current revenues, expenses, and income estimate, as well as a future projection of the revenues, expenses, and income associated with an income producing property, is therefore at the very core of an investor's analysis. These revenues, expenses, and income estimates, known as a property's *reconstructed operating statement*, form the basis of the investor's one-year estimate or multiple-year forecast for the property.

Although each component of revenues and expenses are of interest to investors, the property's' operating income—the difference between revenues and expenses—determines both the rate of return of capital and the rate of return on capital. And operating income can be quantified monetarily.

## Advantages of Commercial Real Estate as an Investment

The advantages of investing in commercial real estate are both intangible and tangible. The intangible, or unmeasurable, advantages include pride of ownership, a sense of accomplishment, and ego gratification. The tangible, or measurable, advantages can be quantified monetarily. These monetary benefits fall into the category of either return of capital or return on capital and include cash flow, tax shelter, property depreciation, reduction of property debt financing, increases in property value, and equity buildup.

Every investor should consider these measurable advantages prior to investing. To determine if a particular property will provide measurable advantages, the investor must first understand, then analyze, the financial statements of the property.

## Basic Financial Statements

When analyzing revenues, expenses, and income for commercial real estate, two basic financial statements must be considered: the balance sheet and the profit and loss statement.

### *Balance Sheet*

A **balance sheet** is a financial statement that summarizes the total assets, total liabilities, and net worth of an individual or business entity. An individual may utilize a balance sheet for the purposes of qualifying for a loan. A business or "entity" that owns a real estate asset uses a balance sheet to measure assets and liabilities. The difference between assets and liabilities is *net worth.*

Net Worth =
Assets – Liabilities

**Net worth is the difference between total assets and total liabilities.** Net worth represents the ownership claim on property after all claims and liens have been deducted. It is also referred to as equity.

Assets =
Liabilities + Net Worth

**Assets are any owned property that has value.** Assets may be tangible, having a physical dimension, such as real estate, also known as real property. Property other than real property is known as personal property, which includes tangible financial assets such as automobiles, boats, and gold coins. Assets may also be intangible; examples include cash, bonds, and mortgage notes receivable. Total assets are obtained by adding the equity claim to the debt claim.

Liabilities =
Assets – Net Worth

**Liabilities are financial obligations, debts, and claims.** A liability is a debt owed to another person or entity that is obligated to be paid by a specified date (maturity). Liabilities may be secured or collateralized debt, such as a mortgage note payable, or unsecured debt such as a credit card balance.

Balance sheets are sometimes referred to as a "snapshot" of the property. They present a summarized financial picture of a property as of a specific date. Types of balance sheets include reconstructed balance sheets and pro forma balance sheets.

**Figure 1.1**

Simplified Balance Sheet

| **Assets** | | | **Liabilities and Equity** | | |
|---|---|---|---|---|---|
| Current Assets | | | Current Liabilities | | |
| Cash | | $20,000 | Accounts Payables | | $4,750 |
| Rent Receivable | | $3,000 | | | |
| Total Current Assets | | $23,000 | | | |
| | | | | | |
| Fixed Assets | | | Long-Term Debt | | |
| Land | | $70,000 | 1st Mortgage | $262,500 | |
| Building | $280,000 | | *less:* Debt Reduction | $(87,219) | |
| *less:* Depreciation | $(101,818) | | Balance Outstanding | | $175,281 |
| Depreciated Building | | $178,182 | | | |
| Net Fixed Assets | | $248,182 | Total Liabilities | | $180,031 |
| | | | | | |
| | | | Net Worth | | |
| | | | Partnership Equity | | $91,151 |
| | | | | | |
| Total Assets | | $271,182 | Liabilities and Equity | | $271,182 |

Figure 1.1 presents a simplified balance sheet.

### *Profit and Loss Statement*

A **profit and loss statement**, also known as a P&L or an operating statement, summarizes the revenues, expenses, and net operating income or loss of an investment during a defined period of time. There are different types of operating statements.

A *reconstructed operating statement* is prepared by an appraiser, investor, accountant, etc., and represents an opinion of a real estate investment's prior or current year revenues, expenses, and income. In preparing these reconstructed operating statements, the analyst usually references accountants', auditors', or sellers' financial statements, referred to as source documentation. Reconstructed P&Ls are used to estimate the historical or current financial benefits of an investment.

Another type of operating statement is the *pro forma operating statement*. A pro forma operating statement, also known as a pro forma P&L, is used to forecast a property's future revenues, expenses, and net operating income during a defined period based on specific assumptions and projections. Pro formas provide an estimation of the future financial benefits that an investment is anticipated to generate.

If an investor is acquiring a property, the profit and loss statement is the most important financial statement. However, if an investor must first acquire a business entity that owns the property to acquire the property, then the balance sheet gains in importance. Regardless of what must be done to gain control of the property, the profit and loss statement is generally considered the core financial statement required for conducting a meaningful evaluation.

### *Don't Worry, We'll Send You the Numbers!*

Many sellers, anxious to sell their properties, will offer to provide prospective purchasers with the financial statements pertaining to the property. Although this gesture may seem like a sign of good faith on the seller's part, caveat emptor! (Buyer beware!) Financial "information" is subject to a wide range of interpretations and presentations. For example, information may be accidentally or purposefully omitted or included in an attempt to conceal or misrepresent the facts. Also, the standards used to prepare financial statements vary. Accordingly, the most reliable financial statements are those that are audited and certified by professional accounting and tax counsel, such as a certified public accounting or real estate tax law firm.

Consider the balance sheet presented in Figure 1.1. The land value is stated as $70,000, and the building value, before depreciation, is stated as $280,000. What is the basis for these amounts? Is the land value based on the owner's estimate, the appraised value, or the acquisition price (book value)? How was the land price split out from the total price? Was it based upon accepted accounting methods or the owner's own estimate?

Now let's consider the profit and loss statement. Prospective purchasers consider the information contained within the profit and loss statement, the "must have" financial information to analyze an income-producing property properly. The three issues of interest when looking at P&Ls are:

1. The classification and terminology used to describe the revenues, expenses, and income within the P&L is not always consistent.
2. The source of the information is not always obvious.
3. Care must be taken to ensure that essential information that should be included is in fact present.

## Basic Income Estimates and Terminology

### *Income Refers to Net Operating Income, Not Cash Flow*

Net Operating Income = Revenues – Expenses

The terms *net operating income* and *cash flow* are often confused. **Net operating income (NOI)** is the income that remains after all operating expenses are deducted from adjusted gross revenues, but before mortgage debt service and depreciation are deducted. Net operating income is available to be allocated to the interests in real estate. For example, if an investor decides to purchase property with only cash, then the only party with an interest in the property is the owner. As such, the NOI would be allocated in its entirety to the owner's interest.

NOI is the income that is allocated to the interests in the real estate.

If, however, the investor decides to purchase the property with a combination of debt and cash, then both the lender and the investor have an interest in the property's income. Both the lender and the investor are obtaining at least a portion of their return of, and return on, their respective investments from the property's cash flow, and the NOI would be allocated to both lender's and the investor's interest. Once the debt service was deducted from the NOI, the remaining amount would be considered cash flow.

**Figure 1.2**

Simplified Real Estate Profit and Loss Statement

| | | |
|---|---|---|
| Potential Gross Income | | $100,000 |
| *less:* | | |
| Vacancy and Collection Losses @ | 5% | $5,000 |
| *equals:* | | |
| Effective Gross Income | | $95,000 |
| *less:* | | |
| Operating Expenses (Including Reserves) | | $40,000 |
| *equals:* | | |
| Net Operating Income | | $55,000 |
| *less:* | | |
| Mortgage Interest Expense | $ - | |
| Mortgage Principal Reduction | $ - | |
| Total Mortgage Payments | | $0 |
| *equals:* | | |
| Pretax Cash Flow | | $55,000 |

Cash Flow = Net Operating Income – Debt Service

**Cash flow (CF)** is the income that remains after the cost of financing, or debt service, is deducted from net operating income.

Cash flow can be measured on both a pretax basis and an after-tax basis. *Pretax cash flow (PTCF)* is the portion of net operating income that remains after total mortgage debt service (financing) is paid but before ordinary income tax on operations is deducted. *After-tax cash flow (ATCF)* is the portion of pretax cash flow that remains after all income tax liabilities have been deducted. Cash flow is typically measured in monthly, quarterly, or annual accounting periods.

What if there is no financing to consider and the investor is evaluating the property before any tax considerations? Then pretax cash flow would equal net operating income.

### *Measuring Net Operating Income*

The following discussion pertaining to net operating income is summarized in Figure 1.2. We'll be introducing a number of new terms. It may be helpful to refer to Figure 1.2, also referred to as the cash flow "stack," to understand how these terms fit into our discussion.

### *Potential Gross Income*

Let's say that an investor acquired a ten-unit, multifamily rental apartment that has a potential gross income of $100,000 per year. **Potential gross income (PGI)** is the total income that a real estate investment could generate, if the property was operating

1. at full occupancy;
2. before vacancy and collection losses are considered and deducted; and
3. before operating expenses are considered and deducted.

Potential gross income includes income attributable to *all* of the leaseable area, regardless if the space is actually leased, occupied, and generating rent.

Potential gross income includes scheduled base income from existing leases. *Scheduled base income* is the portion of potential gross income that is based upon the existing leases. Scheduled base income is also known as scheduled base rent, base income, base rent, contract rent, and existing rent. The scheduled base rent may consist of flat rent and, if applicable, income from leases with rent escalation.

What if there is vacant space? Potential gross income also includes market rent for vacant space (units) that could be leased in the near term. Potential gross income may also include income from sources other than the leases; for example, income derived from a common area laundry operation in a multifamily rental property. In this case, income would be generated from the washers, dryers, and vending machines, not from the rental unit leases.

### *Vacancy and Collection Losses*

Although management's goal is to operate property at full occupancy with no loss in collectable rent, this goal is usually not achievable. For example, consider a tenant who accepts employment in another part of town and decides to relocate. If that occurred, one of the units in the ten-unit, multifamily rental apartment would become vacant until a new replacement tenant could be found. PGI would decline because vacancy loss increased. In another example, this same tenant may lose his existing employment and be unable to pay their rent. PGI would decline because collection loss increased. So reductions in PGI may originate from vacancy losses, collection losses, or both.

**Vacancy and collection loss (V&C)** is an allowance for reductions in potential gross income attributable to unit vacancies, tenant turnover, and nonpayment of rents. The allowance amount represents the typical V&C loss for the particular property's type within the property's market area. For a proposed property, or when a market valuation is sought, V&C is based upon stabilized market conditions.

Vacancy and collection loss may be stated as a fixed percent of PGI. It may be further segregated into the vacancy component and the collection component. For example, let's say a total of 5 percent, or $5,000, is deducted from the potential gross income depicted in Figure 1.2. The V&C could be stated as 5 percent. Alternatively, the vacancy could be stated as 3 percent, and the collection losses could be stated as 2 percent.

Vacancy and collection losses are directly influenced by a property's type; the age, quality, and condition of the property; the overall supply of competitive property; and economic conditions. Generally, properties do not operate at potential gross income levels. Occasionally, at least one rental unit will be vacant due to a premature vacancy or renovation. Even when a unit is rented, rent is not always collectable. For existing properties, the actual historical and current vacancy and collection loss is the most accurate indicator of the property's potential.

What if a profit and loss statement shows no deduction for vacancy and credit? Then either the property is operating at its potential gross income level, the V&C has already been netted out against the income, or the statement is in error.

### Effective Gross Income

Deducting vacancy and collection loss from potential gross income produces the effective gross income for the property. **Effective gross income (EGI)** is the expected income from all operations of real property after an allowance is made for vacancy and collection losses. Effective gross income includes lease income from space or units and other income from sources such as parking, washers, dryers, or vending machines. Effective gross income is sometimes referred to as gross operating income (GOI).

The EGI for the property presented in Figure 1.2 comes to $95,000. Because the income statement is presented in a simplified format, it is not clear if items of "other income" are included.

### Categories of Operating Expenses

As presented in Figure 1.2, operating expenses for the year total $40,000. **Operating expenses (OE)** are the periodic expenditures necessary to operate and maintain the real property and continue the production of effective gross income, assuming prudent and competent management. As with the entire financial presentation of a property, as a general rule, the more detail in operating expenses, the better the financial and investment analysis of the property.

Operating expenses are further classified as fixed expenses, variable expenses, and replacement allowances. However, because the income statement in Figure 1.2 is presented in a simplified format, this additional level of detail is not available to us for review.

### Fixed Expenses

**Fixed expenses (FE)** are those operating expenses that are usually unaffected by the level of occupancy and would continue even if the property were totally vacant. Traditional examples of fixed operating expenses include real estate (property) taxes and property insurance.

Although the amount of fixed expenses may vary over time, the expenses themselves are constant, or fixed. For example, real estate taxes are paid annually, although the exact amount is subject to adjustment. Similarly, insurance policy premiums must be paid regularly, although not necessarily annually. If an expense is recurring but not paid each year, its cash amount must be restated on an accrual basis for consistency. Cash and accrual accounting methods are discussed later.

### Variable Expenses

**Variable expenses (VE)** are those operating expenses that usually vary in direct relation to the level of occupancy and would decline or even stop if the property were totally vacant. Traditional examples of variable expenses include management fees, administrative charges, payroll, advertising and promotion, telephone, utilities (including water, sewer, and electric), trash removal, repairs and maintenance, general supplies, pool maintenance, landscape maintenance, and pest control, among others.

Following is additional information about typical variable expenses:

- *Management fees.* Whether management services are provided by a management services firm or by the owner personally, management fees are considered a variable expense. Management fees are typically determined by allocating a percentage of effective gross income and are strongly influenced by the "typical" range of fees within the competitive market of the property's type.
- *Advertising and promotion.* These expenses are associated with marketing the property. Expenses in this category can include advertising in newspapers, magazines, proprietary Web sites, and other media.
- *Telephone.* Business-related telephone charges are typically presented as a separate line item category. Alternatively, telephone charges are sometimes added to another expense category such as administrative and general expenses or utility expenses.
- *Utilities.* Utility expenses include charges for water; sewer; electric; gas; and heating, ventilation, and air-conditioning (HVAC). Ownership expense for utilities generally applies to common and public areas. Utility expenses vary based on property type, as follows:
    - Utility costs associated with the lighting and cooling of apartment building corridors are the owner's responsibility. However, rental units are normally individually metered with the utility expense being the tenants' responsibility.
    - In the case of office buildings, the terms of the lease may indicate that the owner is responsible for the current (base) year utilities expenses attributable to leased space as well as common areas, with any increases over the current (base) year to be prorated and charged back to the tenant in occupancy.
    - For a retail property, the terms of the lease may indicate that the current year's property operating expenses attributable to the common areas are to be charged back to the tenant in occupancy on a prorated basis.
- *Trash removal.* Trash removal for larger investment properties is usually based on a contract. Often, a vendor will offer a discount for services based upon a multiple-year contact. These expenses, therefore, may be accounted for on either a cash or accrual basis.
- *Repairs and maintenance.* This expense category covers the broad area of property repairs and maintenance items that are normally considered part of the current period's operations. Charges in this category may be further detailed as structural repair and maintenance, grounds repair and maintenance, and landscaping repair and maintenance. Alternatively, all repair and maintenance expenses may be summarized. This expense category is also impacted by a related expense account, replacement reserves.

  Repairs and maintenance expenses are not considered capital expenditures. *Capital expenditures* are investments made to acquire, improve, or replace a real estate asset. Examples of capital expenditures are the acquisition of land and buildings, expenditures associated with building renovations and expansions, site improvements such as the installation of an underground irrigation system for landscaping, the replacement of a building's air-conditioning system, and the replacement of a building's elevator system. Capital expenditures are expenditures for long-term real estate components that, being permanent in nature, are considered income-producing assets. Capital expenditures are related to replacement reserves, discussed in the next section.

- *Unit interior decorating.* Expenses in this category include the cost of redecorating units, such as multifamily units, after one tenant moves out and before another tenant can move in. Typical charges include painting; carpet repair, cleaning, or replacement; and repair or replacement of window treatments. For an office or retail property, this expense may be considered as a "TI," real estate jargon that translates to "tenant's improvement allowance." For office and retail properties, TIs include such items as installation or repositioning of electrical outlets, installation or removal of non-load-bearing walls, installation or removal of doors from non-load-bearing walls, extending HVAC duct work, and installing dropped acoustical ceiling tiles. Depending on the amount and extent of the TI, this expense may be classified as a capital expenditure. The total cost would then be amortized over the term of the tenant's lease.
- *Landscape, lawn, and grounds.* The expense of maintaining landscaping, lawn, and grounds varies significantly based on the type of property, total site area, and location. Professionally designed and coordinated landscaping and lawns have always had great "curb appeal" for residential properties. Today, landscape architects often play a significant role in designing such areas for commercial properties as well. One-time costs include the design, irrigation systems, and the landscaping itself; these may actually be classified as capital expenditures. Recurring repairs and maintenance costs may include landscape maintenance contracts, supplies, and fertilizers. Low-maintenance landscaping is popular today, as is landscaping that that requires less water, a utility expense.
- *Pest control.* Pest control services are ordinarily contracted. Often, a vendor will offer a discount for services based upon a multiple-year contract. These expenses, therefore, may be accounted for on either a cash or accrual basis.
- *Leasing commissions.* Leasing commissions are paid to leasing agents or brokers who act as either an owner's representative or tenant's representative. Leasing commissions are usually associated with properties that are larger or have multiple tenants. Depending on the location, leasing commissions may either be paid out during the first year of the lease or allocated over the life of the lease. In either case, leasing commissions must be deducted as an expense. Leasing commissions are often classified as capital expenditures. The total cost would then be amortized over the term of the tenant's lease.
- *Miscellaneous.* Because operating expenses should be clearly categorized, this expense category should always be minimal. This category is sometimes erroneously used to account for expense contingencies. If a contingency expense category is desired, it should be so labeled.

### *Replacement Reserves*

**Replacement reserves (RR)** are based on a combination of the estimated useful lives of various building components and the recognition that certain building components wear out faster than others. Land does not depreciate or wear out; accordingly, the allocated costs are excluded from a replacement reserve. Replacement reserves are also known as replacement allowances, reserves for replacements, and reserves.

Replacement reserves consist of the annual average cost of replacing various building components and are reflected in the operating statement on an accrual basis. However, replacement reserves are not considered capital expenses, because allocating the cost over the life of the asset has the effect of creating a cash outflow for those expense items that are normally considered part of the current period's operations. Although reserves are not necessarily a cash expense in the year of recognition, they are a recognition of inevitable expense, allocated annually, over the life of the asset. Prudent property owners should not only account for the replacement reserve, they should fund the replacement reserve from available income to ensure the funds to replace the item will actually be available in the year of replacement.

A property management's repairs and maintenance program directly influence replacement reserves. Overly burdening the property with both liberal repairs and maintenance expense and a reserve category penalizes the property with an artificially low net operating income. Alternatively, artificially lowering (underfunding) the replacement reserve results in overstating the net operating income. This is not only true for the property being analyzed but for all comparable properties being analyzed as well.

Replacement reserves are strongly influenced by the size and type of property. For our ten-unit, multifamily rental property, we should take the following under consideration:

- Apartment unit property:
    - Kitchen items such as fixtures, sinks, plumbing, refrigerators, dishwashers, microwaves, ranges, and certain built-in cabinets
    - Bathroom items such as showers, bathtubs, fixtures, sinks, plumbing, toilets, and bidets
    - Carpeting and window treatments
    - Air-conditioning units and HVAC units
- Apartment common area property:
    - Common area washers and dryers
    - Hallway artwork and furniture
- Nonstructural site improvements:
    - Walkways, driveways, and parking lots
    - Pools and hot tubs
    - Landscaping and fencing

- Short-lived building components:
  - Roofs
- Nonstructural building components:
  - Exterior paint

The level of detail to provide in a replacement reserve is subject to judgment. It should be based on cost guides and useful lives established by industry norms. For example, appraisers employ nationally recognized cost guides as a regular part of their appraisal practice. These guides also serve as excellent references for investors and others for current costs and useful life calculations.

A replacement reserves expense is an accrual amount deducted as an operating expense from effective gross income to determine net operating income. However, this accrual amount is added back for calculation of taxable income. Investors can deduct *depreciation*, an accounting concept recognizing the "wasting away" of a real estate asset, to arrive at taxable income. Depreciation is calculated after debt service but before taxable income. Investors should not confuse these two concepts, replacement reserves and depreciation, as they impact the relative desirability of a investment very differently.

### Total Operating Expenses

Remember that total operating expenses are the sum of all fixed and variable operating expenses and replacement allowances. Deducting total operating expenses from effective gross income results in the property's net operating income. Expenses related to financing a property acquisition, such as interest expenses and loan principal amortization, are considered part of the property's debt service. Debt service is not considered an operating expense because it is not, as explained earlier, "a periodic expenditure necessary to operate and maintain the real property and continue the production of the effective gross income." Debt service is a periodic expenditure necessary to repay a loan used to acquire a property, not operate a property.

### Net Operating Income

Remember, too, that net operating income is the income that results from a property's operations. Subtracting *operating* expenses from *operating* revenue results in a net income, thus net *operating* income. NOI does not consider the effects of mortgage debt service and depreciation. It can be calculated before or after deducting replacement reserves. It can be calculated on the basis of a property's actual or projected profit and loss statement.

Net operating income represents the actual or projected profit generated by a real estate investment. NOI is an important consideration for lenders and borrowers, as it represents the amount of money available to pay debt service. It is an important consideration for buyers and sellers, too, as it is the amount of money used to determine the value of the property by "capitalizing" the NOI. NOI is affected by the inclusion or exclusion of the degree of vacancy and collection loss as well as operating expenses. For example, lowering operating expenses will increase NOI. When the increased NOI is capitalized, it results in a higher value.

### Net Operating Income versus Cash Flow

In Figure 1.2, we presented a summary presentation of the basic information required to calculate a net operating income of $55,000. Although line items were presented for mortgage interest expense and principal reduction, a mortgage was not considered. Accordingly, pretax cash flow also equaled $55,000. However, although net operating income and pretax cash flow are the same amount in this example, they do not represent the same concept. NOI represents income before debt consideration, while PTCF represents income after debt consideration.

### Cash or Accrual Basis

It is also important to know if the financial information presented has been prepared on a cash or accrual basis. **Cash basis** is a method of accounting in which income and expenses are recognized when they are actually received or paid out. **Accrual basis** is a method of accounting in which income and expenses are recorded on the books in the fiscal period when they are earned or incurred, regardless of when they are actually received or paid. For income tax purposes, taxpayers use either a cash basis or an accrual basis and recognize and report their income accordingly.

## Case Study: One-Year Analysis of Income and Expenses

Thus far, we have shown a simplified operating statement. However, a detailed review and analysis of the operating expenses of a property is important for many reasons. When available, historical operating statements provide factual information that should be reviewed to determine if trends, patterns, efficiencies, or inefficiencies exist.

As mentioned, the three issues of concern for historical P&Ls are:

1. The classification and terminology used to describe the income and expenses within the P&L is not always consistent.
2. The source of the information presented is not always obvious.
3. Care must be taken to ensure that essential information that should be included is in fact present.

These are some of the reasons that an investor should reconstruct the P&L and develop a market-oriented presentation of the property.

Let's now reanalyze the income and expenses for the ten-unit, multifamily rental property introduced earlier, employing a detailed profit and loss statement. Our goal is to present the information in a way that will be useful in evaluating the property for decision-making purposes. Our initial investigations will focus on the revenues, expenses, and net income of the property.

### Property Overview

**Property characteristics.** The ten-unit rental apartment property consists of a two-story multifamily rental apartment building containing 10,500 square feet of living/rentable area. We are evaluating the property as of December 31 of the current year. Our reconstructed P&L will be for the current year and result in a current-year presentation of revenues, expenses, and net income.

**Figure 1.3**

Summary of Property Unit Mix, Square Footages, and Rents

| Unit Type | No. | % | Livable SF | Total SF | $/Month | $/SF/ Month | Annual Rent |
|---|---|---|---|---|---|---|---|
| Studio | 3 | 30% | 790 | 2,370 | $699.50 | $0.89 | $25,182 |
| 1Bd-1Ba | 3 | 30% | 990 | 2,970 | $809.25 | $0.82 | $29,133 |
| 2Bd-2Ba | 4 | 40% | 1,290 | 5,160 | $939.25 | $0.73 | $45,084 |
| Total/Avg. | 10 | 100% | 1,050 | 10,500 | $828.32 | $0.79 | $99,399 |
| **Base Rent** | | | | | | **Rounded** | **$99,400** |

**Potential gross income.** There are ten units, including studio units, one-bedroom units, and two-bedroom units. The unit sizes are considered comparable to those in the market area. Based on the unit mix, the property has a total of 10,500 square feet of "livable" (air-conditioned) square footage. Base rent from unit rentals accounts for $99,400. The owner has provided a summary of the unit mix, square footages, and current rents, and based on this information, we prepare the Figure 1.3.

Other income, derived from a laundry facility for the tenants' use, accounts for $600 for the year, or $50 per month. Some potential additional income in this category has been lost due to a coin laundry retailer located within walking distance. However, this retail facility is expected to close within 12 months.

Neither base rent nor other income has been raised during the last 12 months. The potential gross income of the property for the year, at 100 percent occupancy, is $100,000.

**Vacancy and collection losses.** Vacancy and collection losses for the property have historically ranged from 2 percent to 6 percent of PGI, as follows:

- The current year's V&C has been estimated at 5 percent, or $5,000.
- Half (2.5%) of this amount was the amount of income loss attributable to market vacancy.
- The other half (2.5%) was attributable temporary vacancies of two of the two-bedroom, two-bathroom units, which were vacated by the existing tenants for approximately one and one-third months due to water damage caused by a storm. (Note: The owner's property insurance policy paid for all repairs to the property and all costs associated with the temporary relocation of the tenants to a hotel. As such, the expenses associated with this insured loss were not included in the reconstructed operating statement. However, the owner was not reimbursed for the $2,500 income loss from the two units during the repair.)

**Fixed operating expenses.** These include:

- *Real estate taxes.* The current year's tax bill is $11,000, inclusive of any discounts available to the owner for timely payment. This amount is expected to be stable in the short term.
- *Insurance.* The property owner carries $2 million in fire and casualty coverage and currently pays $1,750 per year. The coverage and policy amount increased from $1.75 million the year before. The current policy amount is not expected to be adjusted in the near term.

**Variable operating expenses.** These include:

- *Management fee.* The current owner of the property also manages the property. He charges the property a management fee based on 4 percent of effective gross income. Based upon your investigations into the marketplace, you determine that the management fee for similarly sized properties ranges from 3 percent to 5 percent of effective gross income. You conclude that 4 percent is reasonable.
- *Advertising and promotion.* The current owner advertises regularly in local newspapers and area brochures at a cost ranging from $0 to $100 per month, or $825 for the year.
- *Telephone expenses.* The telephone expense for the current year has been consistent at $75 per month, or $900 for the year.
- *Utilities expenses.* Utility expenses for the property for the current year are $1,600, or about $133 per month. This amount includes the utility expenses for the common areas of the property, including the laundry room, and covers water, sewer, and electric charges.
- *Trash removal.* Trash removal at the property is based on a biannual contract, with allocated annual amounts of $1,000. This is the first year of a two-year contract, with the same amount expected to be paid next year.
- *Repairs, maintenance, and supplies.* Recurring property repairs and maintenance and supplies are accounted for as a single line item amount of $11,000. Further investigation reveals that the amount breaks down into the following components:
    - *Permanent part-time maintenance.* The owner has a part-time general maintenance person budgeted at 300 hours per year, or 25 hours per month, at an hourly rate of $15 per hour. This comes to $4,500 per year.
    - *Supplies.* This category includes all the miscellaneous supplies that the part-time maintenance person requires for normal repairs. Included are paint, hardware, plumbing supplies, lightbulbs, and electrical wiring. The current year's cost, similar to the previous year's cost, is $3,600.
    - *Contractor repairs.* This category includes the cost of contractors for major repairs and maintenance such as air-conditioning, electrical, and plumbing issues. The current year's cost, similar to that of the prior year, is $2,900.
- *Unit interior decorating.* Interior unit decorating costs for the year amounted to $1,475, or about $123 per month. Because the property has historically maintained a high occupancy rate, with resulting low turnover of units, interior decorating has been kept to a minimum. However, the owner sometimes uses interior decorating as an inducement for lease renewal.
- *Landscape, lawn, and grounds.* Maintenance in this category is based on a $1,200 annual contract, which has remained unchanged for the last year.
- *Pest control.* Maintenance in this category is based on a two-year contract with annual payments of $450. This is the first year of the contract, with the same amount expected to be paid the following year.

**Replacement reserves.** The current owner has an annual accrual for replacement reserves of $5,000. This amount is based upon the owner's consultation with his appraiser, a nationally recognized cost guide, and the owner's accountant. The replacement reserves consider all of the short-lived components at the property, such as:

- *Rental units.* Such items as the kitchen appliances; bathroom fixtures; and individual, high-efficiency air-conditioning units. The cost new for these items has been estimated at $20,000, or $2,000 per unit. Their useful life has been estimated at 15 years.
- *Washers and dryers.* Two heavy-duty, commercial-grade washers and dryers. The cost new for these items has been estimated at $2,500, or $625 per unit. Their useful life has been estimated at eight years.
- *Artwork and furniture.* A ground floor and second floor corridor, both decorated with artwork and ornamental tables. The cost new for these items has been estimated at $1,500. Their useful life has been estimated at 15 years.
- *Site improvements.* A private, circular drive of asphalt paving that is maintained by the owner; paved concrete walkways in the front and along the sides and rear of the building; lush tropical landscaping with an extensive irrigation system, shrubbery, perimeter fencing, and security lighting; an on-site asphalt paved parking area for ten cars. The cost new for these items has been estimated at $60,000. Their blended useful life has been estimated at 40 years.
- *Roof.* A flat roof of built-up tar with gravel overlay over a concrete deck. The cost new for this item has been estimated at $15,000. Its useful life has been estimated at 20 years.
- *Exterior paint.* Based on bids provided by contractors, the cost new for painting has been estimated at $5,000. Its useful life has been estimated at five years.

Based on the information the owner has provided, we prepare Figure 1.4.

**Figure 1.4**

Replacement Reserve Calculations

| Component | Cost New | Useful Life | Annual Reserve |
|---|---|---|---|
| Unit Property | $20,000 | 15 | $1,333 |
| Washers and Dryers | $2,500 | 8 | $313 |
| Artwork and Furniture | $1,500 | 15 | $100 |
| Site Improvements | $60,000 | 40 | $1,500 |
| Roof | $15,000 | 20 | $750 |
| Exterior Painting | $5,000 | 5 | $1,000 |
| **Total** | | | **$4,996** |
| **Rounded to** | | | **$5,000** |

## Preparing a Reconstructed Profit and Loss Statement

With the additional detail provided in the case study, we can now reconstruct the information in a profit and loss statement. This presentation will be different from the simplified P&L presented in Figure 1.2. We will, however, arrive at the same answer.

The reconstructed profit and loss is significantly more relevant than the simplified presentation for several reasons. The format is standardized, employing a computer-based spreadsheet software, and the income and expenses are presented in the following relative units of measure:

- Total dollars
- Dollars per unit
- Dollars per square foot
- Percent of either income or expense

Relative units of measure are an important tool for effectively analyzing the property, comparing the property to other properties, and comparing the property to industry standards (benchmarking). Using a standard format and benchmarking allow comparisons with other properties as well as further analysis.

The reconstructed profit and loss statement is presented in Figure 1.5.

## Analysis

The reconstructed operating statement presented in Figure 1.5 provides a significant amount of detail about the revenue, expense, and income components of the ten-unit apartment building. It includes the property results on the basis of total dollars, dollars per unit, dollars per square foot, and percent of income or expense. Each of these units of measure provides a basis for an analysis of the property. As mentioned, the tangible, or measurable, advantages of investing in commercial real estate can be quantified monetarily.

### *Amount*

The total dollars—either by subcategory or in total revenues, expenses, and income—is key to estimating the total net operating income of a property. This in turn provides the owner or investor with a measure of both the return on, and return of, the invested capital.

### *Amount per Unit*

The dollar amount per unit is determined by dividing the total dollar amount by the number of apartment units. For example, the unit interior redecorating expense per unit would be obtained as follows:

$1,475 expense ÷ 10 units = $148 per unit

Many investors focus on the amount per unit to identify and quantify understatements, overstatements, or misstatements of financial information. For example, investors in multifamily apartments may want to know the other

**Figure 1.5**

Current Year's Reconstructed Operating Statement

**Ten-Unit Apartment Building—Income and Expense Analysis**

Units 10
Living Area Square Feet 10,500

| *Period* | *Current Year* | | | |
|---|---|---|---|---|
| **REVENUES** | | | | |
| Category | Amount | Amount per Unit | Amount per SF | % Total PGI |
| Scheduled Base Rent | $96,900 | $9,690 | $9.23 | 96.90% |
| **Market Rent for Vacant Units** | $2,500 | $250 | $0.24 | 2.50% |
| ***Subtotal: Adjusted Base Rent*** | $99,400 | $9,940 | $9.47 | 99.40% |
| **Other Income** | | | | |
| Laundry | $600 | $60 | $0.06 | 0.60% |
| ***Subtotal: Other Income*** | $600 | $60 | $0.06 | 0.60% |
| **Potential Gross Income @ 100% Occupancy** | $100,000 | $10,000 | $9.52 | 100.00% |
| **Vacancy and Collection Loss @ 5% PGI** | $5,000 | $500 | $0.48 | 5.00% |
| **Effective Gross Income** | $95,000 | $9,500 | $9.05 | 95.00% |
| **EXPENSES** | | | | |
| **Operating Expenses** *Fixed* | Amount | Amount per Unit | Amount per SF | % Total EGI |
| Real Estate Taxes | $11,000 | $1,100 | $1.05 | 11.58% |
| Insurance | $1,750 | $175 | $0.17 | 1.84% |
| ***Subtotal Fixed*** | $12,750 | 1,275 | $1.21 | 13.42% |
| *Variable* | | | | |
| Management Fee @ 4% EGI | $3,800 | $380 | $0.36 | 4.00% |
| Advertising and Promotion | $825 | $83 | $0.08 | 0.87% |
| Telephone | $900 | $90 | $0.09 | 0.95% |
| Utilities (Water, Sewer, Electric) | $1,600 | $160 | $0.15 | 1.68% |
| Trash Removal | $1,000 | $100 | $0.10 | 1.05% |
| Repairs, Maintenance, and Supplies | $11,000 | $1,100 | $1.05 | 11.58% |
| Unit Interior Redecorating | $1,475 | $148 | $0.14 | 1.55% |
| Landscape, Lawn, and Grounds | $1,200 | $120 | $0.11 | 1.26% |
| Pest Control | $450 | $45 | $0.04 | 0.47% |
| ***Subtotal Variable*** | $22,250 | $2,225 | $2.12 | 23.42% |
| ***Replacement Reserves*** | | | | |
| ***Subtotal Replacement Reserves*** | $5,000 | $500 | $0.48 | 5.26% |
| **Total Operating Expenses** | $40,000 | $4,000 | $3.81 | 42.11% |
| **OPERATING INCOME** | | | | |
| **Net Operating Income** | $55,000 | $5,500 | $5.24 | 57.89% |

income for the property on a per unit basis. Other income is often an overlooked component of PGI, which can often be increased faster than base rents, thereby increasing revenues and income.

Other important per-unit categories are fixed, variable, and replacement reserve expenses. For example, investors will want to know the amounts of repairs, maintenance, and supplies and replacement reserves, both by category and in relationship to each other. If the repairs, maintenance, and supplies expenses are overstated and the reserves are correctly stated, then operating expenses are overstated and NOI is understated. However, if the replacement reserves are understated, or not included at all, then NOI is overstated.

NOI per unit is important because the capitalized NOI per unit equals the value or price per unit. The value or price per unit can be referenced to other comparable sales transactions as a benchmark test of reasonableness as supported by the marketplace.

### *Amount per Square Foot*

Investors are also interested in the dollar amount per square foot. For example, as it pertains to revenues, from a competitive market analysis perspective, scheduled base rent and market rent are compared based on dollars per square foot, per month. Other income is another category that is measured on a dollar-per-square-foot basis.

Fixed expenses and replacement reserves are also typically benchmarked based on the dollar amount per square foot.

### *Percentages and Ratios*

Percentages and ratios are another key analytical tool for analyzing a property's operating statement.

**Revenues.** Percentages or ratios are calculated to compare adjusted base rent, other income, potential gross income, vacancy and collection losses, and effective gross income to potential gross income. Remember that the potential gross income percentage or ratio should always reflect the potential income at 100 percent occupancy. Following are some ratios commonly used in analysis:

- The ratios of scheduled base rent and market rent to adjusted base rent indicate the income risk associated with vacant units and the rent differential risk associated with contract and market rent.
- V&C percentage measures the ratio of vacancy and collection loss to the potential gross income. Recall that the vacancy and collection loss percentage or ratio should reflect actual property operating results, and this percentage should be supported by the competitive market. Lenders or investors may, however, change the V&C percentage to coincide with a typical or conservative (larger) amount to match their investor or lender underwriting criteria. (Any changes to actual reconstructed operating results change the P&L to a pro forma statement.)

- The effective gross income percentage measures the ratio of EGI to PGI. Remember that potential gross income is the total income attributable to real property at full occupancy, before vacancy and collection losses are deducted. Effective gross income is the anticipated income from all operations of the property after an allowance is made for vacancy and collection losses. Stated differently, effective gross income is the actual income available, from which all other deductions are made.

**Expenses.** Percentages or ratios of the categories of fixed expenses, variable expenses, replacement allowances, and total operating expenses are calculated to show these categories' relationships to effective gross income. Following are some ratios commonly used in analysis:

- The fixed operating expense percentage measures the ratio of fixed expenses to effective gross income.
- The variable operating expense percentage measures the ratio of variable expenses to effective gross income.
- The replacement reserves expense percentage measures the ratio of replacement reserves expense to effective gross income.
- The total operating expense percentage measures the ratio of total operating expenses to effective gross income. For example, an investor may focus on the total operating expense ratio to ascertain if the total percentage amount is reasonable, given comparable market information and industry standards. Based on these comparative benchmarks, an investor contemplating an acquisition may conclude that total operating expenses greater than, say, 45 percent are too high, while total operating expenses of, say, 37.5 percent are too low. Both conditions impact NOI and value.

## The Importance of Benchmarking

Local, regional, and national studies of the various property types are regularly prepared by leading professional, trade, and academic organizations. These studies provide general and specific information that can be referenced for benchmarking revenue, expense, and income ratios. Based on property type, these ratios tend to cluster within relatively narrow ranges. Ratios that fall outside these defined ranges require further analysis to determine why the ratio falls outside the range and how it might be corrected.

While these studies provide a framework for analysis, they are often global and not representative of a given local market. Therefore, investors must corroborate the validity of these ratios by looking at a local market analysis of comparable and competitive properties.

## Summary

Investors in real estate expect the recovery of all their invested capital, as well as a payment for the use of their capital. Return of capital and return on capital are based on the income and expense profile of the contemplated investment. Analytical tools help investors understand and develop a supportable current income and expense estimate of commercial real estate being considered for investment. The property's operating income determines both the rate of return of capital and the rate of return on capital, and operating income can be quantified monetarily. This is important, because every investor should consider *measurable* benefits prior to investing.

When analyzing income and expenses, one must examine two basic financial statements, the balance sheet and the profit and loss statement. A balance sheet is an itemized listing of the total assets, total liabilities, and net worth of a person or business entity. A profit and loss statement reflects the gross revenues, expenses, and net operating income profit or loss of an investment over a period of time. If an investor is acquiring a property, the profit and loss statement is most important. However, if an investor must first acquire a business entity that owns the property so as to acquire the property, then the balance sheet gains in importance. Standards used to prepare financial statements vary. As a result, financial information is subject to a wide range of interpretation.

### *Profit and Loss Statements*

P&Ls consist of three category classifications: revenues, expenses, and income. Potential gross income, also referred to as PGI, is the total income attributable to real property at full occupancy, before vacancy and collection losses and operating expenses are deducted. PGI consists of income attributable to the entire leaseable area, regardless of whether the space is actually occupied. Vacancy and collection loss, also referred to as V&C, is an allowance for reductions in potential gross income attributable to vacancies, tenancy turnover, and nonpayment of rents. Effective gross income, also referred to as EGI, is the anticipated income from all operations of the real property after an allowance is made for vacancy and collection losses.

Expenses for real property are called operating expenses. Operating expenses, also known as OE, are the periodic expenditures necessary to maintain the real property and continue production of the effective gross income, assuming prudent and competent management. Operating expenses are further classified as fixed expenses, variable expenses, or replacement reserves.

Fixed expenses, also known as FE, are those operating expenses that are usually unaffected by the level of occupancy and would continue even if the property were vacant. On the other hand, variable expenses, also known as VE, usually vary in direct relation to the level of occupancy and would decline or possibly discontinue if the property were vacant. Replacement reserves, also known as RR, are based on a combination of the estimated useful lives of various components and the recognition that certain building components wear out faster than others.

Total operating expenses are the sum of all fixed and variable operating expenses and the replacement reserves.

Net operating income, also known as NOI, is the actual or anticipated net income that remains after all operating expenses are deducted from effective gross income, but before mortgage debt service and book depreciation are deducted.

Another important consideration is whether the information has been accounted for on a cash or accrual basis. Cash basis is a method of accounting in which income and expenses are recognized when they are actually received or paid out. Accrual basis is a method of accounting in which income and expenses are recorded on the books in the fiscal period when they are earned or incurred, regardless of when they are actually received or paid. For income tax purposes, taxpayers use either a cash basis or an accrual basis and recognize and report their income accordingly.

When analyzing revenues, expenses, and income, employing a case study format often simplifies the process by providing a framework or template into which the available information may be placed. For smaller properties, these templates may be created in computer spreadsheets, which will perform calculations and analyze information rapidly. Analyzing historical information is also important. The three areas of concern for historical P&Ls are:

1. The classification and terminology used to describe the income and expenses within the P&L is not always consistent.
2. The source of the information presented is not always obvious.
3. Care must be taken to ensure that essential information that should be included is in fact present.

Once all available information has been reviewed and verified for relevancy, investors should prepare a reconstructed P&L of the property employing a computer-based spreadsheet to develop a market-oriented presentation of the property. Formats can be standardized with selected relevant units of measures, including total dollars, dollars per unit, dollars per square foot, and percent of either income or expense. Relative units of measure are an important tool for effectively analyzing the property, comparing it to other properties, and comparing the property to industry standards (benchmarking). Using a standard format and benchmarking provide a basis for comparison with other properties as well as further analysis.

A reconstructed P&L provides a significant amount of detail, which, thanks to the use of units of measure, allows for a relevant analysis. Local, regional, and national studies of the various property types are regularly prepared by leading professional, trade, and academic organizations. These studies provide both general and specific information, which can be referenced for benchmarking revenue, expense, and income ratios. Based on property type, these ratios tend to cluster within relatively narrow ranges. Ratios that fall outside these defined ranges require further analysis to determine why the ratio falls outside the range and how it might be corrected. While these studies provide a framework for analysis, they are often global and not representative of the local market. Investors must corroborate their validity by examining a local market analysis of comparable and competitive properties.

## Review Questions

1. Real estate investors expect payment for the use of their capital as well as the recovery of all their invested capital. These amounts will be derived from the
   a. return on capital.
   b. reversion.
   c. return of capital.
   d. all of the above.

2. Which of the following, if any, are advantages of investing in commercial real estate?
   a. Cash flow and equity build-up
   b. Tax shelter and depreciation
   c. Reduction of property debt financing and increases in property value
   d. All of the above

3. Balance sheets measure
   a. assets, liabilities, and net worth.
   b. revenues, expenses, and income.
   c. cash flow, either on a pretax or after-tax basis.
   d. all of the above.

4. Profit and loss statements measure
   a. assets, liabilities, and net worth.
   b. revenues, expenses, and income.
   c. appreciation, reversion, and leverage.
   d. all of the above.

5. Potential gross income
   a. may be measured on a pretax or after-tax basis.
   b. is the anticipated income from all operations of real property after an allowance is made for vacancy and collection losses.
   c. is the anticipated income from all operations of real property before an allowance is made for vacancy and collection losses.
   d. includes a reduction attributable to vacancies, tenant turnover, and nonpayment of rents.

6. Effective gross income may be referred to as
   a. potential gross income less vacancy and collection losses.
   b. equity build-up less debt service.
   c. owner's equity plus assets.
   d. appreciation less vacancy and collection losses.

7. Net operating income is equal to
   a. PGI less EGI.
   b. EGI less PGI.
   c. EGI less OE.
   d. PGI less OE.

8. Vacancy and collection loss is an allowance for reductions in
   a. potential gross income.
   b. effective gross income.
   c. net operating income.
   d. debt service payments.

9. Total operating expenses usually include
   a. fixed expenses.
   b. variable expenses.
   c. replacement reserves.
   d. all of the above.

10. Operating expenses
    a. are expenditures associated with selecting one investment opportunity as compared to another.
    b. are expenditures to maintain the real property and production of income.
    c. include expenditures to amortize a loan.
    d. include expenditures for depreciation.

### *Case Study of One-Year Analysis of Income and Expenses*

The following case study provides information to answer questions 11 through 15.

**Property overview.** We are evaluating a two-story rental apartment building containing 20 rental units. The property features a walk-up covered porch area located along the north side of the building. Entry double doors open to a wide interior corridor with five rental apartment units on each side of the corridor, ten units per floor. The rear of the property features a covered rear porch area located along the south side of the building, which has been renovated into an enclosed laundry facility. There are four washers, four dryers, and a soap vending machine, all on separate "laundry room" electric and water meters. A service company pays a flat fee of $150 per month for the right to operate at the property and has installed the washers, dryers, and vending machine. The owner receives this amount net of all expenses and has no obligations whatsoever for the utility expenses, maintenance, and repair of this equipment.

The ground floor interior corridor has two staircases leading to the second floor. A staircase/exit is on both the east and west side of the corridor; each is located approximately midway along the corridor. The exits lead to side entryways/exits. Each of the staircase/exits has enough area to accommodate a vending machine. One staircase/exit area has a soda/juice/water vending machine. The other staircase/exit area has a snack food vending machine. A service company pays a flat fee of $50 per month for the right to operate at the property and has installed the vending machines. The owner receives this amount net of all expenses and has no obligations whatsoever for the utility expenses, maintenance, and repair of this equipment.

**Unit mix and unit revenues.** There are 20 rental apartments, consisting of studio units, one-bedroom units, and two-bedroom units. The unit sizes are considered comparable to others in the market area. Based on the unit mix, there is a total of 20,000 square feet of "livable" (air-conditioned) square footage. Base rent from unit rentals comes to $253,920. The owner has provided a summary of the unit mix, square footages, and current rents, and based on this information, we prepare Figure 1.6.

**Figure 1.6**

Case Study: Summary of Property Unit Mix, Square Footages, and Rents

| Unit Type | No. | % | Livable SF | Total SF | $/Month | $/SF/ Month | Annual Rent |
|---|---|---|---|---|---|---|---|
| Studio | 4 | 20% | 750 | 3,000 | $900.00 | $1.20 | $43,200 |
| 1Bd-1Ba | 8 | 40% | 950 | 7,600 | $1,045.00 | $1.10 | $100,320 |
| Rear: 2Bd-2Ba | 4 | 20% | 1,100 | 4,400 | $1,100.00 | $1.00 | $52,800 |
| Front: 2Bd-2Ba | 4 | 20% | 1,250 | 5,000 | $1,200.00 | $0.96 | $57,600 |
| Total/Avg. | 20 | 100% | 1,000 | 20,000 | $1,058.00 | $1.06 | $253,920 |
| **Base Rent** | | | | | | **Rounded** | **$253,920** |

Demand for rentals in this market area are very strong with 5 percent per annum rent increases the norm. Accordingly, next year's rental unit income can safely be estimated to increase by 5 percent.

**Other income.** As mentioned, a service company pays the property owner a flat fee of $150 per month for the right to operate washers, dryers, and a soap vending machine. Additionally, the property owner is paid a flat fee of $50 per month for the right to operate food and beverage vending machines. The total other income amounts to $200 per month, or $2,400 per year. This income is neither variable nor subject to vacancy and collection losses.

**Vacancy and collection loss.** Vacancy and collection losses for the property have historically averaged 5 percent of EGI. However, the current year vacancy and collection losses are running at about 25 percent. This is due to a city public works "upgrade and beautification" project that has closed off the street to through-traffic. The "upgrade" part of the project calls for the installation of new water and sewer lines and street asphalt paving. The "beautification" part of the project calls for improved streetlighting and landscaping. The project commenced at the beginning of this year and will conclude by the end of this year.

**Rental concession program.** To maintain occupancy during construction, the owner has put in place a temporary rental concession program whereby all tenants' rents are discounted by 20 percent per month. This concession program commenced at the beginning of this year and will conclude at the end of the year, at the same time the upgrade and beautification project is completed. The current owner has a waiting list of prospective tenants who are ready, willing, and able to take occupancy as soon as the work is completed. Accordingly, next year's occupancy is expected to rise to 100 percent.

**Figure 1.7**

Case Study: Operating Expenses

| Type of Expense | Unit of Measure |
|---|---|
| *Fixed Expenses* | |
| Real Estate Taxes: | $1,100.00 per unit |
| Insurance: | $ 0.20 per square foot |
| | |
| *Variable Expenses* | |
| Management Fees: | 4% Of EGI |
| Advertising and Promotion: | $0.07 per square foot |
| Telephone: | $75 per unit |
| Utilities: | 1.50% EGI |
| Trash: | $0.10 per square foot |
| Repairs and Maintenance: | $0.80 per square foot |
| Unit Interior Redecorating: | $100.00 per unit |
| Landscape, Lawn, and Grounds: | $2,400.00 per annum |
| Pest Control: | $0.05 per square foot |
| | |
| *Replacement Reserves* | |
| Reserves: | $350.00 per unit |

**Operating expenses.** Figure 1.7 shows a summary of the operating expenses for the property. All expenses are quoted on an annual basis. A number of benchmarks are used to present this information. Some of the operating expenses are quoted on a total dollar basis, while others are quoted on an amount per unit or amount per square foot per annum basis. Finally, some of the expenses are quoted as a percentage of EGI. All fixed expenses are growing at an average of 2 percent per year. All variable expenses, other than percentage expenses, are growing at an average of 3 percent per year.

Based upon the preceding case study information, prepare a current-year reconstructed operating statement and answer questions 11 through 15.

**11.** What is the current year's effective gross income, in total and per unit?

- **a.** $154,752 in total and $7,738 per unit
- **b.** $152,352 in total and $7,618 per unit
- **c.** $190,440 in total and $9,522 per unit
- **d.** $253,920 in total and $12,696 per unit

**12.** What are the current year's fixed expenses, in total and per unit?

- **a.** $22,000 in total and $1,100 per unit
- **b.** $4,000 in total and $200 per unit
- **c.** $26,000 in total and $1,300 per unit
- **d.** $8,000 in total and $400 per unit

**13.** What are the current year's variable expenses, in total and per unit?

- **a.** $41,810 in total and $2,091 per unit
- **b.** $34,810 in total and $1,741 per unit
- **c.** $27,810 in total and $1,391 per unit
- **d.** $20,810 in total and $1,041 per unit

**14.** What are the current year's replacement reserve expenses, in total and per unit?

- **a.** $9,000 in total and $450 per unit
- **b.** $8,000 in total and $400 per unit
- **c.** $7,000 in total and $350 per unit
- **d.** $6,000 in total and $300 per unit

**15.** What will the current year's net operating income come to, in total and per unit?

- **a.** $96,942 in total and $4,847 per unit
- **b.** $92,942 in total and $4,647 per unit
- **c.** $86,942 in total and $4,347 per unit
- **d.** $82,942 in total and $4,147 per unit

chapter two

# VALUING COMMERCIAL REAL ESTATE VIA DIRECT CAPITALIZATION

## Key Terminology

| | | |
|---|---|---|
| "As Is" Cap Rate | "In-House" Cap Rate | "Reversionary" Cap Rate |
| Capitalization | IRV Formula | Risk |
| Capitalization Rate | Net Operating Income | Ro |
| Direct Capitalization | Overall Rate (OAR) | "Stabilized" Cap Rate |
| Direct Cap Formula | Return | Uncertainty |

## Overview

In this chapter, the first of the two methods of capitalization is discussed. The importance of direct capitalization as a credible method of estimating value is emphasized, and both the benefits and shortcomings of this simple valuation method are described. The derivation of the overall rate, its other names, and its applications are introduced. The IRV formula and the direct capitalization formula are explained, and variations of the formulas and their applications are presented in detail. The concepts of risk, return, and their relationship to the capitalization formula are discussed.

As we explore the process of direct capitalization, we introduce numerous new terms, and the importance of applying practical mathematics to business decisions becomes apparent. Multistep calculations for determining income, value, and rate are introduced. The ability to employ overall rates (OARs) to a reconstructed or forecasted operating statement as a tool for investing is emphasized as fundamental to the decision-making process.

## Learning Objectives

After completing this chapter, you should be able to accomplish the following:

- Define the term *capitalization*
- Discuss the process of direct capitalization
- List the three alternative names for *capitalization rates*
- Explain the components of the IRV Formula
- Differentiate between *return on capital* and *return of capital*, as these terms apply to direct capitalization
- Discuss the relationship between risk and return
- Explain the relationship between OARs and risk
- Describe the relationship between rates and values
- Discuss the sources of capitalization rates
- Explain the process of direct capitalization of current year's income
- Describe the process of direct capitalization of forecasted income

## What Is Capitalization?

Widely used within the context of financial and investment analysis, as it applies to real estate, **capitalization** is the conversion of income into an estimate of value. Although there are various capitalization methods, processes, and techniques, the most well-known among real estate investors are direct capitalization and yield capitalization. In this chapter, we focus on direct capitalization. In the following chapter, we'll focus on yield capitalization.

## Direct Capitalization

**Direct capitalization** is a method used to convert an estimate of a single year's expected income into an indicator of value in one direct step; hence, the term *direct capitalization*. Direct capitalization converts income into value by dividing the estimated income by a rate or by multiplying the estimated income by a factor. These rates and factors are known as **capitalization rates**. The most widely recognized direct capitalization technique is dividing the estimated income by a rate. Direct capitalization is often referred to as direct cap, and capitalization rates are often referred to as caps.

The preferred sources of capitalization rates and/or multipliers are "extracted" from sales. Extracting capitalization rates from sales is preferred for two reasons.

1. Sales provide evidence as to currently acceptable capitalization rates in the marketplace.
2. They are considered relatively simple to extract.

Capitalization rates may also be derived by various mathematical techniques that account for such factors as the anticipated return on and of equity and debt; anticipated changes in revenue, expenses, and income; anticipated growth and yield; and so on. Regardless of the source of the capitalization rate, only a single year's income is considered. An income's growth, yield, and value changes are all implied, but not identified, in a direct capitalization rate.

At first glance, direct capitalization appears simple enough. After all, how difficult can it be to find an appropriate capitalization rate? Using information gained from a combination of Internet-based search engines and "knowledgeable individuals" such as real estate investors, brokers, and appraisers, you could obtain all the cap rates you could desire. However, these cap rates must be further evaluated as market-, investor-, or speculative-oriented or not appropriate at all. Whereas information pertaining to capitalization rates abounds, finding the correct capitalization rate is another issue entirely.

Another consideration is the concept of income. What type of income are we capitalizing? Is it this year's actual income, this year's reconstructed income, next year's pro forma income, or a future year's pro forma income? And what kind of income? Is it the property's net operating income before or after capital expenses have been considered? And what do investors and the marketplace consider to be capital expenses? The answer is: "It depends."

### *I'm Not Buying Your Cap!*

I had the opportunity to be on the "buy side" of a real estate transaction. As a buyer's broker, our firm was employed by the principal (the buyer) to acquire Class A office buildings based on all-cash offers and a 10 percent rate of return on current income. In one such transaction, a property had a current income of $1,000,000. The seller employed a brokerage firm to represent them. During the negotiations for the property acquisition, a three-way, long-distance conference call took place. On our end of the telephone were the buyer, the buyer's broker, and the broker's staff. Also on the conference call, at another location, were the seller's broker and that broker's staff. Additionally, at still another location was the seller. The conference call went something like this:

*Seller's Broker*: Everybody on?

*Seller:* Yes.

*Buyer:* Yes.

*Buyer's Broker:* Yes.

*Seller's Broker*: On behalf of the seller, thank you for your Letter of Intent.

*Buyer's Broker:* You're welcome. Is it acceptable to the seller?

*Seller's Broker:* We are close. Your offer is based on a 10½ cap. The seller prefers a 9½ cap sale.

*Buyer's Broker*: We think the 10½ cap is fair, given the condition of the property, fine asset that it is.

*Seller's Broker*: Let me discuss this privately with the seller. (Call placed on hold)

*Seller's Broker*: The seller would accept a 9¾ cap.

*Buyer's Broker:* Let me discuss this privately with the buyer. (Call placed on hold)

*Buyer's Broker:* The buyer will stretch to a 10¼ cap.

*Seller's Broker*: That's not acceptable.

*Buyer's Broker*: But we agreed that the property needs work! Are we supposed to pay a market cap and also pay for the renovation on top of that cap?

*Buyer*: Stop, both of you! You are both talking about caps. Am I buying clothing from you? No! Are you my haberdashers? No! *I'm not buying your cap!* If I want a cap, I'll go to my haberdashery, thank you. Where is the seller? Is he there?

*Seller*: Yes, I'm here.

*Buyer:* How much longer do we have to do this?

*Seller:* You tell me—hopefully not much longer.

*Buyer:* I like the property, but it needs work. I require a 10 percent rate of return on my money. That is fair, you know it's fair, and it's the best I can do.

*Seller*: All cash?

*Buyer:* Yes.

*Seller:* And a 45-day closing?

*Buyer:* Better than that. Say, a 30-day closing after inspections.

*Seller*: Done deal!

*Buyer:* Yes! Done deal!

*Seller:* *And I'll throw in a cap!*

*Buyer:* That's not funny.

What the buyer and seller are doing is establishing the price of the property, based on a negotiated cap rate. Notice that a dollar amount for the property never entered the conversation. Both the buyer and the seller were aware of the currently acceptable capitalization rates demanded by the real estate marketplace for this type of property. Stated differently, both the buyer and seller were aware of the currently acceptable rates of return demanded by real estate investors in the marketplace. With this information, the buyer and seller could negotiate in terms of rate of return. Because they have agreed on income, when they negotiate a rate of return, they are also negotiating the price of the real estate investment. Once income is known, price is determined by the rate of return.

Investors who are less cash constrained in deal making are more concerned about the return on their investments.

Let's revisit the conversation between the buyer and the seller. This time, however, let's say the buyer and seller are negotiating in terms of price. The size of the property, 100,000 square feet, is also a consideration, as the price will also be discussed in terms of price per square foot. Because they have agreed on income, as they negotiate a price, they are also negotiating a rate of return on the real estate investment. When income is known, rate of return is determined by price.

The conference call would go something like this:

*Seller's Broker*: Everybody on?

*Seller:* Yes.

*Buyer:* Yes.

*Buyer's Broker:* Yes.

*Seller's Broker*: On behalf of the seller, thank you for your Letter of Intent.

*Buyer's Broker:* You're welcome. Is it acceptable to the seller?

*Seller's Broker:* We are close. Your offer is based on $95.25 per square foot. The seller prefers $105.25 per square foot.

*Buyer's Broker*: We think the $95.25 per square foot is fair, given the condition of the property, fine asset that it is.

*Seller's Broker*: Let me discuss this privately with the seller. (Call placed on hold)

*Seller's Broker*: The seller would accept $102.50 per square foot.

*Buyer's Broker:* Let me discuss this privately with the buyer. (Call placed on hold)

*Buyer's Broker:* The buyer will stretch to $97.50 per square foot.

*Seller's Broker*: That's not acceptable.

*Buyer's Broker*: But we agreed that the property needs work! Are we supposed to pay a market rate for square footage and also pay for the renovation on top of that?

*Buyer:* Stop, both of you! Where is the seller? Is he there?

*Seller:* Yes, I'm here.

*Buyer:* How much longer do we have to do this?

*Seller:* You tell me—hopefully not much longer.

*Buyer:* I like the property, but it needs work. Reasonably similar buildings in this market are trading for around $100 per square foot. I am willing to pay a comparable sales price per square foot. So I can pay $100 per square foot or $10,000,000 for the entire building and no more. That is fair, you know its fair, and it's the best I can do.

*Seller:* All cash?

*Buyer:* Yes.

*Seller:* And a 45-day closing?

*Buyer:* Better than that. Say, a 30-day closing after inspections.

*Seller:* Done deal!

*Buyer:* Yes! Done deal!

What the buyer and seller are doing is establishing the cap rate of the property, based on a negotiated price. Notice that the cap rate for the property never entered the conversation. Both the buyer and the seller were aware of currently acceptable prices per square foot in the marketplace. Stated differently, both the buyer and seller were aware of currently acceptable prices per square foot demanded by the real estate marketplace for this type of property. With this information, the buyer and seller could negotiate in terms of price per square foot. Because they have agreed on income, when they negotiate a purchase price, they are also negotiating a rate of return on the real estate investment. When income is known, rate of return is determined by price.

**Figure 2.1**

Relationship between Income, Cap Rates, and Price

| Income | Divided By | Cap Rate | Equals | Price Rounded |
|---|---|---|---|---|
| $1,000,000 | / | 10.50% | = | $9,525,000 |
| $1,000,000 | / | 10.25% | = | $9,750,000 |
| $1,000,000 | / | 10.00% | = | $10,000,000 |
| $1,000,000 | / | 9.75% | = | $10,250,000 |
| $1,000,000 | / | 9.50% | = | $10,525,000 |

Investors who are more cash constrained in deal making are more concerned about the price of their investment.

In both scenarios, what is known is the property's income. When the buyer and seller were negotiating on the basis of cap rate, they were establishing the purchase price. When the buyer and seller were negotiating on the basis of price, they were establishing the cap rate. So there is a clear relationship between income, cap rate, and price. This relationship is presented in Figure 2.1.

For a given income stream, as the capitalization rate increases, the price decreases, and as the capitalization rate deceases, the price increases.

Figure 2.1 presents an important mathematical relationship for all income-producing properties and property valuation. The income is being converted into price by using various capitalization rates. Given an income stream, as the capitalization rate increases, the price decreases; as the capitalization rate deceases, the price increases.

### Types of Direct Capitalization

Few terms are as readily recognized and yet as misunderstood as *direct capitalization rates*, or "cap rates" as they are often called. A capitalization rate is a rate that is used to convert income into value. However, because there are different types of income at different periods during an investment, there are different types of cap rates. Following are some of the different types:

- **"As-is" cap rate.** Used to convert existing or "as is" income into an actual or expected price or value of a property. "As-is" income may or may not be considered stabilized. "As-is" cap rates are also referred to as going-in or acquisition cap rates.
- **Stabilized cap rate.** Used to convert stabilized income into an actual or expected price or value of a property, which is operating under stabilized operating conditions, including occupancy, revenues, and expenses.
- **Reversionary cap rate.** Used to convert projected future stabilized income into an actual or expected price or value of a property at the conclusion of an investment's holding period. Reversionary rates are used to estimate the resale price or value of a property. Reversionary cap rates are also referred to as exit, terminal, disposition, or going-out capitalization rates.

When discussing "as is," stabilized, or reversionary cap rates, we also need to know from whose perspective are we considering them. Are we considering these cap rates from a seller's, buyer's, lender's, or market perspective? Perspective is important because, as the following shows, each party's expectations are different given the same income stream:

- From a seller's perspective, cap rate expectations are usually lower, because lower cap rates result in higher capitalized prices for property.
- From a buyer's perspective, cap rate expectations are usually higher, because higher cap rates result in lower capitalized prices for property.
- From a lender's perspective, their underwriting requirements addressing loan-to-value ratios and debt coverage ratios usually temper both the buyer's and seller's cap rate expectations. From a lender's perspective, the property's capitalization rate reflects the weighted cost of capital in the investment.

  Lenders sometimes rely on **in-house capitalization** rates to support their lending decisions. Utilizing this method, lenders consider the traditional terms of lending such as the interest rate, loan-to-value ratio, amortization term, maturity and payment period, and other constraining factors such as the debt coverage ratio. The in-house cap rate is estimated by a mathematical process whereby the debt coverage ratio is multiplied by the mortgage capitalization rate and the loan-to-value ratio.

- From the market's perspective, cap rate expectations are usually a composite of sellers', buyers', and lenders' perspectives and return requirements. So the market reflects a distillation of all market participants involved in the buying, selling, and financing of real estate.

So defining a capitalization rate is straightforward. Unfortunately, determining what should be capitalized, and by what rate, is a bit vague.

## Shortcomings of Direct Capitalization

A shortcoming of the simplistic direct cap process is that it does not clearly differentiate between the return on capital and the return of capital. The cap rate implicitly contains an acceptable rate of return on capital and a satisfactory rate of recovery of invested capital. Another concern is "the numbers": What is included and excluded in the P&L? What is price: Is it the sales price or the adjusted acquisition price? What about operating expenses: Are fixed expenses, variable expenses, and reserves allowances considered?

Consider the three multifamily rental apartment properties presented in Figure 2.2. The three recently sold properties are located in the same market area, are all apartments, and all contain between 10 and 25 units. The properties' sales prices, net operating incomes, and extracted capitalization rates (OARs) are summarized in Figure 2.2.

The cap rate, also known as an overall rate, implicitly contains an acceptable rate of return on capital and a satisfactory rate of recovery of invested capital. Let's consider each of our examples:

- For Property A, the invested capital would be $550,000 (price), and the return on capital and return of invested capital would be $55,000 (NOI). The rate of return on/of capital would be calculated by dividing the NOI by the price, which for Property A would be 10 percent.
- For Property B, the invested capital would be $990,000 (price), and the return on capital and return of invested capital would be $108,000 (NOI). The rate of return on/of capital would be calculated by dividing the NOI by the price, which for Property B would be 10.91 percent.
- For Property C, the invested capital would be $1,478,125 (price), and the return on capital and return of invested capital would be $137,500 (NOI). The rate of return on/of capital would be calculated by dividing the NOI by the price, which for Property C would be 9.30 percent.

**Figure 2.2**

Analysis of Multifamily Apartment Transactions

| Property/Units | A/10 | B/18 | C/25 |
|---|---|---|---|
| Price | $550,000 | $990,000 | $1,478,125 |
| Net Operating Income | $55,000 | $108,000 | $137,500 |
| OAR | 10.00% | 10.91% | 9.30% |

### *OARs*

The **overall rate**, also expressed as either **OAR** or **Ro**, is an income rate for a total real property interest. It reflects the relationship between the expected single year's net operating income and the total property sales price or value. This relationship is summed up in the OAR for the following purposes:

- An OAR can be extracted from a property as an indicator of the currently acceptable capitalization rates in the marketplace.
- An OAR can be used to convert a single year's income expectancy into an indicator of a property's sales price or value.
- An OAR that is extracted from one property can then be used to convert another property's income into an indicator of that property's sales price or value.

The OAR formula is represented by the IRV equation:

$$\text{OAR (R)} = \frac{\text{NOI (I)}}{\text{Value or Price (V)}}$$

We employed this formula to determine the OARs for property sales A, B, and C in Figure 2.2. The OAR contains the rate of return on the investment as well as the rate of return of the investment. Because it encompasses both without clearly differentiating between the return on capital and the return of capital, it is an *overall* rate. The OAR implicitly contains both an acceptable rate of return on capital and a satisfactory rate of recovery of invested capital but does not distinguish between them.

### *They Called It Income, but Is It Income?*

In simpler times, "income" referred to net operating income. **Net operating income** was generally regarded as effective gross income less all operating expenses. Some investment sectors held that operating expenses included both fixed and variable expenses but excluded some or all replacement allowances, tenant improvement costs, and leasing commissions. The reasoning for these exclusions was their tendency to distort NOI in a given year when substantial nonrecurring capital repairs were required, or significant amounts of space were turning over and incurring improvements expenses and leasing commissions (re-leasing costs), that distorted that year's income. Unfortunately, calculating income gets more complicated.

Reflecting the current disagreement in the marketplace, one widely read investor survey currently describes NOI as *either*

1. income after capital replacement reserves but before tenant improvements and leasing commissions; or
2. income before capital reserves, tenant improvements, and leasing commissions; or
3. income after all capital replacement reserves, tenant improvements, and leasing commissions.

**Figure 2.3**

IRV Formula Icon

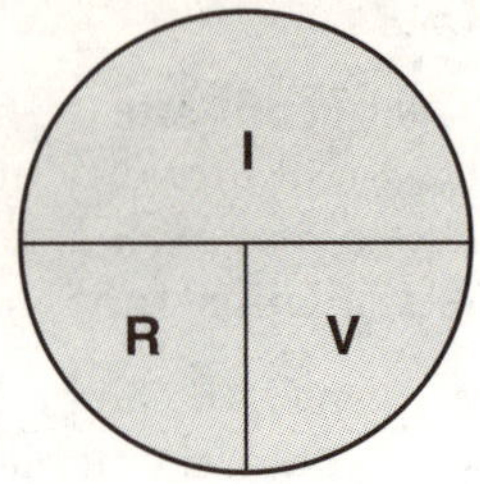


Where:
I = Income, as in net operating income
R = Rate, as in capitalization rate
V = Value, as in sales price, price, or appraised value

***Be Consistent***

Most real estate valuation experts agree that operating expenses include all fixed expenses and variable expenses. They also agree that operating expenses should include replacement allowances. However, regardless of how the properties are analyzed, the key is to be consistent and apply the same methodology to each property.

## The IRV Formula

One of the simplest and most powerful valuation formulas is the **IRV formula**. The formula is so simple, it is deceiving. If you understand the IRV formula, you are well on your way to understanding direct capitalization. The IRV formula can be presented simply, with the use of the IRV icon, as shown in Figure 2.3.

In this presentation, IRV is deceptively simple. Using the IRV formula, we can solve for income, rate, or value by knowing the remaining two elements.

Income = Rate × Value
Rate = Income ÷ Value
Value = Income ÷ Rate

Some individuals remember these three equations by using the formula summary in Figure 2.3 and "covering up" what they are solving for. For example:

- If we know rate and value and want to solve for income, we could simply place our finger on the I portion of the formula summary. What we are left with is the formula to solve for I: I = R multiplied by V.

$$R \times V$$

- If we know income and value and want to solve for rate, we could simply place our finger on the R portion of the formula summary. What we are left with is the formula to solve for R: R = I divided by V.

$$\frac{I}{V}$$

- If we know income and rate and want to solve for value, we could simply place our finger on the V portion of the formula summary. What we are left with is the formula to solve for V: V = I divided by R.

$$\frac{I}{R}$$

For example, let's say we wanted to solve for the overall rate for Property A, presented in Figure 2.2. We know that the invested capital of $550,000 would be its value, and the net operating income of $55,000 would be its income. We place our finger on the R portion of the formula summary in Figure 2.3. What we are left with is the formula to solve for R: R = I divided by V. In this case, our formula would yield $55,000 divided by $550,000, which equals 10 percent. The overall rate for this property sale would be 10 percent.

## Direct Capitalization Formula

### *Expanding the IRV Formula into a Direct Capitalization Formula*

The IRV formula and the direct capitalization formula employ the same methodology. The **direct capitalization formula** is sometimes referred to as IRV, IRV the Investor, or IRV the Appraiser. Here is the direct capitalization formula:

$$\text{Value (V)} = \frac{\text{Net Operating Income (I)}}{\text{Overall Capitalization Rate (R)}}$$

The above formula will solve for the property's value, if the net operating income and the overall capitalization rate are provided. For example, in Figure 2.2, Property A has a net operating income of $55,000 and an overall rate of 10 percent. Using the direct capitalization formula, the value would be $550,000, calculated as follows:

$$\$550{,}000 = \frac{\$55{,}000}{0.10}$$

### *Variations of the Direct Capitalization Formula*

The IRV formula is very versatile. If you know any two of the property components, you can solve for the third. The following formula solves for OAR:

$$\text{OAR (R)} = \frac{\text{NOI (I)}}{\text{Value or Price (V)}}$$

This formula solves for the OAR, if the net operating income and either the value or price are provided. For example, in Figure 2.2, Property A has a net operating income of $55,000 and a price of $550,000. Using the direct capitalization formula, the OAR would be 10 percent, calculated as follows:

$$10\% = \frac{\$55{,}000}{\$550{,}000}$$

The formula can be varied to solve for the NOI, if the OAR and the value or price is provided:

$$\text{NOI (I)} = \text{OAR (R)} \times \text{Value or Price (V)}$$

For example, in Figure 2.2, Property A has an OAR of 10.00% and a price of $550,000. Using the direct capitalization formula, the NOI would be $55,000, calculated as follows:

$$\$55{,}000 = 0.10 \times \$550{,}000$$

## Case Study: Risk, Return, and Direct Capitalization Formula

Ideally, commercial real estate investors will have alternative properties to analyze and consider before selecting one to bid on and purchase. However, while many properties will look similar, their anticipated rates of return (OARs) and the risk associated with those returns will most certainly differ. Accordingly, investors must first determine their desired level of **risk** associated with their desired level of **return**. Risk and return normally move in the same direction.

The greater the anticipated risk associated with a monetary return, the greater the monetary return necessary to induce an investor to accept the risk.

Consider the following example, which is based on actual events. An investor has selected an area to invest in and decides he would like to purchase a freestanding building leased to a national drugstore chain. The lease must be a minimum of 20 years, with the tenant responsible for all expenses, including property taxes, insurance, structural repair, and maintenance. Therefore, the rent actually paid to the investor-landlord is net of all expenses, and the predictability of the periodic net rent payments is similar to a dividend or an annuity. The net rent payments are the investor's anticipated returns. The predictability of the rent payments addresses risk.

The combination of risk and return becomes an investment objective.

The investor finds two such properties to analyze and consider before selecting one to bid on and purchase. These two properties, Drugstores #1 and #2, are presented in Figure 2.4.

The investor desires the tenant occupying the property to pay a lease rate of a minimum of $25 per square foot, net of all expenses. The investor desires a high degree of certainty that the payment of rent will occur as promised within the lease. The higher the degree of certainty, the lower the degree of risk. And the lower the degree of risk, the lower the required return. The investor will accept returns as evidenced in the market (that is, the investor will accept a return consistent with the market's OAR).

**Figure 2.4**

Alternative Investment Locations

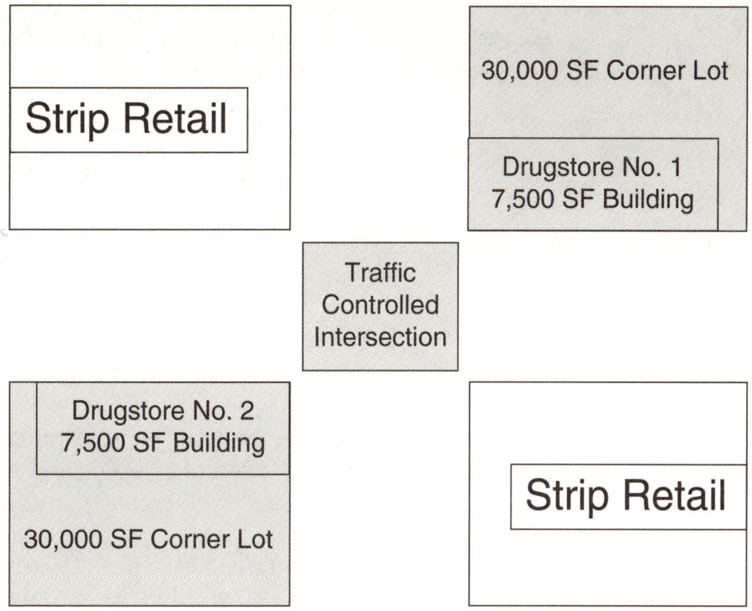


Both prospective tenants are national pharmacy drugstore chains. They are located on opposite and equally desirable corners of the main intersection in the area and are similar in every way. Both buildings are 7,500 square feet and located on 30,000-square-foot corner lots. Both investment properties have 20 years remaining on their leases with the tenants paying identical lease rates of $25 per square foot net of all expenses. Because the properties are the same size, their total rent payments are the same, $187,500 a year.

The investor learns that Drugstore #1 is wholly owned by a major U.S. corporation. This corporation has had a profitable business year, and its credit worthiness is rated AAA+ (excellent) by a national rating agency. Because the corporation guarantees the lease, the rent default risks associated with this lease are minimal. Based upon the review of a number of comparable sales of this drugstore chain within the investor's region, investors are willing to accept a return of 8 percent on current rent payments.

Upon further investigation, the investor finds that Drugstore #2 is also wholly owned by a major U.S. corporation. This corporation has had financial problems, and its creditworthiness has been rated BBB- (fair to poor) by a national credit rating agency. Because this corporation also guarantees the drugstore's lease, the rent default risk associated with this lease is considered greater than the risk associated with Drugstore #1. Based upon the review of a number of comparable sales of this drugstore chain within the investor's region, investors are willing to accept a return of 9.75 percent on current rent payments.

With this information, the investor prepares Figure 2.5.

Figure 2.5 summarizes the investment alternatives available to the investor. This investor prefers less risk and more safety. Therefore, the investor prefers the AAA+ credit-rated tenant and must accept the lower return of 8

**Figure 2.5**

Alternative Investments, OARs, and Price

| Description | Drugstore No. 1 | Drugstore No. 2 |
|---|---|---|
| Sq. Ft. Building | 7,500 | 7,500 |
| Rent Per Sq. Ft. | $25.00 | $25.00 |
| Annual Rent | $187,500 | $187,500 |
| Credit Rating | AAA+ | BBB– |
| Return Rates | 8.00% | 9.75% |
| Total Bid Price | $2,343,750 | $1,923,077 |
| Bid Price Sq. Ft. | $312.50 | 256.41 |

percent. This means that the investor can bid, or offer to pay, $2,343,750 for an annual rent stream of $187,000 and still receive an 8 percent return on the investment.

Because investing in Drugstore #1 would require $2,343,750, while investing in Drugstore #2 would require only $1,923,075, the investor must spend $420,673 more for the same income stream, given his risk-return preferences. This additional $420,675, shown in Figure 2.6, represents an *opportunity cost*, because these additional funds are no longer available for alternative investments.

Principal Deposited × Simple Interest Rate per Annum = Interest Income per Annum.

The real estate investor's analysis can be compared to that of someone considering opening a savings account. If the investor has $2,343,750 to deposit at the local bank and desires to put it into an account paying 8 percent simple interest per year, the investor would receive a total of $187,500 in interest at the end of one year, as shown by the following calculation using the IRV formula:

$$V \times R = I$$
$$\$2{,}343{,}750 \times 0.08 = \$187{,}500$$

In the case of our real estate investor, because he knew the amount of income he would receive and the rate of interest (the rate of return), he simply solved for the principal by the following calculation:

Interest Income per Annum ÷ Simple Interest Rate per Annum = Principal Deposited.

$$I \div R = V$$
$$\$187{,}500 \div 0.08 = \$2{,}343{,}750$$

**Figure 2.6**

Opportunity Cost—Unleveraged Basis

| Description | Equity |
|---|---|
| Drugstore No. 1—Unleveraged | $2,343,750 |
| *less:* | $1,923,075 |
| Drugstore No. 2—Unleveraged | $187,500 |
| *equals:* | |
| **Opportunity Cost—Unleveraged** | **$420,675** |

### *When the Rate Goes Up, the Value Goes Down*

How can an income stream of $187,500 have two different capitalized values? By employing two different capitalization rates. Why employ two different capitalization rates? Because each capitalization rate measures a different risk associated with the $187,500 return.

Given an income stream:

When the Rate (OAR) goes up, the Value goes down.

When the Rate (OAR) goes down, the Value goes up.

Consider our income stream of $187,500. When this income stream is capitalized employing an OAR of 8 percent, the value is $2,343,750. However, when this same income stream is capitalized employing an OAR of 9.75 percent, the value declines to $1,923,077. The income stream has not changed, but the risk associated with the income stream has changed.

## Deriving Capitalization Rates from Property Sales

As we have seen, capitalization rates contain a tremendous amount of information, assumptions, and expectations. As would be expected, the actual capitalization rate is determined by a host of property factors. Knowing those factors and circumstances assist an investor in ascertaining the market's perception of property by type, class, and risk, among other categories.

The preferred method of deriving capitalization rates is to look at similar properties. A real estate investment analyst, broker, or appraiser might refer to these properties as comparable to, and competitive with, the subject property. Essentially, examining the revenues, expenses, and income characteristics of these similar properties provides a solid basis for a real comparison and, as appropriate, adjustments to this information. The revenues, expenses, and income characteristics of these similar properties are provided by their operating statements.

Following is a summary of the minimum information required to determine if one property is really similar to another:

- Sales price
- Revenues, by component
- Expenses, by category
- Financing considerations, including loan-to-value ratio, term, and rate
- Motivations of the buyer and the seller to the transaction
- General market conditions at the time of sale
- Method by which net operating income is calculated

An experienced real estate analyst named Robert is always telling me, "You can never have enough information." The three sales and extracted OARs discussed earlier provide a good example of why more information is always better. As Figure 2.7 summarizes, Property A contains 10 apartments, Property B contains 18 apartments, and Property C contains 25 apartments. If we were considering the purchase of Property D, a 25-unit apartment building, we would probably focus on the comparable Property C, because it also has 25 apartments.

**Figure 2.7**

Analysis of Multifamily Apartment Transactions

| Property/Units | A/10 | B/18 | C/25 |
|---|---|---|---|
| Price | $550,000 | $990,000 | $1,478,125 |
| Net Operating Income | $55,000 | $108,000 | $137,500 |
| OAR | 10.00% | 10.91% | 9.30% |

If the NOI for Property D is $125,000, we could estimate its value and the price we might pay for it by employing the direct capitalization formula, as follows:

$$\text{Value} = \text{NOI} \div \text{OAR}$$
$$\$1{,}344{,}086 = \$125{,}000 \div 0.093$$

To summarize, based on the capitalization rates extracted from property sales, we might conclude that we could offer $1,345,000 (rounded) for the 25 units, or $53,800(rd) per unit, and still obtain a rate of return of 9.3 percent.

### *It Looks Like a Duck, and It Quacks Like a Duck, So Why Isn't It a Duck?*

What if the information presented above represented someone's interpretation of the information but not necessarily all of the information? Or what if the information presented above was really only a summary of the pertinent information? Or what if a sales price had been "adjusted" based on additional transaction costs that the buyer added in? Or what if certain operating expenses, say replacement reserves, had been omitted? Or what if each property was presented differently? If so, how would we know?

Figure 2.8 presents an expanded profit and loss statement analysis of the same three multifamily apartment transactions that first appeared in Figure 2.2 and were reintroduced in Figure 2.7. It would appear that my real estate analyst friend Robert was correct when he said, "You can never have enough information." Examining each of the three sales a bit closer will reveal some fundamental concerns regarding the information we receive when analyzing real estate transactions. As the expanded analysis of multifamily apartment transactions reveals, the information we received was not as consistent as first believed.

### *Analysis of the Ten-Unit, Multifamily Apartment Transaction*

This transaction represents our ten-unit, multifamily apartment building introduced in Chapter 1. The financial information pertaining to the sale of this property presented in Figure 2.8 is significantly more detailed than the same information presented in Figure 2.7. However, it is significantly less detailed than the same information presented in Figure 1.5. Employing the IRV formula and solving for rate (OAR) provides us with an extracted capitalization rate of 10 percent. Because this transaction incorporates all the financial information we require, the remaining multifamily apartment transactions should be presented on a comparable and consistent basis.

**Figure 2.8**

Expanded P&L Analysis of Multifamily Apartment Transactions

| Units | 10 | Per Unit | 18 | Per Unit | 25 | Per Unit |
|---|---|---|---|---|---|---|
| Sales Price | $550,000 | $55,000 | $990,000 | $55,000 | $1,375,000 | $55,000 |
| Transaction Costs | $- | $- | $- | $- | $103,125 | $4,125 |
| Adjusted Sales Price | $550,000 | $55,000 | $990,000 | $55,000 | $1,478,125 | $59,125 |
| | | | | | | |
| Potential Gross Income | $100,000 | $10,000 | $180,000 | $10,000 | $250,000 | $10,000 |
| V&C @ 5% | $5,000 | $500 | $9,000 | $500 | $12,500 | $500 |
| Effective Gross Income | $95,000 | $9,500 | $171,000 | $17,100 | $237,500 | $23,750 |
| Operating Expenses | | | | | | |
| Fixed Expenses | $12,750 | $1,275 | $22,950 | $1,275 | $31,875 | $1,275 |
| Variable Expenses | $22,250 | $2,225 | $40,050 | $2,225 | $55,625 | $2,225 |
| Replacement Reserves | $5,000 | $500 | $- | $- | $12,500 | $500 |
| | | | | | | |
| Total Operating Expenses | $40,000 | $4,000 | $63,000 | $3,500 | $100,000 | $4,000 |
| Net Operating Income | $55,000 | $5,500 | $108,000 | $6,000 | $137,500 | $5,500 |
| | | | | | | |
| **OAR** | **10.00%** | | **10.91%** | | **9.30%** | |

### *Analysis of the 18-Unit, Multifamily Apartment Transaction*

This transaction represents the sale of an 18-unit, multifamily apartment building. Taking the available information and restating it in the format with which we are comfortable reveals that the prospective seller and/or buyer did not consider replacement reserves in the financial information presented. Because we are considering replacement reserves as an operating expense, the relative expenses of these two transactions are not comparable. Specifically, this transaction has understated operating expenses and overstated net operating income, resulting in an overstated OAR.

### *Analysis of the 25-Unit, Multifamily Apartment Transaction*

This transaction represents the sale of a 25-unit, multifamily apartment building. Taking the available information and restating it in the format with which we are comfortable reveals that the buyer considered the transaction costs (for example, acquisition due diligence cost, brokerage fees, etc.) as part of the total acquisition price. Because we are not considering transaction costs as part of the purchase price, the relative adjusted sales prices of these two transactions are not comparable. Specifically, this transaction has an overstated sales price, resulting in an understated OAR.

For an investor to make use of the information presented, it would have to be adjusted to a comparable basis. If we adjusted the 18-unit building informa-

**Figure 2.9**

Restated P&L Analysis of Multifamily Apartment Transactions

| Units | 10 | Per Unit | 18 | Per Unit | 25 | Per Unit |
|---|---|---|---|---|---|---|
| Sales Price | $550,000 | $55,000 | $990,000 | $55,000 | $1,375,000 | $55,000 |
| Transaction Costs | $- | $- | $- | $- | $- | $- |
| Adjusted Sales Price | $550,000 | $55,000 | $990,000 | $55,000 | $1,375,000 | $55,000 |
| Potential Gross Income | $100,000 | $10,000 | $180,000 | $10,000 | $250,000 | $10,000 |
| V&C @ 5% | $5,000 | $500 | $9,000 | $500 | $12,500 | $500 |
| Effective Gross Income | $95,000 | $9,500 | $171,000 | $17,100 | $237,500 | $23,750 |
| Operating Expenses | | | | | | |
| Fixed Expenses | $12,750 | $1,275 | $22,950 | $1,275 | $31,875 | $1,275 |
| Variable Expenses | $22,250 | $2,225 | $40,050 | $2,225 | $55,625 | $2,225 |
| Replacement Reserves | $5,000 | $500 | $9,000 | $500 | $12,500 | $500 |
| Total Operating Expenses | $40,000 | $4,000 | $72,000 | $4,000 | $100,000 | $4,000 |
| Net Operating Income | $55,000 | $5,500 | $99,000 | $5,500 | $137,500 | $5,500 |
| **OAR** | **10.00%** | | **10.00%** | | **10.00%** | |

tion for reserves, and the 25-unit building for transaction costs, the restated apartment transactions would be presented as shown in Figure 2.9.

After the adjustments, the restated multifamily apartment transactions have adjusted OARs of 10 percent each. This is important, because in our earlier analysis of Property D, we applied the most "comparable" property's capitalization rate of 9.3 percent, resulting in a capitalized value of $1,344,086 or $53,763 per unit, determined as follows:

Value = NOI ÷ OAR
$1,344,086 = $125,000 ÷ 0.093

However, because our adjusted capitalization rate is 10 percent, our capitalized value of the $125,000 income stream of Property D would be $1,250,000 or $50,000 per unit, determined as follows:

Value = NOI ÷ OAR
$1,250,000 = $125,000 ÷ 0.10

The difference between these two values is significant.

**Figure 2.10**

Seller's Pricing Matrix

| Income | Divided By | Cap Rate | Equals | Price Rounded |
|---|---|---|---|---|
| $125,000 | / | 9.00% | = | $1,389,000 |
| $250,000 | / | 9.00% | = | $2,778,000 |
| $375,000 | / | 9.00% | = | $4,167,000 |
| $500,000 | / | 9.00% | = | $5,556,000 |
| $750,000 | / | 9.00% | = | $8,333,000 |
| $2,000,000 | / | 9.00% | = | $22,223,000 |

Consider the following example. Let's say a buyer and seller are negotiating the acquisition of various income-producing properties to be sold as a portfolio. They prepare a reconstructed profit and loss statement for each property and agree on the revenues, expenses, and income. They prepare a completely error-free and realistic P&L for each property but use an inappropriate or biased cap rate to convert income into price or value. Both the properties and portfolio would be either overpriced or underpriced and would not represent true market value.

The seller wants to "sell high" and uses a 9 percent cap rate to convert income into value. The seller wants to sell the $2,000,000 portfolio income stream on a 9 percent cap basis, which comes to a price of $22,223,000. She prepares Figure 2.10, a pricing matrix.

The buyer wants to "buy low" and uses a 10 percent cap rate to convert income into value. The buyer desires to acquire the $2,000,000 portfolio income stream on a 10 percent cap basis, which comes to a price of $20,000,000. He prepares the pricing matrix in Figure 2.11.

Comparing the prices desired by the seller and buyer, as shown in Figure 2.12, reveals how powerfully a small change in capitalization rates can impact value.

Each 1 percent change in the Cap Rate will cause a 10 percent change in Price or Value.

Comparing the seller's and buyer's pricing models reveals that a 1 percent change in the cap rate will cause a 10 percent change in price or value.

**Figure 2.11**

Buyer's Pricing Matrix

| Income | Divided By | Cap Rate | Equals | Price Rounded |
|---|---|---|---|---|
| $125,000 | / | 10.00% | = | $1,250,000 |
| $250,000 | / | 10.00% | = | $2,500,000 |
| $375,000 | / | 10.00% | = | $3,750,000 |
| $500,000 | / | 10.00% | = | $5,000,000 |
| $750,000 | / | 10.00% | = | $7,500,000 |
| $2,000,000 | / | 10.00% | = | $20,000,000 |

**Figure 2.12**

Pricing Difference Based on 1 Percent Change in Cap Rate

| Income | @ 9%Cap | @ 10%Cap | $ Change % | Change $ |
|---|---|---|---|---|
| $125,000 | $1,389,000 | $1,250,000 | 10.0% | $139,000 |
| $250,000 | $2,778,000 | $2,500,000 | 10.0% | $278,000 |
| $375,000 | $4,167,000 | $3,750,000 | 10.0% | $417,000 |
| $500,000 | $5,556,000 | $5,000,000 | 10.0% | $556,000 |
| $750,000 | $8,333,000 | $7,500,000 | 10.0% | $833,000 |
| $2,000,000 | $22,223,000 | $20,000,000 | 10.0% | $2,223,000 |

## Deriving Capitalization Rates from Other Sources

Today in the "information age," many credible sources are available for acquiring current information about capitalization rates. Published reports are available from varied local, regional, and national appraisal, brokerage, and market research firms as well as national trade organizations. These reports range from general to highly specialized and are offered on either a free or fee basis. Also, vast resources are available on the Internet. Regardless of the source, it is not only important to obtain creditable capitalization rates but also to obtain credible supporting information, which provides insight into the market trends affecting the direction of these capitalization rates. These sources include:

- Commercial investment property listings, including "asking" capitalization rates
- Brokerage, appraisal, valuation, and market research firm directories
- Investment counseling firm directories
- Financing firm directories
- National and regional real estate investor surveys
- Real estate investor Web sites
- National and regional geographic overviews
- News on international, national, and regional economic issues
- News on international, national, and regional capital markets issues
- International, national, and regional market overviews by property type
- Capitalization rates for institutional and noninstitutional property types
- Quarterly surveys, semiannual surveys, and annual surveys

An abundance of information is available for real estate investors to support their decision-making processes. Selection of the "best" sources of information is a personal decision, but a source's track record and references are an important consideration.

## Case Study: Direct Capitalization of the Current Year's Income

We can now capitalize the current year's reconstructed operating statement, shown again in Figure 2.13, for our property.

**Figure 2.13**

Current Year's Reconstructed Operating Statement

**Ten-Unit Apartment Building—Income and Expense Analysis**

| | |
|---|---|
| Units | 10 |
| Living Area Square Feet | 10,500 |

| *Period* | *Current Year* | | | |
|---|---|---|---|---|
| **REVENUES** | | | | |
| Category | Amount | Amount per Unit | Amount per SF | % Total PGI |
| Scheduled Base Rent | $96,900 | $9,690 | $9.23 | 96.90% |
| **Market Rent for Vacant Units** | $2,500 | $250 | $0.24 | 2.50% |
| ***Subtotal: Adjusted Base Rent*** | $99,400 | $9,940 | $9.47 | 99.40% |
| **Other Income** | | | | |
| Laundry | $600 | $60 | $0.06 | 0.60% |
| ***Subtotal: Other Income*** | $600 | $60 | $0.06 | 0.60% |
| **Potential Gross Income @ 100% Occupancy** | $100,000 | $10,000 | $9.52 | 100.00% |
| **Vacancy and Collection Loss @ 5%PGI** | $5,000 | $500 | $0.48 | 5.00% |
| **Effective Gross Income** | $95,000 | $9,500 | $9.05 | 95.00% |
| **EXPENSES** | | | | |
| **Operating Expenses** | | | | |
| *Fixed* | Amount | Amount per Unit | Amount per SF | % Total EGI |
| Real Estate Taxes | $11,000 | $1,100 | $1.05 | 11.58% |
| Insurance | $1,750 | $175 | $0.17 | 1.84% |
| ***Subtotal Fixed*** | $12,750 | 1,275 | $1.21 | 13.42% |
| *Variable* | | | | |
| Management Fee @ 4% EGI | $3,800 | $380 | $0.36 | 4.00% |
| Advertising and Promotion | $825 | $83 | $0.08 | 0.87% |
| Telephone | $900 | $90 | $0.09 | 0.95% |
| Utilities (Water, Sewer, Electric) | $1,600 | $160 | $0.15 | 1.68% |
| Trash Removal | $1,000 | $100 | $0.01 | 1.05% |
| Repairs, Maintenance, and Supplies | $11,000 | $1,100 | $1.05 | 11.58% |
| Unit Interior Redecorating | $1,475 | $148 | $0.14 | 1.55% |
| Landscape, Lawn, and Grounds | $1,200 | $120 | $0.11 | 1.26% |
| Pest Control | $450 | $45 | $0.04 | 0.47% |
| ***Subtotal Variable*** | $22,250 | $2,225 | $2.12 | 23.42% |
| ***Replacement Reserves*** | | | | |
| ***Subtotal Replacement Reserves*** | $5,000 | $500 | $0.48 | 5.26% |
| **Total Operating Expenses** | $40,000 | $4,000 | $3.81 | 42.11% |
| **OPERATING INCOME** | | | | |
| **Net Operating Income** | $55,000 | $5,500 | $5.24 | 57.89% |

Based upon the reconstructed operating statement presented in Figure 2.13, the net operating income for the property is $55,000. Based on the analysis of multifamily apartment transactions presented, a stabilized OAR for the income stream of $55,000 is 10 percent. We now know the I and the R required for direct capitalization of income into value:

$$\$550{,}000 \text{ Value (V)} = \frac{\text{Net Operating Income (I) } \$55{,}000}{\text{Overall Capitalization Rate (R) } 0.10}$$

Based on our analysis of the property, we could pay $550,000 for the ten units and expect to receive a 10 percent return on our investment. Thus, our prospective purchase price is $55,000 per unit.

### *Test of Reasonableness*

Two ways to test the reasonableness of our conclusion are as follows:

1. Obtain current or recent sales transactions for similar multifamily properties and compare these transaction prices to our purchase price. The OAR and price per unit should be relatively similar.
2. Obtain current or recent offers for sale of similar multifamily properties and compare these offers to our purchase price. The OAR should be relatively lower, and price per unit of the properties offered for sale should be relatively higher.

## Case Study: Direct Capitalization of Forecasted Income

Let's say we are considering the acquisition of the same ten-unit property described above. Everything about the property, including its current year's revenues, expenses, and net operating income remain the same. As discussed in Chapter 1, we are evaluating the property as of December 31 of the current year. Therefore, our reconstructed P&L will be for the current year and result in a current year's presentation of revenues, expenses, and income.

Because we are reconstructing the current year, we do not receive all the requested and required information to complete our analysis of this property until, say, March of the next year. The seller receives our offer of $550,000 to purchase the property. The seller reviews the offer and tells us that $550,000 would be agreeable if we were buying it last year, but because it is now a new year and income is increasing, the seller wants a price based on the forecasted performance of the property during the new year. The seller is correct.

Figure 2.14 shows a current year's reconstructed and future year's forecast of revenue, expenses, and income for the subject property.

Forecasting anticipated revenues, expenses, and operating income is as much an art as a science. As we proceed from one-year forecasts to multiple-year forecasts, we proceed from the realm of direct capitalization to yield capitalization. Yield capitalization is discussed at length in Chapter 3. Suffice it to say at this point that multiple years' forecasted projections are a very important component in determining an offering price for a property.

**Figure 2.14**

Current Year's Reconstructed and Following Year's Forecasted Operating Statement

**Ten-Unit Apartment Building—Income and Expense Analysis**

| | |
|---|---|
| Units | 10 |
| Living Area Square Feet | 10,500 |

| *Period* | *Current Year 2004* | | | | *Forecast 2005* | | | | *Forecast 2006* | | | |
|---|---|---|---|---|---|---|---|---|---|---|---|---|
| **REVENUES** | | | | | | | | | | | | |
| Category | Amount | Amount per Unit | Amount per SF | % Total PGI | Amount | Amount per Unit | Amount per SF | % Total PGI | Amount | Amount per Unit | Amount per SF | % Total PGI |
| Scheduled Base Rent | $99,400 | $9,940 | $9.47 | 99.40% | $102,382 | $10,238 | $9.75 | 99.39% | $107,245 | $10,725 | $10.21 | 99.36% |
| **Market Rent for Vacant Units** | $- | $- | $- | 0.00% | $- | $- | $- | 0.00% | $- | $- | $- | 0.00% |
| ***Subtotal: Adjusted Base Rent*** | $99,400 | $9,940 | $9.47 | 99.40% | $102,382 | $10,238 | $9.75 | 99.39% | $107,245 | $10,725 | $10.21 | 99.36% |
| **Other Income** | | | | | | | | | | | | |
| Laundry | $600 | $60 | $0.06 | 0.60% | $630 | $63 | $0.06 | 0.61% | $690 | $69 | $0.07 | 0.64% |
| ***Subtotal: Other Income*** | $600 | $60 | $0.06 | 0.60% | $630 | $63 | $0.06 | 0.61% | $690 | $69 | $0.07 | 0.64% |
| **Potential Gross Income @ 100% Occupancy** | $100,000 | $10,000 | $9.52 | 100.00% | $103,012 | $10,301 | $9.81 | 100.00% | $107,935 | $10,793 | $10.28 | 100.00% |
| **Vacancy and Collection Loss @ 5%PGI** | $5,000 | $500 | $0.48 | 5.00% | $5,151 | $515 | $0.49 | 5.00% | $5,397 | $540 | $0.51 | 5.00% |
| **Effective Gross Income** | $95,000 | $9,500 | $9.05 | 95.00% | $97,861 | $9,786 | $9.32 | 95.00% | $102,538 | $10,254 | $9.77 | 95.00% |
| **EXPENSES** | | | | | | | | | | | | |
| **Operating Expenses** | | | | | | | | | | | | |
| *Fixed* | Amount | Amount per Unit | Amount per SF | % Total PGI | Amount | Amount per Unit | Amount per SF | % Total PGI | Amount | Amount per Unit | Amount per SF | % Total PGI |
| Real Estate Taxes | $11,000 | $1,100 | $1.05 | 11.58% | $11,000 | $1,100 | $1.05 | 11.24% | $11,165 | $1,117 | $1.06 | 10.89% |
| Insurance | $1,750 | $175 | $0.17 | 1.84% | $1,750 | $175 | $0.17 | 1.79% | $1,500 | $150 | $0.14 | 1.46% |
| ***Subtotal Fixed*** | $12,750 | 1,275 | $1.21 | 13.42% | $12,750 | 1,275 | $1.21 | 13.03% | $12,665 | 1,267 | $1.21 | 12.35% |
| *Variable* | | | | | | | | | | | | |
| Management Fee @ 4% EGI | $3,800 | $380 | $0.36 | 4.00% | $3,914 | $391 | $0.37 | 4.00% | $4,102 | $410 | $0.39 | 4.00% |
| Advertising and Promotion | $825 | $83 | $0.08 | 0.87% | $800 | $80 | $0.08 | 0.82% | $700 | $70 | $0.07 | 0.68% |
| Telephone | $900 | $90 | $0.09 | 0.95% | $900 | $90 | $0.09 | 0.92% | $800 | $80 | $0.08 | 0.78% |
| Utilities (Water, Sewer, Electric) | $1,600 | $160 | $0.15 | 1.68% | $1,600 | $160 | $0.15 | 1.63% | $1,575 | $158 | $0.15 | 1.54% |
| Trash Removal | $1,000 | $100 | $0.01 | 1.05% | $1,000 | $100 | $0.10 | 1.02% | $1,030 | $103 | $0.10 | 1.00% |
| Repairs, Maintenance, and Supplies | $11,000 | $1,100 | $1.05 | 11.58% | $11,000 | $1,100 | $1.05 | 11.24% | $10,000 | $1,000 | $0.95 | 9.75% |
| Unit Interior Redecorating | $1,475 | $148 | $0.14 | 1.55% | $1,425 | $143 | $0.14 | 1.46% | $1,275 | $128 | $0.12 | 1.24% |
| Landscape, Lawn, and Grounds | $1,200 | $120 | $0.11 | 1.26% | $1,200 | $120 | $0.11 | 1.23% | $1,250 | $125 | $0.12 | 1.22% |
| Pest Control | $450 | $45 | $0.04 | 0.47% | $450 | $45 | $0.04 | 0.46% | $400 | $40 | $0.04 | 0.39% |
| ***Subtotal Variable*** | $22,250 | $2,225 | $2.12 | 23.42% | $22,289 | $2,229 | $2.12 | 22.78% | $21,132 | $2,113 | $2.01 | 20.61% |
| ***Replacement Reserves*** | | | | | | | | | | | | |
| ***Subtotal Replacement Reserves*** | $5,000 | $500 | $0.48 | 5.26% | $5,000 | $500 | $0.48 | 5.11% | $5,000 | $500 | $0.48 | 4.88% |
| **Total Operating Expenses** | $40,000 | $4,000 | $3.81 | 42.11% | $40,039 | $4,004 | $3.81 | 40.91% | $38,797 | $3,880 | $3.69 | 37.84% |
| **OPERATING INCOME** | | | | | | | | | | | | |
| **Net Operating Income** | $55,000 | $5,500 | $5.24 | 57.89% | $57,822 | $5,782 | $5.51 | 59.09% | $63,742 | $6,374 | $6.07 | 62.16% |

### Analysis of the Current Year as Compared to the Forecast Year 2005

Based on the information in Figure 2.14, potential gross income (PGI) is anticipated to increase from $100,000 to $103,012, or a one-year increase of 3.01 percent. This percentage relationship is also the same for estimated gross income (EGI). Total operating expenses are anticipated to increase from $40,000 to $40,039, a one-year increase of only 0.10 percent. These changes in the patterns of revenues and expenses have the effect of increasing NOI from $55,000 to $57,822, a one-year increase of 5.13 percent. Accordingly, by stabilizing expenses and increasing revenues, the NOI increases by a significant percentage.

### Direct Capitalization of the Forecast Year's Income

If we were satisfied that the underlying forecast was credible and supported by evidence extracted from the market, and if we were also satisfied that a direct capitalization rate of 10 percent would be appropriate for this income stream, then we would capitalize the forecasted income stream into value and ascertain that our offer price for our ten-unit property would be $578,220, calculated as follows:

$$\$578{,}220 \text{ Value (V)} = \frac{\text{Net Operating Income (I) } \$57{,}822}{\text{Overall Capitalization Rate (R) } 0.10}$$

Based on our analysis of the property, we could pay $578,220 for the ten units, or $57,822 per unit, and expect to receive a 10 percent return on our investment.

### Analysis of Next Forecast Year 2005 as Compared to Future Forecast Year 2006

PGI is anticipated to increase from $103,012 to $107,935, a one-year increase of 4.78 percent. This percentage relationship is the same for EGI. Total operating expenses are anticipated to decrease from $40,039 to $38,797, a one-year decrease of 3.10 percent. These changes in the patterns of revenues and expenses cause NOI to increase from $57,822 to $63,742, a one-year increase of 10.24 percent. Accordingly, reducing expenses and increasing revenues causes the NOI to increase dramatically.

### Direct Capitalization of the Future Forecast Year's Income

If we were satisfied that the underlying forecast was credible and supported by evidence extracted from the market, and if we were also satisfied that a direct capitalization rate of 10 percent would be appropriate for this income stream, then we would capitalize the forecasted income stream into value and ascertain that our offer price for our ten-unit property would be $637,420, calculated as follows:

$$\$637{,}420 \text{ Value (V)} = \frac{\text{Net Operating Income (I) } \$63{,}742}{\text{Overall Capitalization Rate (R) } 0.10}$$

Based on our analysis of the property, we could pay $637,420 for the ten units, or $63,742 per unit, and expect to receive a 10 percent return on our investment.

Real estate investments consist of historical and current years' revenues, expenses, and operating income patterns as well as future years' revenues, expenses, and operating income patterns. The difference between historical and forecasted future performance of real estate assets can be significant. Investors pay a price today for the right to receive all of the anticipated future economic benefits of ownership. In evaluating what rate of return they should select to capitalize income into value, investors in the marketplace consider the various risks associated with their expected financial returns.

## Economic, Market, and Property-Related Risk

Capitalization is the process of converting income into value. Today's property value always represents the present value of anticipated future economic benefits. Although investors would like all forecasted future events to occur, they know that forecasts are rarely perfect. However, the better they are at preparing forecasts, the higher the likelihood that the forecasted results will occur, and the lower their risk will be.

All real estate investments have some degree of risk. Risk is the probability that anticipated events will not occur. Stated differently, risk is the probability that what we expect to happen during a real estate investment does not happen. Investors demand that as an investment's risk increases, so should the investment's return. Different conditions cause risk to enter a real estate investment:

- *Economic conditions.* For example, the general economy may move into a recession, or increasing interest rates may affect the investment performance or the ability to buy or sell a property.
- *Market conditions.* For example, an unexpected increase in the competitive supply of new properties in the surrounding market area may affect the investment's performance or the ability to buy or sell a property.
- *Property condition.* For example, a property suffering from underfunded repairs and maintenance or neglected capital replacements will eventually result in a loss of building desirability, occupancy, revenues, and value. The resultant costs to correct these problems will affect either the investment's performance or the investor's ability to buy or sell the property.
- *Management conditions.* For example, poor strategic planning, the inability to implement a management plan, or the inability to put management controls in place may affect investment performance or the ability to buy or sell a property.

Economic, market, and property-related risks are important factors in market analysis. The higher the likelihood that the forecasted events will not occur, the higher the perceived uncertainty associated with that forecast. **Uncertainty** is the probability that unforeseen events will occur. Stated differently, uncertainty is the probability that what we do not expect to happen during a real estate investment happens after all.

Ideally, commercial real estate investors analyze and consider alternative properties before selecting one to bid on and purchase. However, while many properties look similar, their anticipated rates of return, and the risk associated with those returns, most certainly differ. Accordingly, investors must first determine their desired level of risk associated with their desired level of return. Remember: Risk and return normally move in the same direction.

## Summary

Capitalization is the conversion of income into value. Of the various capitalization methods and techniques, the most well-known among real estate investors are direct capitalization and yield capitalization. Direct capitalization is a method used to convert an estimate of single year's expected income into an indicator of value in one direct step, hence, the term "direct" capitalization. Direct capitalization converts income into value either by dividing the estimated income by a rate or by multiplying the estimated income by an appropriate factor. The most widely recognized direct capitalization technique is dividing the estimated income by a rate.

Whereas information pertaining to capitalization rates abounds, finding the correct capitalization rate is another issue entirely. Few terms are as simple yet as misunderstood as direct capitalization rates, or "cap rates" as they are often called. While the cap rate implicitly contains an acceptable rate of return on capital and a satisfactory rate of recovery of invested capital, it does not clearly differentiate between the return on capital and the return of capital.

The OAR contains the rate of return on the investment as well as the rate of return of the investment. The OAR implicitly contains an acceptable rate of return on capital and a satisfactory rate of recovery of invested capital. Because it encompasses both without clearly differentiating between the return on capital and the return of capital, it is an overall rate. All cap rates are not alike. Cap rates may be differentiated as "as is," "stabilized," or "reversionary" cap rates. When discussing any cap rate, we need to know from whose perspective we are considering it. Are we considering the cap rates from a seller's, buyer's, lender's, or market perspective?

One of the simplest and most powerful valuation formulas is the IRV formula. The formula is so simple, it is deceiving. If you understand the IRV formula, you are well on your way to understanding direct capitalization. The IRV formula and the direct capitalization formula employ the same methodology. The direct capitalization formula is sometimes referred to as IRV, IRV the Investor, or IRV the Appraiser.

The preferred method of deriving capitalization rates is to work from similar properties. Examining the revenues, expenses, and income characteristics of similar properties provides a concrete basis for a real comparison and, as appropriate, adjustments to this information. The revenues, expenses, and income characteristics of similar properties are provided by the operating statement.

Today in the "information age," many credible sources of current information about capitalization rates are available. Regardless of the source, credible capitalization rates and supportive information about trends, patterns, and direction of capitalization rates are critical data for any property we are considering. A small change in the capitalization rate can significantly affect the property's value.

Forecasting anticipated revenues, expenses, and operating income is as much an art as a science. As we proceed from one-year forecasts to multiple-year forecasts, we proceed from the realm of direct capitalization to yield capitalization. Multiple years of projections are very important to determine an offering price for a property.

While probably not all forecasted events will occur, the investor hopes that most forecasted events will take place. The higher the likelihood that forecasted results will occur, the lower the perceived risk associated with the forecast. Similarly, the higher the likelihood that the forecasted events will not occur, the higher the perceived uncertainty. Economic, market, and property-related risks are important factors addressed in market analysis.

Ideally, commercial real estate investors analyze and consider alternative properties before selecting one to bid on and purchase. However, while many properties will look similar, their anticipated rates of return (OARs), and the risk associated with those returns, will most certainly differ. Accordingly, investors must first determine their desired level of risk associated with their desired level of return. Risk and return normally move in the same direction.

For a real estate investor, the greater the anticipated risk associated with a monetary return, the greater the return necessary to induce an investor to accept the risk. The combination of risk and return that the investor selects becomes part of the investor's investment objectives.

## Review Questions

1. Capitalization
   a. is the conversion of value into income.
   b. is the reversion of value into income.
   c. is the conversion of income into value.
   d. is the reversion of income into value.

2. Direct capitalization
   a. converts one year's income to value.
   b. is also referred to as "direct cap."
   c. employs rates and factors.
   d. does all of the above.

3. Capitalization rates are also known as
   a. cap rates.
   b. OARs.
   c. Ros.
   d. all of the above.

4. The IRV formula may be stated as
   a. Income equals Rate multiplied by Value.
   b. Rate equals Income divided by Value.
   c. Value equals Income divided by Rate.
   d. all of the above.

5. Which of these statements about risk is *TRUE?*
   a. The greater the risk, the greater the return necessary to induce investment.
   b. The greater the risk, the lower the return necessary to induce investment.
   c. The lower the risk, the greater the return necessary to induce investment.
   d. The greater the risk, the greater the safety of the investment.

6. Which of these statements about the OAR is *TRUE?*
   a. The greater the risk, the higher the OAR necessary to induce investment.
   b. The greater the risk, the lower the OAR necessary to induce investment.
   c. The lower the risk, the greater the OAR necessary to induce investment.
   d. The greater the risk, the greater the safety of the OAR.

7. Generally speaking,
   a. when the cap rate goes up, the value goes down.
   b. when the value goes down, the cap rate goes up.
   c. the greater the risk, the higher the OAR necessary to induce investment.
   d. all of the above are true.

8. Capitalization rates can be derived from
   a. property sales.
   b. property listings.
   c. surveys.
   d. all of the above.

9. Direct capitalization of the current year's income is
   a. usually based on a reconstructed "as is" operating statement.
   b. oriented toward the future anticipated value, not the current value.
   c. usually based on a forecasted operating statement.
   d. oriented toward the past performance, not the current performance, of the property.

10. Direct capitalization of forecasted income is
    a. usually based on a forecasted pro forma operating statement.
    b. oriented toward the present anticipated value, not the future value.
    c. usually based on a reconstructed "as is" operating statement.
    d. oriented toward the past performance, not the current performance, of the property.

### *Case Study of Income and Capitalization Rates*

The following case study provides information to answer questions 11 through 15.

**Property summary.** We are considering the purchase of a two-story rental apartment building containing 20 rental units. The property features a walk-up covered porch area located along the north side of the building. Double entry doors open to a wide interior corridor. Five rental apartment units are located on each side of the corridor, with ten units per floor. The rear of the property features a covered porch area along the south side of the building, which has been renovated into an enclosed laundry facility. Four washers, four dryers, and a soap vending machine all operate on separate "laundry room" electric and water meters. A service company pays the property owner a flat fee of $150 per month for the right to operate at the property and has installed the washers, dryers, and vending machine. The owner receives this amount net of all expenses and has no obligations whatsoever for the utility expenses, maintenance, and repairs of this equipment.

**Figure 2.15**

Case Study: Reconstructed Operating Statement

| Reconstructed Operating Statement | PGI | Total | Per Unit |
|---|---|---|---|
| Base Rents/Potential Gross Income | | $253,920 | $12,696 |
| *less:* | | | |
| Vacancy and Collection Loss @ | 25% | $(63,480) | $(3,174) |
| *equals:* | | | |
| Subtotal | | $190,440 | $9,522 |
| *less:* | | | |
| Rental Concessions @ | 20% | $(38,088) | $(1,904) |
| *equals:* | | | |
| Subtotal | | $152,352 | $7,618 |
| *add:* | | | |
| Other Income | | $2,400 | $120 |
| *equals:* | | | |
| Effective Gross Income | EGI | $154,752 | $7,738 |
| *less:* | | | |
| Total Operating Expenses | 44% | $(67,810) | $(3,391) |
| *equals:* | | | |
| Net Operating Income | 56% | $86,942 | $4,347 |

The ground floor interior corridor has two staircases leading to the second floor. There is a staircase/exit on the east and west side of the corridor; each located approximately midway along the corridor. The exits lead to side entryways/exits. Each of the staircases/exits can accommodate a vending machine. One staircase/exit area has a soda/juice/water vending machine. The other staircase/exit area has a snack food vending machine. A service company pays the property owner a flat fee of $50 per month for the right to operate at the property and has installed the vending machines. The owner receives this amount net of all expenses and has no obligations for the utility expenses, maintenance, and repairs of this equipment.

**Reconstructed profit and loss statement.** Based on the information provided, we prepare the following current year's reconstructed operating statement, shown in Figure 2.15.

Information used in our current year's reconstructed operating statement is presented in the following sections.

**Unit mix and unit revenues.** There are 20 rental apartments, consisting of studio units, one-bedroom units, and two-bedroom units. The unit sizes are considered comparable to others in the market area. Based on the unit mix, there is a total of 20,000 square feet of "livable" (air-conditioned) square footage. Base rent from unit rentals comes to $253,920.

Demand for rentals in this market area is very strong with 5 percent per year rent increases the norm. Accordingly, next year's rental unit income is forecast to escalate by 5 percent.

**Other income.** As mentioned, a service company currently pays the property owner a flat fee of $150 per month for the right to operate washers, dryers, and a soap vending machine. Additionally, the property owner is paid a flat fee of $50 per month for the right to operate food and beverage vending machines. Based on the service contract between the vendor and property owner, the vendor has the right to maintain these vending machines at the property on an annual basis, subject to an annual increase to the monthly fees to the property owner of 10 percent per annum.

The owner receives these amounts net of all expenses and has no obligations whatsoever for the utility expenses, maintenance, and repairs of this equipment. The total current year's other income amounts to $200 per month or $2,400 per year. This other income is neither variable nor subject to vacancy and collection losses.

**Vacancy and collection losses.** Vacancy and collection losses for the property have historically averaged 5 percent of EGI. However, the current year's vacancy and collection losses are running at about 25 percent. This is due to a city public works "upgrade and beautification" project that has closed off the street to through-traffic. The "upgrade" part of the project calls for the installation of new water and sewer lines and street asphalt paving. The "beautification" part of the project calls for improved street lighting and landscaping. The project commenced at the beginning of this year and will be completed by the end of this year.

**Rental concession program.** To maintain occupancy during the project's construction, the owner has put in place a temporary rental concession program whereby all tenants' rents are discounted by 20 percent per month. This concession program commenced at the beginning of this year and will conclude at the end of the year, when the upgrade and beautification project is complete. The current owner has a waiting list of prospective tenants who are ready, willing, and able to take occupancy as soon as the work is completed. Accordingly, next year's occupancy is expected to rise to 100 percent, before vacancy and collection loss considerations.

**Operating expenses.** All operating expenses for the property are quoted on an annual basis. The operating expenses are quoted on a total dollar and per unit basis, with the exception of management fees, which are quoted on the basis of 4 percent of EGI. The following assumptions are in place:

- All fixed expenses are increasing at an average of 2 percent per year.
- All variable expenses, other than management fees, are increasing at an average of 3 percent per year.
- The reserves expense will remain unchanged.

**Figure 2.16**

Case Study: Summary of the Current Year's Operating Expenses

| Current Year Operating Expense | Total per Annum | Total per Unit/Annum |
|---|---|---|
| *Fixed Expenses* | | |
| Real Estate Taxes: | $22,000 | $1,100 |
| Insurance: | $4,000 | $200 |
| *Variable Expenses* | | |
| Management Fees: | $6,190 | $310 |
| Advertising and Promotion: | $1,400 | $70 |
| Telephone: | $1,500 | $75 |
| Utilities: | $2,320 | $116 |
| Trash: | $2,000 | $100 |
| Repairs and Maintenance: | $16,000 | $800 |
| Unit Interior Redecorating: | $2,000 | $100 |
| Landscape, Lawn, and Grounds: | $2,400 | $120 |
| Pest Control: | $1,000 | $50 |
| *Replacement Reserves* | | |
| Reserves: | $7,000 | $350 |
| **Total Operating Expenses** | **$67,810** | **$3,391** |

Figure 2.16 shows a summary of the property's operating expenses.

Based upon the preceding case study information, answer questions 11 through 15.

**11.** Using the IRV formula, what is the current year's price or value if income is capitalized at 9 percent?

**a.** $2,821,333

**b.** $1,719,466

**c.** $966,022

**d.** $753,444

**12.** Using the IRV formula, what is the current year's price or value if income is capitalized at 10 percent?

**a.** $2,539,200

**b.** $1,547,520

**c.** $869,420

**d.** $678,100

13. Comparing your answers from questions 11 and 12, what conclusions can be drawn about cap rates?
    a. Given a particular NOI, a 1 percent increase in a cap rate will result in a 10 percent decrease in price or value.
    b. Given a particular NOI, an increase in a cap rate will result in a decrease in price or value.
    c. Given a particular NOI, a decrease in a cap rate will result in an increase in price or value.
    d. All of the above are true.

14. Using the information contained within the case study, prepare a one-year pro forma operating statement based on next year's anticipated revenues, expenses, and income. What is the pro forma NOI?
    a. $92,289
    b. $182,690
    c. $82,690
    d. $192,289

15. Using your answer from question 14, if pro forma income is capitalized at 8.5 percent, what is the forecast year's price or value?
    a. $1,085,750
    b. $2,149,295
    c. $972,825
    d. $2,262,225

chapter three

# VALUING COMMERCIAL REAL ESTATE VIA YIELD CAPITALIZATION

3

## Key Terminology

- Annuity
- Annuity Capitalization
- Basis Point
- Capital Recapture
- Discounted Cash Flow Analysis (DCFA)
- Future Value
- Future Value of a Dollar
- Future Value of an Annuity
- Internal Rate of Return (IRR)
- Net Present Value (NPV)
- Present Value
- Present Value of a Dollar
- Present Value of an Annuity
- Projection Period
- Property Forecast
- Reversion
- Time Value of Money
- Yield Rates
- Yield Capitalization

## Overview

In this chapter, the second of the two methods of capitalization is discussed, emphasizing the importance of yield capitalization as a credible method of estimating value. The benefits and burdens of this complex valuation method are described. The important concept of the time value of money is introduced. The present and future value interest factors, of both a dollar and of an annuity, are explained. Variations of the formulas and their applications are presented in great detail. The concepts of time and its relationship to yield capitalization are discussed.

As we explore the process of yield capitalization, numerous new terms are introduced, and the importance of applying advanced financial and investment analysis skills becomes apparent. Multistep calculations for determining the discounted present value of future projected cash flows and projected net sales proceeds from a property sale are introduced. The ability to apply various combinations of yield and reversion rates to a reconstructed or forecasted operating statement as a tool for investing is emphasized as fundamental to the decision-making process.

## Learning Objectives

After completing this chapter, you should be able to accomplish the following:

- Define yield capitalization
- List the four broad areas of consideration of yield capitalization
- Discuss projection periods
- Explain why forecasting is such an important consideration in yield capitalization
- Differentiate between reversion, gross sales proceeds, and net sale proceeds as they apply to yield capitalization
- Discuss the relationship between yield rates and reversionary rates
- Explain the concept of time value of money
- Describe the relationship between the present and future value of a dollar
- Discuss the relationship between the present and future value of an annuity
- Explain the process of discounted cash flow analysis

## Yield Capitalization—An Overview

As previously discussed, capitalization is the conversion of income into value. Whereas direct capitalization converts one year's income into an estimate of value, yield capitalization converts all of the income associated with the investment into an estimate of value. **Yield capitalization** converts a property's future income into a value today. The value today represents a discounted value of the sum total of all the anticipated future income streams associated with the investment during the anticipated investment period.

A discount rate is a rate of return. Investors require a rate of return that addresses the risk associated with that investment. So investors demand different rates of return for different property types. Essentially, the desired rate of return is applied to each year's income and then discounted to arrive at today's present value. So two investors could analyze the identical income streams and arrive at two different present value conclusions, by selecting discount rates that reflect their individual requirements. *Discount rates* are rates of return used to adjust a future income stream (the property's future value) to yield a desired return today (the present value). That is why discount rates are also known as **yield rates**.

The discounted value today is called the **present value**. The property's future income is called the **future value**. When discussing terms such as *present value* and *future value*, we are addressing the financial concept of the *time value of money*. Yield capitalization encompasses all of these concepts. Some of these concepts are rather technical and mathematically complex. Because of the complexities associated with yield capitalization, many investors simply stay away from it and utilize direct cap instead. Ideally, however, investors should use both methods to support the price or value of real estate, as the two methods are interrelated and mutually supportive techniques.

## Why Use Yield Capitalization?

Some real estate investments may be acquired on a stabilized revenue, expense, and income basis. Other real estate investments may be acquired on a nonstabilized revenue, expense, and income basis. Still other real estate investments may be "from the ground up": new construction that needs to be completed, then brought to a stabilized revenue, expense, and income basis. As any one year's income becomes less stable, direct capitalization becomes less reliable. Investors seek to determine the overall return or yield on the investment during the investment period, and they can accomplish this by yield capitalization.

Yield capitalization brings together different and complementary disciplines and techniques, which are used in conjunction with one another to create a sophisticated form of real estate investment analysis. So yield capitalization is significantly more involved than direct capitalization. Yield capitalization consists of four broad areas of consideration:

1. *Projection period.* The **projection period** is also known as a "holding period."
2. *Property forecast.* The **property forecast** is a reconstruction of the current year's and a forecast of future years' revenues, expenses, and operating income, consistent with the projection period.
3. *Yield rate.* A yield rate is selected consistent with the type of rate of return sought, being either investor specific or market oriented.
4. *Yield capitalization.* Yield capitalization is the capitalization of future income into a present value. In a multiple-year forecast, this process is referred to as **discounted cash flow analysis (DCFA)**.

Following is an overview of each of these four components.

### *Projection Periods*

Yield capitalization considers an investor's expected ownership period, referred to as the *anticipated holding period*. Holding periods are also referred to as projection periods. A *projection period* is the expected period of property ownership. A projection period is important to establish, because it represents the period of time during which a forecast will be prepared for the current and future years' revenues, expenses, and operating income for the property. Usually, real estate ownership periods are for a number of years. Some consider the long-term nature of real estate investment to be a disadvantage. However, for a number of reasons, long-term investment is actually advisable.

To maximize its total return, acquired property must generally be held for a number of years. It usually takes from three to five years to obtain optimal increases in cash flow and property value from the combination of property enhancement and property appreciation. As a rule of thumb, investors hold property for five to ten years to meet their investment and capital recapture objectives. **Capital recapture** is the return of equity in an investment as distinguished from the return on equity. Invested capital may be recaptured through annual income, or it may be recaptured all or in part through resale of the property. The tax laws on capital gains income also encourage long-term investments.

**Figure 3.1**

Projection Period

| | |
|---|---|
| Acquisition | January 1, 2005 |
| First Year of Holding Period | January 1–December 31, 2005 |
| Second Year of Holding Period | January 1–December 31, 2006 |
| Third Year of Holding Period | January 1–December 31, 2007 |
| Fourth Year of Holding Period | January 1–December 31, 2008 |
| Fifth Year of Holding Period | January 1–December 31, 2009 |
| Disposition | December 31, 2009 |

For example, let's say that we are considering the acquisition of the ten-unit, multifamily rental apartment property already discussed. We have determined that our holding period will be for five years. We have the historical information for 2004, the prior year. It is now January 1, 2005. If we acquire the property on January 1, 2005, our holding period would terminate on December 31, 2009, as detailed in Figure 3.1.

### *Forecast of Revenues, Expenses, and Operating Income*

Now that we have a projected holding period, we will have to reconstruct the historical or prior year's (2004) and forecast of future years' (2005 through 2009) revenues, expenses, and operating income, consistent with the projection period. We also need to forecast the *disposition* (sale) of the property at the end of our holding period. Because we have already reconstructed the prior year (refer to Chapter 2), what remains is the forecast, or projection, of future revenues, expenses, and operating income. Also remaining is the forecast of the property disposition, also known as **reversion**.

The following forecast is based upon our continuing analysis of the property. The prior year and the first two years of our forecasted holding period are presented in Figure 3.2. Based upon our review of the property, we conclude that we can implement meaningful adjustments during the first two years of our holding period that will significantly increase NOI. Figure 3.2 presents those adjustments and resulting changes in great detail for the first three years of our analysis. It uses the following units of measure:

- Total dollars
- Dollars per unit
- Dollars per square foot
- Percent of either income or expense

"A property goes, as its market flows, and a property went, as its market was spent."—Joseph Petrole

After the first two years of the forecasted holding period, we anticipate that the property will be fully adjusted to market and become a stabilized asset, essentially moving in the same direction ("drafting off") as the market in general. And this is why market analysis is so important in forecasting. A property is a portion of the market in which it is located.

**Figure 3.2**

Historical 2004 and Forecasted 2005 through 2006 Operating Statement

**Ten-Unit Apartment Building—Income and Expense Analysis**

Units 10
Living Area Square Feet 10,500

| *Period* | *Current Year 2004* | | | | *Forecast 2005* | | | | *Forecast 2006* | | | |
|---|---|---|---|---|---|---|---|---|---|---|---|---|
| **REVENUES** | | | | | | | | | | | | |
| Category | Amount | Amount per Unit | Amount per SF | % Total PGI | Amount | Amount per Unit | Amount per SF | % Total PGI | Amount | Amount per Unit | Amount per SF | % Total PGI |
| Scheduled Base Rent | $99,400 | $9,940 | $9.47 | 99.40% | $102,382 | $10,238 | $9.75 | 99.39% | $107,245 | $10,725 | $10.21 | 99.36% |
| **Market Rent for Vacant Units** | $- | $- | $- | 0.00% | $- | $- | $- | 0.00% | $- | $- | $- | 0.00% |
| ***Subtotal: Adjusted Base Rent*** | $99,400 | $9,940 | $9.47 | 99.40% | $102,382 | $10,238 | $9.75 | 99.39% | $107,245 | $10,725 | $10.21 | 99.36% |
| **Other Income** | | | | | | | | | | | | |
| Laundry | $600 | $60 | $0.06 | 0.60% | $630 | $63 | $0.06 | 0.61% | $690 | $69 | $0.07 | 0.64% |
| ***Subtotal: Other Income*** | $600 | $60 | $0.06 | 0.60% | $630 | $63 | $0.06 | 0.61% | $690 | $69 | $0.07 | 0.64% |
| **Potential Gross Income @ 100% Occupancy** | $100,000 | $10,000 | $9.52 | 100.00% | $103,012 | $10,301 | $9.81 | 100.00% | $107,935 | $10,793 | $10.28 | 100.00% |
| **Vacancy and Collection Loss @ 5%PGI** | $5,000 | $500 | $0.48 | 5.00% | $5,151 | $515 | $0.49 | 5.00% | $5,397 | $540 | $0.51 | 5.00% |
| **Effective Gross Income** | $95,000 | $9,500 | $9.05 | 95.00% | $97,861 | $9,786 | $9.32 | 95.00% | $102,538 | $10,254 | $9.77 | 95.00% |
| **EXPENSES** | | | | | | | | | | | | |
| **Operating Expenses** | | | | | | | | | | | | |
| *Fixed* | Amount | Amount per Unit | Amount per SF | % Total PGI | Amount | Amount per Unit | Amount per SF | % Total PGI | Amount | Amount per Unit | Amount per SF | % Total PGI |
| Real Estate Taxes | $11,000 | $1,100 | $1.05 | 11.58% | $11,000 | $1,100 | $1.05 | 11.24% | $11,165 | $1,117 | $1.06 | 10.89% |
| Insurance | $1,750 | $175 | $0.17 | 1.84% | $1,750 | $175 | $0.17 | 1.79% | $1,500 | $150 | $0.14 | 1.46% |
| ***Subtotal Fixed*** | $12,750 | 1,275 | $1.21 | 13.42% | $12,750 | 1,275 | $1.21 | 13.03% | $12,665 | 1,267 | $1.21 | 12.35% |
| *Variable* | | | | | | | | | | | | |
| Management Fee @ 4% EGI | $3,800 | $380 | $0.36 | 4.00% | $3,914 | $391 | $0.37 | 4.00% | $4,102 | $410 | $0.39 | 4.00% |
| Advertising and Promotion | $825 | $83 | $0.08 | 0.87% | $800 | $80 | $0.08 | 0.82% | $700 | $70 | $0.07 | 0.68% |
| Telephone | $900 | $90 | $0.09 | 0.95% | $900 | $90 | $0.09 | 0.92% | $800 | $80 | $0.08 | 0.78% |
| Utilities (Water, Sewer, Electric) | $1,600 | $160 | $0.15 | 1.68% | $1,600 | $160 | $0.15 | 1.63% | $1,575 | $158 | $0.15 | 1.54% |
| Trash Removal | $1,000 | $100 | $0.01 | 1.05% | $1,000 | $100 | $0.10 | 1.02% | $1,030 | $103 | $0.10 | 1.00% |
| Repairs, Maintenance, and Supplies | $11,000 | $1,100 | $1.05 | 11.58% | $11,000 | $1,100 | $1.05 | 11.24% | $10,000 | $1,000 | $0.95 | 9.75% |
| Unit Interior Redecorating | $1,475 | $148 | $0.14 | 1.55% | $1,425 | $143 | $0.14 | 1.46% | $1,275 | $128 | $0.12 | 1.24% |
| Landscape, Lawn, and Grounds | $1,200 | $120 | $0.11 | 1.26% | $1,200 | $120 | $0.11 | 1.23% | $1,250 | $125 | $0.12 | 1.22% |
| Pest Control | $450 | $45 | $0.04 | 0.47% | $450 | $45 | $0.04 | 0.46% | $400 | $40 | $0.04 | 0.39% |
| ***Subtotal Variable*** | $22,250 | $2,225 | $2.12 | 23.42% | $22,289 | $2,229 | $2.12 | 22.78% | $21,132 | $2,113 | $2.01 | 20.61% |
| ***Replacement Allowances*** | | | | | | | | | | | | |
| ***Subtotal Replacement Allowances*** | $5,000 | $500 | $0.48 | 5.26% | $5,000 | $500 | $0.48 | 5.11% | $5,000 | $500 | $0.48 | 4.88% |
| **Total Operating Expenses** | $40,000 | $4,000 | $3.81 | 42.11% | $40,039 | $4,004 | $3.81 | 40.91% | $38,797 | $3,880 | $3.69 | 37.84% |
| **OPERATING INCOME** | | | | | | | | | | | | |
| **Net Operating Income** | $55,000 | $5,500 | $5.24 | 57.89% | $57,822 | $5,782 | $5.51 | 59.09% | $63,742 | $6,374 | $6.07 | 62.16% |

## Analysis, Projections, and Forecast

### *Revenues*

**Scheduled base rent.** As discussed in Chapter 1, this property's base rents have not been raised during the past year. Moreover, in prior years, the rent increases have not kept up with market rents. Our analysis indicates that base rents are being raised in the market area by 3 percent or more per year. We project this year's increase in rents to be 3 percent and next year's to be 4.75 percent, to bring the rents up to comparable rates in the market area. After that, rents are forecast to increase at a market-oriented 3 percent per year.

**Other income.** As discussed in Chapter 1, other income is derived from a laundry facility for the tenants. The income currently originates from the laundry machines only. This year, the area's only coin laundry retailer will close, boosting demand for the on-site laundry room and causing a 5 percent increase in other income. Next year, we expect a 9.5 percent increase in other income, resulting from additional income from a vendor who will install a vending machine for soap, detergent, fabric softeners, and the like. Beginning in 2007, other income is forecast to increase at 10 percent per year.

**Vacancy and collection losses.** As discussed in Chapter 1, vacancy and collection losses for the property have historically ranged from 2 percent to 6 percent of PGI. During 2004, the property had an actual V&C loss of 5 percent. A 5 percent V&C loss is also projected for 2005 and 2006. Based on projected improving market conditions, increased unit demand, and our projected property management program, we forecast a V&C loss of 4.75 percent for 2007, 4.5 percent for 2008, and stabilizing at 4 percent for 2009 and thereafter.

### *Expenses*

**Fixed expenses.** Real estate taxes for last year were $11,000, including the maximum discount of 4 percent for early payment in November. Real estate taxes for this year are projected to be the same. Every three years, the property is subject to reassessment. Next year, the property is expected to be reassessed by the county property appraiser's office, resulting in an increased tax burden of 1.5 percent during 2006, 2007, and 2008. In 2009, the property is again expected to be reassessed by the county property appraiser's office, resulting in another 1.5 percent tax increase during 2009, 2010, and 2011.

Insurance for last year was $1,750. This amount was based on a two-year policy. Accordingly, this year, the insurance premium expense is expected to be the same. However, beginning next year, the insurance policy is projected to be renegotiated with a new carrier for a five-year term at an annual expense of $1,500 a year for each of the five years.

**Variable expenses.** Management fees have been previously calculated as 4 percent of EGI and will be applied at that rate for the five-year projected holding period.

Advertising and promotion expense last year was $825. We project that, based upon an enhanced property maintenance and management program, along with increasing market demand, expenses in this category can be reduced slightly to $800 this year and reduced slightly again to $700 next year. Beginning in 2007, however, expenses in this category are expected to increase again at, say, 3 percent, or at the rate of the projected consumer price index (CPI) per year.

Telephone expenses last year were $900. We expect this expense to remain unchanged this year. We also expect to switch carriers and, with the "sign-on bonus," project this expense to declining slightly to $800 next year. Based on trends in the telecommunication industry, beginning in 2007, expenses in this category are expected to increase at, say, 3 percent (projected CPI) per year.

Utilities expenses last year were $1,600. We project them to remain unchanged this year, then decline slightly to $1,575 next year. Based on a review of the historical increases for these services at this property, beginning in 2007, expenses in this category are expected to increase at, say, 2 percent (as regulated by the public utilities commission) per year.

Trash removal for last year was $1,000. This amount was based on a two-year contract. Accordingly, this year the trash removal expense is expected to be the same. Beginning next year, a new trash removal contract is projected to be renegotiated with the same company for a two-year (2006 and 2007) term at an annual expense of $1,030 for each of the two years. Based on a review of the historical increases for these services at this property, beginning in 2008, a new trash removal contract is projected to be renegotiated with the same company for a two-year (2008 and 2009) term at an annual expense of $1,060 for each of the two years. Thereafter, the expense is forecasted to increase at, say, 3 percent (projected CPI) per year.

Repairs, maintenance, and supplies for last year were $11,000. This year, this expense is expected to be the same. Based on a review of historical expenses, along with the overall good condition of the property, beginning next year we project to be able to reduce this expense by approximately $1,000 to, say, $10,000. Thereafter, these expenses are projected to increase at, say, 3 percent (projected CPI) per year.

Unit interior redecorating expense last year was $1,475. As discussed in Chapter 1, unit interior decorating was sometimes used by the owner as an inducement for tenant lease renewal. However, our analysis indicates that demand is increasing and this form of concession is no longer required. We project a phasing out of the "concession" part of this expense over a two-year period. This year, this expense is expected to decline slightly from $1,475 to $1,425. Next year, this expense is expected to further decline from $1,425 to $1,275. Based on a review of the historical expenses, along with the overall good condition of the property, beginning in 2007, we project this expense to increase at, say, 3 percent (projected CPI) per year.

Landscape, lawn, and grounds expense for last year was $1,200. This year, this expense is expected to be the same. Based on a review of the historical expenses for this category, along with the required maintenance requirements of the property, we conclude that reductions in this category are not advisable. From requested fee quotes for services, beginning next year, we project this expense to increase by approximately $50 (about 4 percent) per year.

Pest control last year was $450. This amount was based on a two-year policy. Accordingly, this year, pest control expense is expected to be the same. Beginning next year, a new pest control contract is projected to be renegotiated with the same company for a two-year (2006 and 2007) term at an annual expense of $400 for each year. Based on a review of the historical increases for these services at this property, beginning in 2008, expenses in this category are expected to increase at, say, 3 percent (projected CPI) per contract period.

### *Replacement Allowances*

As discussed in Chapter 1, the current owner has an annual accrual for replacement reserves of $5,000. Based on a review of the items to be covered by the reserve, their cost new, and their estimated lives, we conclude that this amount is reasonable and supported. Accordingly, this amount will be applied each year during our projected holding period.

### *Forecast*

Based upon our detailed analysis and projections, we now can prepare a five-year forecast of the property. Based upon our review, we conclude that we can implement some meaningful adjustments during the first two years (2005 and 2006) of our holding period that will significantly increase NOI.

During the last three years (2007, 2008, and 2009) of the forecasted holding period, we anticipate that the property will become a more stabilized asset, essentially moving in the same direction (drafting off) as the market.

The five-year forecasted holding period, along with a one-year forecast for reversion, is presented in Figure 3.3.

## Yield Rates—Rates of Return

### *What Real Estate Investors Expect*

Real estate investors expect:

- *The recovery of all their invested capital, or return of capital.* **Return of capital** is the recovery of the invested capital, usually through a property's income and reversion. The income component of the return of capital consists of the income stream generated by the investment. The reversion component of the return of capital is a lump-sum amount that an investor receives or anticipates receiving at the conclusion of an investment. The reversion component of the return of capital consists of the proceeds from the sale of the investment at the conclusion of the holding period.
- *A payment for the use of the capital, or return on capital.* **Return on capital** is an additional amount received as compensation for the use of an investor's capital until it is returned.

The return on capital and the return of capital together are the investor's rate of return on capital. The *rate of return on capital* is equivalent to an interest rate and, for real estate investments, is known as the yield rate. The **yield rate** is the overall rate of return actually earned, or forecasted to be earned, on the capital invested in a real estate endeavor.

**Figure 3.3**

Forecasted Income and Expense Analysis, for the Period 2005 through 2010

**Ten-Unit Apartment Building—Income and Expense Analysis**

Units 10
Living Area Square Feet 10,500

For the Period 2005–2010

| Period | Forecast 2005 | | Forecast 2006 | | Forecast 2007 | | Forecast 2008 | | Forecast 2009 | | Forecast 2010 | |
|---|---|---|---|---|---|---|---|---|---|---|---|---|
| | Holding Year 1 | | Holding Year 2 | | Holding Year 3 | | Holding Year 4 | | Hclding Year 5 | | Reversion | |
| **REVENUES** | | | | | | | | | | | | |
| Category | Amount | Amount per Unit | Amount | Amount per Unit | Amount | Amount per Unit | Amount | Amount per Unit | Amount | Amount per Unit | Amount | Amount per Unit |
| Scheduled Base Rent | $102,382 | $10,238 | $107,245 | $10,725 | $110,462 | $11,046 | $113,776 | $11,378 | $117,190 | $11,719 | $120,705 | $12,071 |
| **Market Rent for Vacant Units** | $- | $- | $- | $- | $- | $- | $- | $- | $- | $- | $- | $- |
| ***Subtotal: Adjusted Base Rent*** | $102,382 | $10,238 | $107,245 | $10,725 | $110,462 | $11,046 | $113,776 | $11,378 | $117,190 | $11,719 | $120,705 | $12,071 |
| **Other Income** | | | | | | | | | | | | |
| Laundry | $630 | $63 | $690 | $69 | $759 | $76 | $835 | $83 | $918 | $92 | $1,010 | $101 |
| ***Subtotal: Other Income*** | $630 | $63 | $690 | $69 | $759 | $76 | $835 | $83 | $918 | $92 | $1,010 | $101 |
| **Potential Gross Income @ 100% Occupancy** | $103,012 | $10,301 | $107,935 | $10,793 | $111,221 | $11,122 | $114,611 | $11,461 | $118,108 | $11,811 | $121,715 | $12,172 |
| **Vacancy and Collection Loss @ 5%** | $5,151 | $515 | $5,397 | $540 | $5,283 | $528 | $5,157 | $516 | $4,724 | $472 | $4,869 | $487 |
| **Effective Gross Income** | $97,861 | $9,786 | $102,538 | $10,254 | $105,938 | $10,594 | $109,454 | $10,945 | $113,384 | $11,338 | $116,847 | $11,685 |
| **EXPENSES** | | | | | | | | | | | | |
| **Operating Expenses** | | | | | | | | | | | | |
| *Fixed* | Amount | Amount per Unit | Amount | Amount per Unit | Amount | Amount per Unit | Amount | Amount per Unit | Amount | Amount per Unit | Amount | Amount per Unit |
| Real Estate Taxes | $11,000 | $1,100 | $11,165 | $1,117 | $11,165 | $1,117 | $11,165 | $1,117 | $11,332 | $1,133 | $11,332 | $1,133 |
| Insurance | $1,750 | $175 | $1,500 | $150 | $1,500 | $150 | $1,500 | $150 | $1,300 | $150 | $1,500 | $150 |
| ***Subtotal Fixed*** | $12,750 | 1,275 | $12,665 | 1,267 | $12,665 | 1,267 | $12,665 | 1,267 | $12,332 | 1,283 | $12,832 | 1,283 |
| *Variable* | | | | | | | | | | | | |
| Management Fee @ 4% | $3,914 | $391 | $4,102 | $410 | $4,238 | $424 | $4,378 | $438 | $4,335 | $454 | $4,674 | $467 |
| Advertising and Promotion | $800 | $80 | $700 | $70 | $721 | $72 | $743 | $74 | $765 | $76 | $788 | $79 |
| Telephone | $900 | $90 | $800 | $80 | $824 | $82 | $849 | $85 | $374 | $87 | $900 | $90 |
| Utilities (Water, Sewer, Electric) | $1,600 | $160 | $1,575 | $158 | $1,607 | $161 | $1,639 | $164 | $1,571 | $167 | $1,705 | $170 |
| Trash Removal | $1,000 | $100 | $1,030 | $103 | $1,030 | $103 | $1,060 | $106 | $1,360 | $106 | $1,092 | $109 |
| Repairs, Maintenance, and Supplies | $11,000 | $1,100 | $10,000 | $1,000 | $10,300 | $1,030 | $10,609 | $1,061 | $10,927 | $1,093 | $11,255 | $1,126 |
| Unit Interior Redecorating | $1,425 | $143 | $1,275 | $128 | $1,313 | $131 | $1,353 | $135 | $1,393 | $139 | $1,435 | $144 |
| Landscape, Lawn, and Grounds | $1,200 | $120 | $1,250 | $125 | $1,300 | $130 | $1,350 | $135 | $1,400 | $140 | $1,450 | $145 |
| Pest Control | $450 | $45 | $400 | $40 | $400 | $40 | $412 | $41 | $424 | $42 | $437 | $44 |
| ***Subtotal Variable*** | $22,289 | $2,229 | $21,132 | $2,113 | $21,732 | $2,173 | $22,392 | $2,239 | $23,351 | $2,305 | $23,736 | $2,374 |
| *Replacement Allowances* | | | | | | | | | | | | |
| ***Subtotal Replacement Allowances*** | $5,000 | $500 | $5,000 | $500 | $5,000 | $500 | $5,000 | $500 | $5,200 | $500 | $5,000 | $500 |
| **Total Operating Expenses** | $40,039 | $4,004 | $38,797 | $3,880 | $39,397 | $3,940 | $40,057 | $4,006 | $40,883 | $4,088 | $41,568 | $4,157 |
| **OPERATING INCOME** | | | | | | | | | | | | |
| **Net Operating Income** | $57,822 | $5,782 | $63,742 | $6,374 | $66,541 | $6,654 | $69,397 | $6,940 | $72,500 | $7,250 | $75,278 | $7,528 |

Reversion is usually based on the NOI from the year following the end of the holding period, because it represents the anticipated income to be acquired. In Figure 3.3, the NOI for the year 2010 is $75,278. For us to determine what we should offer for this property, this future income stream, as well as all the other future income streams, have to be converted into a single value estimate effective today. But how can we do that? By employing the yield capitalization method of property valuation.

### *Yield Capitalization and Discounted Cash-Flow Analysis*

*Capitalization* is the conversion of income into value. *Yield capitalization* is the capitalization method used to convert future benefits into a present value by discounting each future benefit at an appropriate yield rate that explicitly reflects the investment's income patterns, value change, and rate of return. Stated differently, yield cap is a capitalization method used to convert expected future cash flows into an equivalent value or price today by discounting each future cash flow at a rate that reflects the investment's income patterns, value change, and desired/required rate of return. Because yield cap involves discounting cash flows, it is also referred to as *discounted cash-flow analysis*.

## The Physical and Financial Architecture of Real Estate

Real estate is all around us. We live, work, shop, and are entertained in various types of real estate, all of which exist in the physical—tangible—world. However, based on the presentation in this textbook, the financial aspect associated with real estate investments should also be apparent. Generally speaking, there are two aspects of a real estate investment: its physical aspects and its financial aspects.

When we discuss the purchase and sale of property, we usually talk in terms of "real estate." For example, consider the statements: "We are in the market to buy real estate," or, "We are in the market to sell real estate." Although everyone knows what is meant, strictly speaking, we are only discussing the physical aspects of property, not the financial.

Let's take a closer look at some of the terms used to define real estate investment:

- Real estate is physical—the physical land and all structures and other improvements attached to the land. However, real estate does not consider any of the rights associated with ownership.
- Real property rights are intangible—the intangible rights associated with the ownership of the physical real estate. Real property rights are referred to as the bundle of rights.
- The *bundle of rights* is a concept that compares property ownership rights to a bundle of sticks, where each stick represents a distinct and separate right, interest, and benefit of ownership, including the right to sell, use, buy, mortgage, pledge, trade, and lease the property and the right not to exercise any of these rights. The bundle of rights concept addresses the legal rights associated with ownership.

The "physical architecture" of real estate consists of its tangible qualities such as the concrete, steel, and glass required to create the physical property. The "financial architecture" of real estate consists of its bundle of rights such as the leases, revenues, expenses, income, mortgage, and other debt service and cash flow, return on investment and return of investment, that are required to create the financial annuity.

The physical architecture of real estate consists of land and improvements; the financial architecture of real estate consists of property rights.

An **annuity** is a schedule of cash payments where the payments occur at regular, fixed intervals. An example of a real estate annuity would be a pro forma forecast of net operating income or cash flows. The physical architecture of real estate can be seen in the physical world and is used for various commercial purposes. The financial architecture of real estate exists in cyberspace, within computer spreadsheets, forecast pro formas, and discounted cash-flow-yield analysis models. This financial architecture is used for various ownership and investment purposes.

## Case Study: Investment in Zero-Coupon Bonds

To understand how the yield capitalization process works, let's compare it to an investment in zero-coupon bonds. This analogy works well, because both real estate investments and bond investments are similar—they both represent annuities. However, real estate is a tangible asset, while a bond is an intangible asset. Stated differently, real estate has both a physical architecture and a financial architecture, while a bond only has a financial architecture.

### *Zero-Coupon Bonds*

Let's say we wanted to make an investment in zero-coupon bonds. *Zero-coupon bonds* are bonds that do not pay any interest during the investment period. An investor can buy a zero-coupon bond today at a discount from its face value. *Face value* is the amount the bond will be worth when it matures or comes due. When the zero-coupon bond matures, we will receive a lump sum equal to the initial investment plus the accrued interest.

So the amount the bond will be worth when it matures or comes due is the bond's future value, while the purchase price paid for the zero-coupon bond today is the bond's discounted present value. We purchase the bond at a discounted price today to yield a certain rate of return.

### *Laddering*

A popular way that bond investors balance risk and return is to use an investment technique called laddering. *Laddering* entails dividing our investment capital into zero-coupon bonds of different but consecutive maturities. For example, we could purchase bonds with maturities of one, two, three, four, and five years. Laddering allows us to diversify our risk by spreading it over a series of different maturities. Laddering our investment capital offers many advantages:

- It diversifies risk while providing ongoing liquidity.
- Its staggered maturities offer a higher degree of income stability.
- A staggered portfolio offers greater returns than those possible from holding only short-term bonds, and it also offers less risk than holding only long-term bonds.

**Figure 3.4**

Laddered Maturity Investment

| Purchase Price Today | Discounted to Yield | Maturity Date | Future Value |
|---|---|---|---|
| ? | 14.37% | One Year | $57,822 |
| ? | 14.37% | Two Years | $63,742 |
| ? | 14.37% | Three Years | $66,541 |
| ? | 14.37% | Four Years | $69,397 |
| ? | 14.37% | Five Years | $770,202 |
| ? | | | |

- The maturing investment capital can be reinvested in other investments.
- We can build a portfolio of laddered maturities for specific time frames.

### *Laddered Maturities*

Let's say we want a five-year laddered investment period. We know the future face value of the zero-coupon bonds. These zero-coupon bonds are priced to yield a rate of return—say 14.37 percent. We now have all the information we need to determine what discounted present value we would pay today to obtain a 14.37 percent yield from the bonds' future values.

Figure 3.4 presents a summary of this laddered investment.

### *Cash-Flow Diagrams*

Cash-flow diagrams are widely used visual tools that often are the first step in solving complex financial problems. A cash-flow diagram can represent any cash-flow problem. Once the diagram is set up, we would identify what is known and unknown about the investment. A horizontal line represents time. Money invested is considered cash payments or outflows, represented as negative with a down arrow. Money returned is considered cash received or inflows, represented as positive with an up arrow. Figure 3.5 shows a cash-flow diagram for our laddered investment.

**Figure 3.5**

Cash-Flow Diagram—Laddered Investment

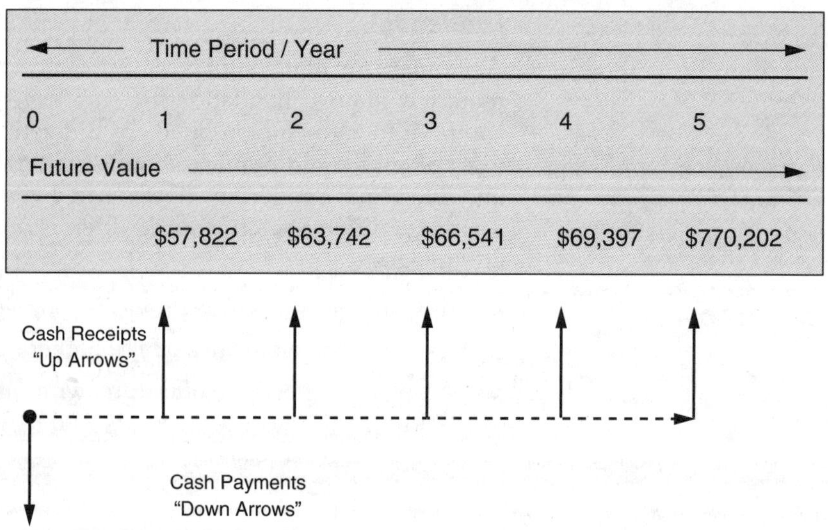

In addition to the cash-flow diagram itself, we have additional information to consider. We know the time period in years and the matching future values associated with those years. We also know that the bonds will be discounted to yield a return of 14.37 percent.

Figure 3.6 is an expanded presentation of the cash-flow diagram in Figure 3.5. In this presentation, each zero-coupon bond's future value is converted into a present value by discounting the future income streams at a 14.37 percent yield rate.

A close look at Figure 3.6 reveals that the zero-coupon bond's future values in years 1, 2, 3, 4, and 5 are the same amounts as the forecasted net operating income and reversion that were presented within Figure 3.3. We are discounting the future values at a 14.37 percent yield rate. The present value of these amounts is $578,000. Separately, via direct capitalization, we capitalized the first year's forecast NOI at a 10 percent overall rate. The capitalized value of this amount is $578,000. This example highlights the relationship between cap rates, yield rates, direct capitalization, and yield capitalization. A discussion of the yield/discount rates used in Figure 3.6 follows.

**Figure 3.6**

Expanded Cash-Flow Diagram—Laddered Investment

| Year | Year 1 | Year 2 | Year 3 | Year 4 | Year 5 |
|---|---|---|---|---|---|
| **Future Value** | $57,822 | $63,742 | $66,541 | $69,397 | $770,202 |
| *multiplied by:* | × | × | × | × | × |
| Yield Rate: 14.37% | 0.874385701 | 0.764550354 | 0.668511897 | 0.584537243 | 0.511111007 |
| *equals:* | | | | | |

**Present Value**

Yr. 1: $50,558.73

Yr. 2: $48,733.97

Yr. 3: $44,483.45

Yr. 4: $40,565.13

Yr. 5: $393,658.72

**Total: $578,000** — ***This total represents the discounted present values of years 1 through 5 of the investment.***

**NOI: $57,800** — ***This NOI represents our ten-unit rental apartments' forecast NOI in Year 1.***

*divided by:*

**Cap @ 10%** — ***This 10% Cap Rate is the Direct Cap Rate we used to convert the forecast NOI into a present value.***

*equals:*

**Total: $578,000** — ***This total represents the present value of the NOI capitalized at 10%.***

**Figure 3.7**

Present Value of Laddered Maturity Investment

| Present Value | Discount @ 14.37% | Maturity Date | Future Value |
|---|---|---|---|
| $50,558.73 | 0.874 | One Year | $57,822 |
| $48,733.97 | 0.765 | Two Years | $63,742 |
| $44,483.45 | 0.669 | Three Years | $66,541 |
| $40,565.13 | 0.585 | Four Years | $69,397 |
| $393,658.72 | 0.511 | Five Years | $770,202 |
| $578,000.00 | | | |

The zero-coupon bonds are priced to yield 14.37 percent, rounded (the exact yield is slightly less than that). Other ways to say, "The zero-coupon bonds were priced to yield 14.37 percent," include:

- "The zero-coupon bonds are discounted to yield 14.37 percent."
- "The discount rate applied to the future zero-bond values is 14.37 percent."
- "The factor applied to discount the future zero-bond values is 14.37 percent."

### *The Present Value of a Future Amount*

As we have seen, the future maturity values of the zero-coupon bonds have an equivalent discounted present value. What determines today's value is

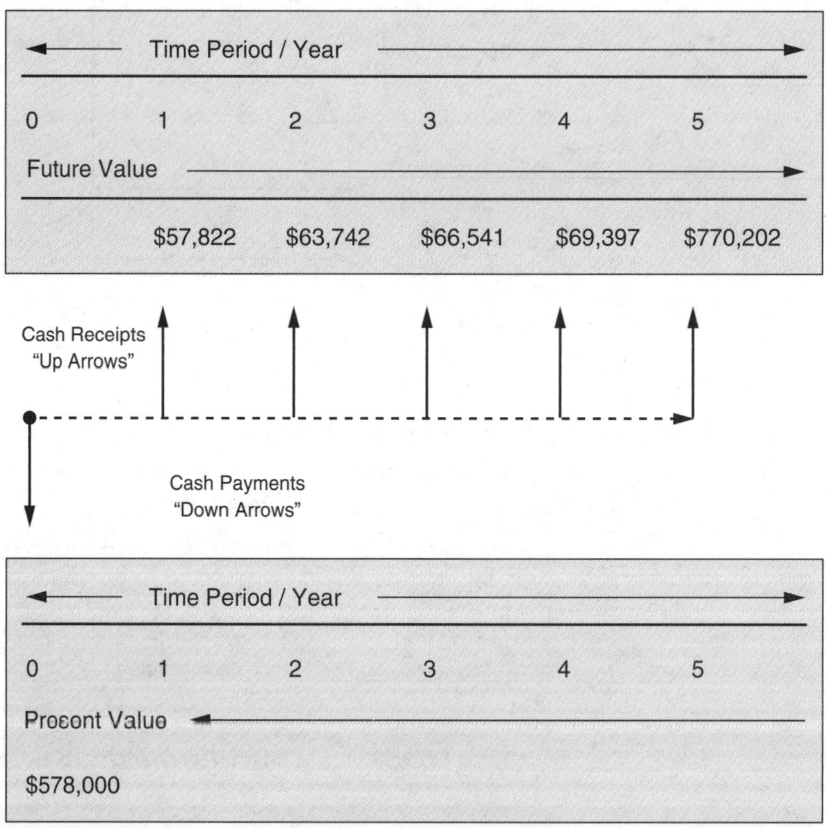


**Figure 3.8**

Cash-Flow Diagram—Laddered Maturity

the yield rate. The greater the yield rate (discount rate), the greater the discount. So a yield rate can be used to discount a future value to arrive at a present value.

A Yield Rate can discount a Future Value to arrive at a Present Value.

Figure 3.7 shows another presentation of our laddered zero-coupon bond investment. In this presentation, the actual discount factors are used to discount the future value to arrive at an equivalent present value, based on an annual time value adjustment of 14.37 percent.

Each future value is discounted to an equivalent present value by multiplying the future value by the discount rate. For example, if we multiply the first year's future value of $57,822 by the discount rate of 0.874385701, then the equivalent present value is $50,558.73. Each year's present value amount is determined the same way. The total of the five present values equates the investment's purchase price today.

Present Value = Future Value × Discount Rate

We can create a picture of this financial problem by using a cash-flow diagram. Figure 3.8 is a cash-flow diagram of the laddered maturity investment presented in Figure 3.7.

### *What Is a Discount Rate?*

A close look at Figure 3.7 reveals that the discount rate converted each future value into an equivalent present value. Discount rates are also known as discount factors or yield rates. A discount rate is also known as a *present value interest factor (PVIF)*. A PVIF is based on a mathematical formula and is used as part of a mathematical process called *discounting*.

The discount rate (PVIF) for any yield rate can be obtained by the following formula:

$$\text{PVIF} = 1 \div (1 + r)^n$$

Where: r = the interest rate
n = the number of periods (how many times the formula is multiplied against itself)

Today PVIFs are readily available in handheld financial calculators and in many financial software packages. So we no longer need to be concerned about the derivation of the formula. However, we could still calculate our PVIFs if we wanted to. For example, the PVIF to discount the first year's zero-coupon bond at a 14.37 percent (rounded) yield rate would be calculated as follows:

$$\text{PVIF} = 1 \div (1 + r)^n$$
$$\text{PVIF} = 1 \div (1 + 0.1436600565)^1$$
$$\text{PVIF} = 1 \div (1.1436600565)$$
$$\text{PVIF} = 0.874385701$$

**Figure 3.9**

Present Value Interest Factors for 14.37 percent—Years 1–5

| Yield Rate | Rounded | N | Factor | X | Factor | X | Factor | X | Factor | X | Factor | = | PVIF |
|---|---|---|---|---|---|---|---|---|---|---|---|---|---|
| Periods=N | | | 1 | | 2 | | 3 | | 4 | | 5 | | |
| 14.36600565% | 14.37% | 1 | 0.874385701 | | | | | | | | | = | 0.874385701 |
| 14.36600565% | 14.37% | 2 | 0.874385701 | X | 0.874385701 | | | | | | | = | 0.764550354 |
| 14.36600565% | 14.37% | 3 | 0.874385701 | X | 0.874385701 | X | 0.874385701 | | | | | = | 0.668511897 |
| 14.36600565% | 14.37% | 4 | 0.874385701 | X | 0.874385701 | X | 0.874385701 | X | 0.874385701 | | | = | 0.584537243 |
| 14.36600565% | 14.37% | 5 | 0.874385701 | X | 0.874385701 | X | 0.874385701 | X | 0.874385701 | X | 0.874385701 | = | 0.511111007 |

Similarly, the PVIF to discount each year's zero-coupon bond at a 14.37 percent (rd) yield rate would be calculated as noted in Figure 3.9.

### *The Future Value of a Present Amount*

The present values of the zero-coupon bonds have an equivalent compounded future value. What determines the future value is the amount of the yield rate. The greater the yield rate, the greater the compounding. A yield rate can be used to compound a present value into a future value.

A Yield Rate can compound a Present Value into an Equivalent Future Value.

For example, consider Figure 3.10.

Figure 3.11 is yet another presentation of our laddered zero-coupon bond investment. In this presentation, we are using compound rates to calculate the equivalent future values of the present values, based on an annual time value adjustment of 14.37 percent.

Future Value = Present Value × Compound Rate

Each present value is compounded to an equivalent future value by multiplying the present value by the compound rate. For example, if we multiply the first year's present value of $50,558.73 by the compound rate of 1.143660057, then the equivalent future value is $57,822. Each year's future value is determined the same way. The total of the five future values equates the maturity values of this investment's future cash flows.

**Figure 3.10**

Future Value of Laddered Maturity Investment

| Purchase Price Today | Compounded to Yield | Maturity Date | Future Value |
|---|---|---|---|
| $50,558.73 | 14.37% | One Year | ? |
| $48,733.97 | 14.37% | Two Years | ? |
| $44,483.45 | 14.37% | Three Years | ? |
| $40,565.13 | 14.37% | Four Years | ? |
| $393,658.72 | 14.37% | Five Years | ? |
| $578,000.00 | | | ? |

**Figure 3.11**

Future Value of Laddered Maturity Investment with Future Value

| Purchase Price Today | Compounded to Yield | Maturity Date | Future Value |
|---|---|---|---|
| $50,558.73 | 1.143660057 | One Year | $57,822.00 |
| $48,733.97 | 1.307958325 | Two Years | $63,742.00 |
| $44,483.45 | 1.495859692 | Three Years | $66,541.00 |
| $40,565.13 | 1.710754980 | Four Years | $69,397.00 |
| $393,658.72 | 1.956522137 | Five Years | $770,202.00 |
| $578,000.00 | | | |

### *What Is a Compound Rate?*

A close look at Figure 3.11 reveals that the compound rate converted each present value into an equivalent future value. Compound rates are also known as *compound factors, yield rates,* or the *future value interest factor (FVIF).* The FVIF is based on a formula and is used as part of a mathematical process called compounding. *Compounding* is the process whereby a principal amount earns interest and that previously earned interest is then added to the principal amount, creating a larger amount of money, which then earns additional interest, occurring over successive time periods. The compound rate, or FVIF, of any yield rate can be obtained by the following formula:

$$\text{FVIF} = (1 + r)^n$$

Where: r = the interest rate
n = the number of periods (how many times the formula is multiplied against itself)

FVIFs are readily available in handheld financial calculators and in many types of financial software. So we no longer need to be concerned about the derivation of the formula. However, we could still calculate our FVIFs if we wanted to.

For example, the FVIF to compound the first year's zero-coupon bond at a 14.37 percent (rd) yield rate would be calculated as follows:

$$\text{FVIF} = (1 + r)^n$$
$$\text{FVIF} = (1 + 0.1436600565)^1$$
$$\text{FVIF} = (1.1436600565)$$
$$\text{FVIF} = 1.1436600565$$

Similarly, the FVIF to compound each year's zero-coupon bond at a 14.37 percent (rd) yield rate would be calculated as shown in Figure 3.12.

## Compound Interest and Time Value of Money Concepts

As discussed within the zero-coupon bond case study, we can discount future values to arrive at a present value. Similarly, we can compound present values into future values. Essentially, these amounts represent equivalent dollar

**Figure 3.12**

Future Value Interest Factors for 14.37 percent—Years 1–5

| Yield Rate | Rounded | N | Factor | X | Factor | X | Factor | X | Factor | X | Factor | = | PVIF |
|---|---|---|---|---|---|---|---|---|---|---|---|---|---|
| Periods=N | | | 1 | | 2 | | 3 | | 4 | | 5 | | |
| 14.36600565% | 14.37% | 1 | 1.143660057 | | | | | | | | | = | 1.143660057 |
| 14.36600565% | 14.37% | 2 | 1.143660057 | X | 1.143660057 | | | | | | | = | 1.307958325 |
| 14.36600565% | 14.37% | 3 | 1.143660057 | X | 1.143660057 | X | 1.143660057 | | | | | = | 1.495859692 |
| 14.36600565% | 14.37% | 4 | 1.143660057 | X | 1.143660057 | X | 1.143660057 | X | 1.143660057 | | | = | 1.710754980 |
| 14.36600565% | 14.37% | 5 | 1.143660057 | X | 1.143660057 | X | 1.143660057 | X | 1.143660057 | X | 1.143660057 | = | 1.956522137 |

values, adjusted for time and yield. This adjustment process is part of what is known as the time value of money concept. Time value of money concepts are based on the notion that, "A dollar received today is worth more than a dollar received in the future."

The **time value of money** is an economic principal. It states that the value of a dollar received today is worth more than a dollar received in the future. The reasoning is that a dollar received today can be invested and earn interest (a rate of return), thereby growing into a larger future amount than the same noninvested dollar will be worth in the future. The concept of time

**Figure 3.13**

Cash-Flow Diagram—Deposit of $1,000

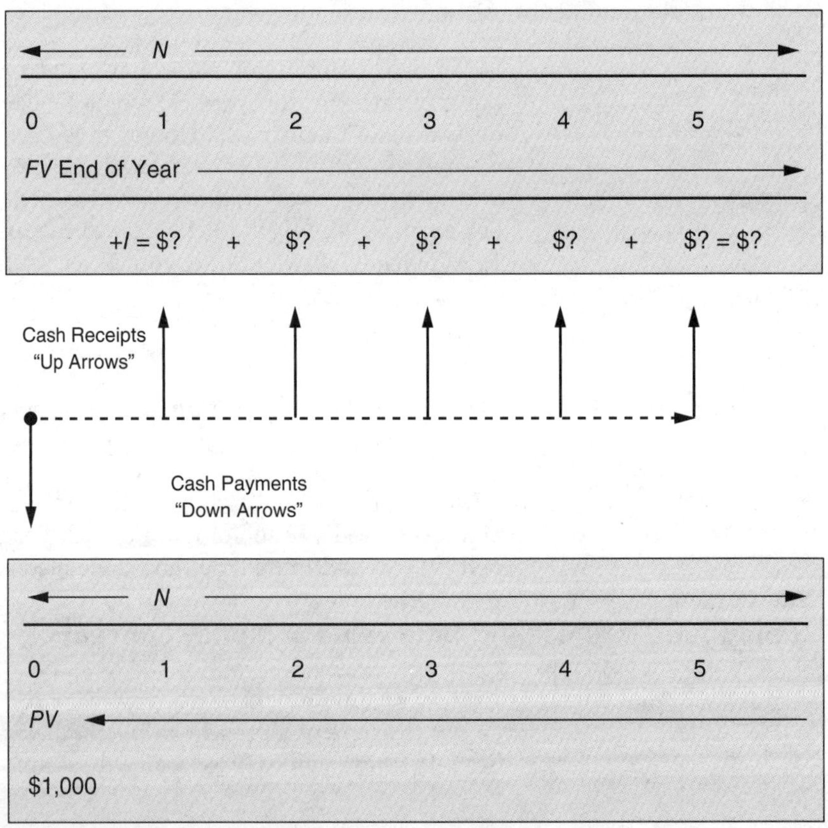

**Figure 3.14**

Compound Interest of $1,000

| Period | Beginning Amount | Rate | Ending Amount |
|---|---|---|---|
| 1 | $1,000.00 | 1.10 | $1,100.00 |
| 2 | $1,100.00 | 1.10 | $1,210.00 |
| 3 | $1,210.00 | 1.10 | $1,331.00 |
| 4 | $1,331.00 | 1.10 | $1,464.10 |
| 5 | $1,464.10 | 1.10 | $1,610.51 |

value of money provides the foundation for all discounted cash-flow analysis. The concept of time value of money includes the future value of a dollar, the present value of a dollar, the future value of an annuity, and the present value of an annuity.

### *Future Value of a Dollar*

Let's say we deposited $1,000 in a savings account at a bank that pays 10 percent interest, compounded annually. How could we determine how much we would have in our account at the end of the year (the **future value of a dollar**)? How about at the end of two years, three years, and so on? By employing the future value concept of the time value of money. To do so, we need to define some terms:

**PV** = the present value, the beginning amount deposited

**R** = the rate of interest earned on the invested capital, expressed as a percentage

**I** = the total amount of interest earned during the year, expressed in dollars

**N** = the year, years, or periods of the investment

**FV** = the future value, the ending amount in the account at the end of a given period, including the total of the beginning amount plus all interest earned

Figure 3.13 shows a cash-flow diagram for our deposit of $1,000.

Figure 3.14 shows our expected income over a forecasted five-year investment period.

Figure 3.14 summarizes the compounding process for determining the beginning amount and ending amount for each period, applying a 10 percent rate of interest to each period's beginning balance. Each year, the beginning amount in the account would earn interest based on the investment's interest rate. A cash-flow diagram modeling the interest earned each year is shown in Figure 3.15.

During the first year, the $1,000 is invested at a rate of 10 percent and earns $100 in interest. The interest earned is then added back to the principal amount to derive a new second-year beginning balance of $1,100. During the second year, the $1,100 is invested at a rate of 10 percent and earns $110 in interest. The interest earned is added back to the principal amount to derive a new third-year beginning balance of $1,210. As time progresses, both the principal and interest earn interest in this compounding process.

**Figure 3.15**

Cash Flow Diagram—Interest Earned

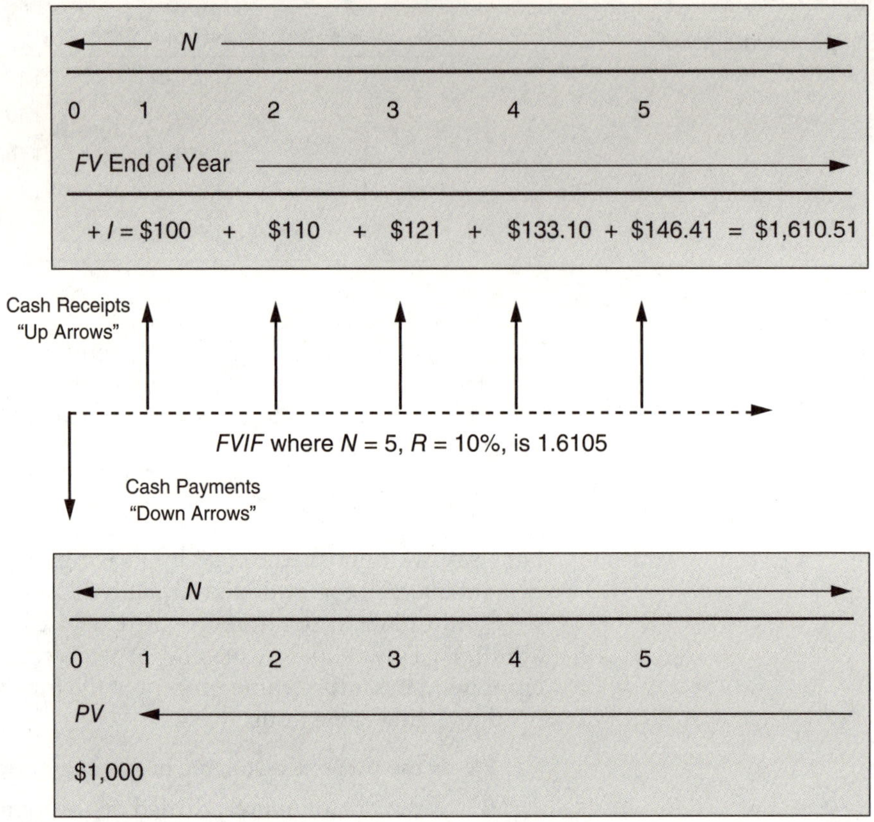


Let's say that we were going to deposit the present value of $1,000 for five years and wanted to know the future value of that $1,000, assuming the same 10 percent rate of interest, per annum, without all those interim calculations. How could we do it? By using the future value factors contained in tables designed for just such a purpose. Alternatively, we can calculate those same factors employing a financial calculator, using a spreadsheet, or by inputting information into financial software designed to model discounted cash-flow analysis.

Figure 3.16 contains the future value interest factors for interest rates ranging from 1 percent to 10 percent and for periods of 0 (the present value) to 15 years.

Using these future value interest factors, we can "cut to the chase" and determine the future value of an amount simply by knowing the length of the investment period and the rate of interest. For example, if we wanted to know the future value of $1,000 deposited for five years at 10 percent, we would use the factor of 1.6101 and multiply it against the deposited amount, as follows:

$$\$1{,}000 \times 1.6105 = \$1{,}610.50$$

**Figure 3.16**

Future Value Interest Factors of a Dollar

| Period | 1.0% | 2% | 3% | 4% | 5% | 6% | 7% | 8% | 9% | 10% |
|---|---|---|---|---|---|---|---|---|---|---|
| 0 | 1.0000 | 1.0000 | 1.0000 | 1.0000 | 1.0000 | 1.0000 | 1.0000 | 1.0000 | 1.0000 | 1.0000 |
| 1 | 1.0100 | 1.0200 | 1.0300 | 1.0400 | 1.0500 | 1.0600 | 1.0700 | 1.0800 | 1.0900 | 1.1000 |
| 2 | 1.0201 | 1.0404 | 1.0609 | 1.0816 | 1.1025 | 1.1236 | 1.1449 | 1.1664 | 1.1881 | 1.2100 |
| 3 | 1.0303 | 1.0612 | 1.0927 | 1.1249 | 1.1576 | 1.1910 | 1.2250 | 1.2597 | 1.2950 | 1.3310 |
| 4 | 1.0406 | 1.0824 | 1.1255 | 1.1699 | 1.2155 | 1.2625 | 1.3108 | 1.3605 | 1.4116 | 1.4641 |
| 5 | 1.0510 | 1.1041 | 1.1593 | 1.2167 | 1.2763 | 1.3382 | 1.4026 | 1.4693 | 1.5386 | 1.6105 |
| 6 | 1.0615 | 1.1262 | 1.1941 | 1.2653 | 1.3401 | 1.4185 | 1.5007 | 1.5869 | 1.6771 | 1.7716 |
| 7 | 1.0721 | 1.1487 | 1.2299 | 1.3159 | 1.4071 | 1.5036 | 1.6058 | 1.7138 | 1.8280 | 1.9487 |
| 8 | 1.0829 | 1.1717 | 1.2668 | 1.3686 | 1.4775 | 1.5938 | 1.7182 | 1.8509 | 1.9926 | 2.1436 |
| 9 | 1.0937 | 1.1951 | 1.3048 | 1.4233 | 1.5513 | 1.6895 | 1.8385 | 1.9990 | 2.1719 | 2.3579 |
| 10 | 1.1046 | 1.2190 | 1.3439 | 1.4802 | 1.6289 | 1.7908 | 1.9672 | 2.1589 | 2.3674 | 2.5937 |
| 11 | 1.1157 | 1.2434 | 1.3842 | 1.5395 | 1.7103 | 1.8983 | 2.1049 | 2.3316 | 2.5804 | 2.8531 |
| 12 | 1.1268 | 1.2682 | 1.4258 | 1.6010 | 1.7959 | 2.0122 | 2.2522 | 2.5182 | 2.8127 | 3.1384 |
| 13 | 1.1381 | 1.2936 | 1.4685 | 1.6651 | 1.8856 | 2.1329 | 2.4098 | 2.7196 | 3.0658 | 3.4523 |
| 14 | 1.1495 | 1.3195 | 1.5126 | 1.7317 | 1.9799 | 2.2609 | 2.5785 | 2.9372 | 3.3417 | 3.7975 |
| 15 | 1.1610 | 1.3459 | 1.5580 | 1.8009 | 2.0789 | 2.3966 | 2.7590 | 3.1722 | 3.6425 | 4.1772 |

### *Present Value of a Dollar*

As we have seen, our potential return of capital will come from forecasted future annual income and reversion. For our ten-unit rental apartment, the annual income during 2005 through 2009 that we forecasted, along with its reversion in 2010, can be converted into an equivalent present worth through the discounting process. As its name implies, *discounting* literally discounts, or reduces, forecasted future incomes into an equivalent **present value of a dollar**. Hence, the term *discounted cash flow analysis*.

Let's say that you are offered a choice of either $1,610.50 at the end of five years or $X today. You know that you could deposit the $X in the bank and earn 10 percent per year. What would $X have to be to make you indifferent to either getting $X today or $1,610.50 after five years?

A cash-flow diagram modeling this problem can be found in Figure 3.17.

If we look at the FVIF table, at 10 percent at period zero (the present), the corresponding present value amount would be $1,000. Figure 3.18 contains the present value interest factors for interest rates ranging from 1 percent to 10 percent and for periods of 0 (present value) to 15 years.

Using these present value interest factors, we can "cut to the chase" and determine the present value of an amount by knowing the length of the

**Figure 3.17**

Cash-Flow Diagram—Discounting

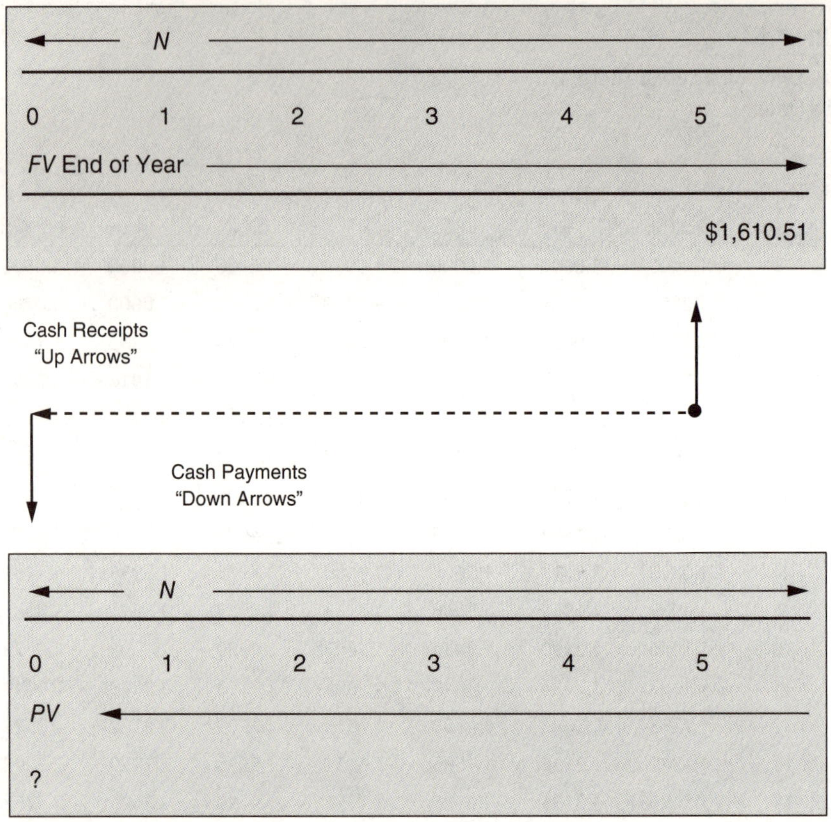


**Figure 3.18**

Present Value Interest Factors of a Dollar

| Period | 1.0% | 2% | 3% | 4% | 5% | 6% | 7% | 8% | 9% | 10% |
|---|---|---|---|---|---|---|---|---|---|---|
| 0 | 1.0000 | 1.0000 | 1.0000 | 1.0000 | 1.0000 | 1.0000 | 1.0000 | 1.0000 | 1.0000 | 1.0000 |
| 1 | 0.9901 | 0.9804 | 0.9709 | 0.9615 | 0.9524 | 0.9434 | 0.9346 | 0.9259 | 0.9174 | 0.9091 |
| 2 | 0.9803 | 0.9612 | 0.9426 | 0.9246 | 0.9070 | 0.8900 | 0.8734 | 0.8573 | 0.8417 | 0.8264 |
| 3 | 0.9706 | 0.9423 | 0.9151 | 0.8890 | 0.8638 | 0.8396 | 0.8163 | 0.7938 | 0.7722 | 0.7513 |
| 4 | 0.9610 | 0.9238 | 0.8885 | 0.8548 | 0.8227 | 0.7921 | 0.7629 | 0.7350 | 0.7084 | 0.6830 |
| 5 | 0.9515 | 0.9057 | 0.8626 | 0.8219 | 0.7835 | 0.7473 | 0.7130 | 0.6806 | 0.6499 | 0.6209 |
| 6 | 0.9420 | 0.8880 | 0.8375 | 0.7903 | 0.7462 | 0.7050 | 0.6663 | 0.6302 | 0.5963 | 0.5645 |
| 7 | 0.9327 | 0.8706 | 0.8131 | 0.7599 | 0.7107 | 0.6651 | 0.6227 | 0.5835 | 0.5470 | 0.5132 |
| 8 | 0.9235 | 0.8535 | 0.7894 | 0.7307 | 0.6768 | 0.6274 | 0.5820 | 0.5403 | 0.5019 | 0.4665 |
| 9 | 0.9143 | 0.8368 | 0.7664 | 0.7026 | 0.6446 | 0.5919 | 0.5439 | 0.5002 | 0.4604 | 0.4241 |
| 10 | 0.9053 | 0.8203 | 0.7441 | 0.6756 | 0.6139 | 0.5584 | 0.5083 | 0.4632 | 0.4224 | 0.3855 |
| 11 | 0.8963 | 0.8043 | 0.7224 | 0.6496 | 0.5847 | 0.5268 | 0.4751 | 0.4289 | 0.3875 | 0.3505 |
| 12 | 0.8874 | 0.7885 | 0.7014 | 0.6246 | 0.5568 | 0.4970 | 0.4440 | 0.3971 | 0.3555 | 0.3186 |
| 13 | 0.8787 | 0.7730 | 0.6810 | 0.6006 | 0.5303 | 0.4688 | 0.4150 | 0.3677 | 0.3262 | 0.2897 |
| 14 | 0.8700 | 0.7579 | 0.6611 | 0.5775 | 0.5051 | 0.4423 | 0.3878 | 0.3405 | 0.2992 | 0.2633 |
| 15 | 0.8613 | 0.7430 | 0.6419 | 0.5553 | 0.4810 | 0.4173 | 0.3624 | 0.3152 | 0.2745 | 0.2394 |

**Figure 3.19**

Cash-Flow Diagram—PVIF

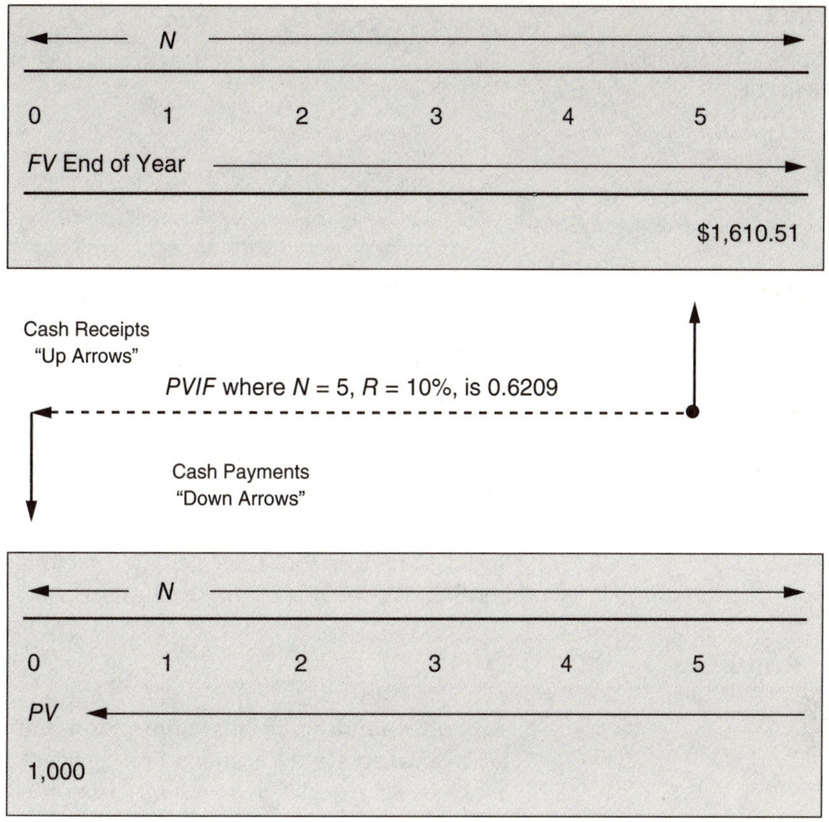


investment period and the rate of interest. A cash-flow diagram modeling this problem can be found in Figure 3.19.

If the PVIFs and the FVIFs seem to involve similar processes, they do—and for good reason. The discounting process is the reciprocal of the compounding process. For any given PVIF:

$$FVIF = 1 \div PVIF$$

For example, from the tables, we know that the FVIF for our $1,000, invested at 10 percent, at the end of period five is 1.6101. As such, the PVIF for five periods at 10 percent is the reciprocal, as follows:

$$PVIF(r,n) = [1 \div FVIF(r,n)]$$
$$0.6209 = [1 \div 1.6101]$$

The PVIF (where the rate [r] equals 10 percent and the discount period [n] is for five years) is equal to one, divided by the FVIF (where the rate [r] equals 10 percent and the compounding period [n] is for five years).

**Figure 3.20**

Reciprocal Relationship of PVIF to FVIF

| Yield Rate | N | PVIF | = | 1 | Divided By | FVIF |
|---|---|---|---|---|---|---|
| 14.37% | 1 | 0.874385701 | = | 1 | / | 1.143660057 |
| 14.37% | 2 | 0.764550354 | = | 1 | / | 1.307958325 |
| 14.37% | 3 | 0.668511897 | = | 1 | / | 1.495859692 |
| 14.37% | 4 | 0.584537243 | = | 1 | / | 1.710754980 |
| 14.37% | 5 | 0.511111007 | = | 1 | / | 1.956522137 |

In other words, the future value of the present sum of $1,000 invested at 10 percent per year, compounded annually for five years, is $1,610.50; and the present value of the future sum of $1,610.50 discounted at 10 percent per year, compounded annually for five years, is $1,000.

Let's apply this mathematical principal of present value and future value to the zero-coupon bond case study presented earlier. Reviewing Figures 3.9 and 3.12 reveals that the calculated factors are, in fact, the reciprocal of one another. We see this clearly in Figure 3.20.

## Annuities

An understanding of what annuities are and how annuities work is important, because yield capitalization is used as part of discounted cash-flow analysis. As discussed, an *annuity* is a schedule of cash payments where the payments occur at regular, fixed intervals. Examples of annuities include

- the purchase of a five-year, laddered portfolio of zero-coupon bonds with income expected to occur periodically;
- the purchase of income-producing real estate expected to be held for five years, with income expected to occur periodically, including the sale of the property;
- the purchase of an amortizing mortgage loan with income expected to occur periodically, including the ballooning of outstanding principal at the end of the fifth year; and
- the investment of $1,000 each year for a five-year period with a lump-sum future income payment expected to occur at the end of the fifth year.

In these examples, the purchase/investment represents a cash outflow, and income represents a cash inflow. Each of these investments can be compared to a program or contract consisting of regular payments of stipulated amounts. These payments do not have to be for equal amounts and can be made monthly, quarterly, annually, or over some other agreed-upon period. However, what all annuities have in common is their scheduled and predictable income. So a feature of an annuity is its expected regularity of payments and predictability of amounts. For all of these reasons, yield capitalization is also referred to as **annuity capitalization**.

### *Future Value of an Annuity*

Let's say we deposit $1,000 a year in a savings account at a bank that pays 10 percent interest, compounded annually. We deposit $1,000 this year, and each and every year, for the next five years. This program of regular annual

**Figure 3.21**

Future Value of $1,000 per Period Annuity, Invested at 10 Percent

| Period | Payment | FVIF ( r,n) | Value Yr 5 |
|---|---|---|---|
| 1 | $1,000 | 1.4641 | $1,464.10 |
| 2 | $1,000 | 1.3310 | $1,331.00 |
| 3 | $1,000 | 1.2100 | $1,210.00 |
| 4 | $1,000 | 1.1000 | $1,100.00 |
| 5 | $1,000 | 1.0000 | $1,000.00 |
| Future Compounded Sum | | | $6,105.10 |

payments would be predictable. In other words, a feature of this annuity is its expected regularity and the predictability of its amounts. How could we determine how much we would have in our account at the end of the five years? By employing the **future value of an annuity**.

Based on the FVIFs for each annual deposit, earning 10 percent interest for the respective periods, our annuity would have a future value of $6,105.10, as calculated in Figure 3.21.

A cash-flow diagram describing this annuity investment is shown by Figure 3.22.

What if all our deposits are equal and for the same amounts? We could determine the future value by employing an annuity factor that considers the term

**Figure 3.22**

Cash-Flow Diagram—Future Value of an Annuity

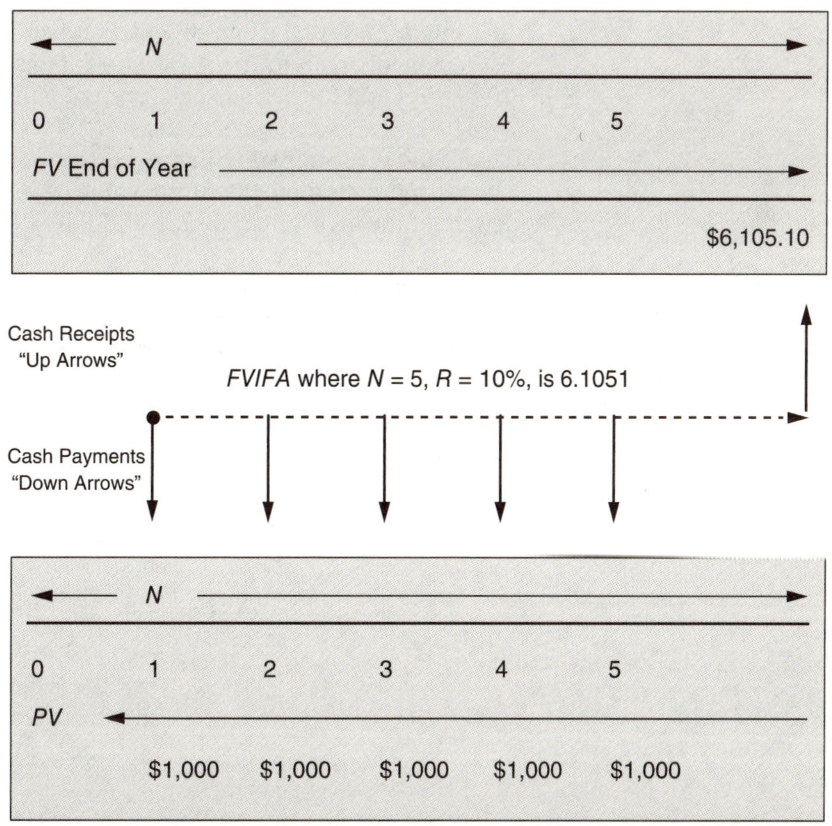

**Figure 3.23**

Future Value Interest Factors of an Annuity

| Period | 1.0% | 2% | 3% | 4% | 5% | 6% | 7% | 8% | 9% | 10% |
|---|---|---|---|---|---|---|---|---|---|---|
| 1 | 1.0000 | 1.0000 | 1.0000 | 1.0000 | 1.0000 | 1.0000 | 1.0000 | 1.0000 | 1.0000 | 1.0000 |
| 2 | 2.0100 | 2.0200 | 2.0300 | 2.0400 | 2.0500 | 2.0600 | 2.0700 | 2.0800 | 2.0900 | 2.1000 |
| 3 | 3.0301 | 3.0604 | 3.0909 | 3.1216 | 3.1525 | 3.1836 | 3.2149 | 3.2464 | 3.2781 | 3.3100 |
| 4 | 4.0604 | 4.1216 | 4.1836 | 4.2465 | 4.3101 | 4.3746 | 4.4399 | 4.5061 | 4.5731 | 4.6410 |
| 5 | 5.1010 | 5.2040 | 5.3091 | 5.4163 | 5.5256 | 5.6371 | 5.7507 | 5.8666 | 5.9847 | 6.1051 |
| 6 | 6.1520 | 6.3081 | 6.4684 | 6.6330 | 6.8019 | 6.9753 | 7.1533 | 7.3359 | 7.5233 | 7.7156 |
| 7 | 7.2135 | 7.4343 | 7.6625 | 7.8983 | 8.1420 | 8.3938 | 8.6540 | 8.9228 | 9.2004 | 9.4872 |
| 8 | 8.2857 | 8.5830 | 8.8923 | 9.2142 | 9.5491 | 9.8975 | 10.2598 | 10.6366 | 11.0285 | 11.4359 |
| 9 | 9.3685 | 9.7546 | 10.1591 | 10.5828 | 11.0266 | 11.4913 | 11.9780 | 12.4876 | 13.0210 | 13.5795 |
| 10 | 10.4622 | 10.9497 | 11.4639 | 12.0061 | 12.5779 | 13.1808 | 13.8164 | 14.4866 | 15.1929 | 15.9374 |
| 11 | 11.5668 | 12.1687 | 12.8078 | 13.4864 | 14.2068 | 14.9716 | 15.7836 | 16.6455 | 17.5603 | 18.5312 |
| 12 | 12.6825 | 13.4121 | 14.1920 | 15.0258 | 15.9171 | 16.8699 | 17.8885 | 18.9771 | 20.1407 | 21.3843 |
| 13 | 13.8093 | 14.6803 | 15.6178 | 16.6268 | 17.7130 | 18.8821 | 20.1406 | 21.4953 | 22.9534 | 24.5227 |
| 14 | 14.9474 | 15.9739 | 17.0863 | 18.2919 | 19.5986 | 21.0151 | 22.5505 | 24.2149 | 26.0192 | 27.9750 |
| 15 | 16.0969 | 17.2934 | 18.5989 | 20.0236 | 21.5786 | 23.2760 | 25.1290 | 27.1521 | 29.3609 | 31.7725 |

and interest rate of the investment. Figure 3.23 contains the future value interest factors of an annuity (FVIFA) for interest rates ranging from 1 percent to 10 percent and for periods of 0 (present value) to 15 years.

Using these future value interest factors of an annuity, we can "cut to the chase" and determine the future value of an amount, simply by knowing the length of the investment period and the rate of interest.

For example, if we wanted to know the future value of $1,000 deposited each year for five years earning 10 percent interest, we would use the factor of 6.1051 and multiply it against the deposited amount, as follows:

$$\$1,000 \times 6.1051 = \$6,105.10$$

The formula for any FVIFA is:

$$\text{FVIFA}(r,n) = \frac{[(1+r)^n] - 1}{r}$$

Where: r = the interest rate
n = the number of periods (how many times the formula is multiplied against itself)

What if our deposits were unequal and for differing amounts? Well, in such a case, although we would still be forecasting a cash flow, it would be in unequal payments, and we could not employ a FVIFA. We would instead use a FVIF(r,n) for each periodic payment to determine its corresponding future value.

FVIFAs are readily available in handheld financial calculators and in many types of financial software. So we no longer need to be concerned about the derivation of the formula. However, we could still calculate our FVIFAs if we wanted to.

For example, the FVIFA for the previous five-year annuity of $1,000 deposited at a 10 percent yield rate would be calculated as follows:

$$\text{FVIFA}(r=10\%, n=5) = \frac{[(1+0.10)^5]-1}{.0.10}$$

$$\text{FVIFA}(r=10\%, n=5) = \frac{[(1.10)^5]-1}{0.10}$$

$$\text{FVIFA}(r=10\%, n=5) = \frac{[(1.10)\times(1.10)\times(1.10)\times(1.10)\times(1.10)]-1}{0.10}$$

$$\text{FVIFA}(r=10\%, n=5) = \frac{[1.61051]-1}{0.10}$$

$$\text{FVIFA}(r=10\%, n=5) = \frac{0.61051}{0.10}$$

$$\text{FVIFA}(r=10\%, n=5) = 6.1051$$

### *Present Value of an Annuity*

Let's say that you are offered a choice of either a five-year annuity of $1,000 per year or a lump-sum payment today. You know that you could deposit the $1,000 payment in the bank and earn 10 percent per year. What would $X today have to be to make you indifferent to either getting $X today or $1,000 per year for the next five years? $X would be the **present value of the annuity** (the five individual payments of $1,000), discounted at 10 percent per year. Based on the PVIFs for each annual deposit, at 10 percent for the respective periods, our annuity would have a present value of $3,790.79, as calculated in Figure 3.24.

**Figure 3.24**

Present Value of $1,000

| Period | Payment | FVIF ( r,n) | Value Yr 5 |
|---|---|---|---|
| 1 | $1,000 | 0.9091 | $909.09 |
| 2 | $1,000 | 0.8264 | $826.45 |
| 3 | $1,000 | 0.7513 | $751.31 |
| 4 | $1,000 | 0.6830 | $683.01 |
| 5 | $1,000 | 0.6209 | $620.92 |
| Present Discounted Sum | | | $3,790.79 |

**Figure 3.25**

Cash-Flow Diagram—Present Value of an Annuity Investment

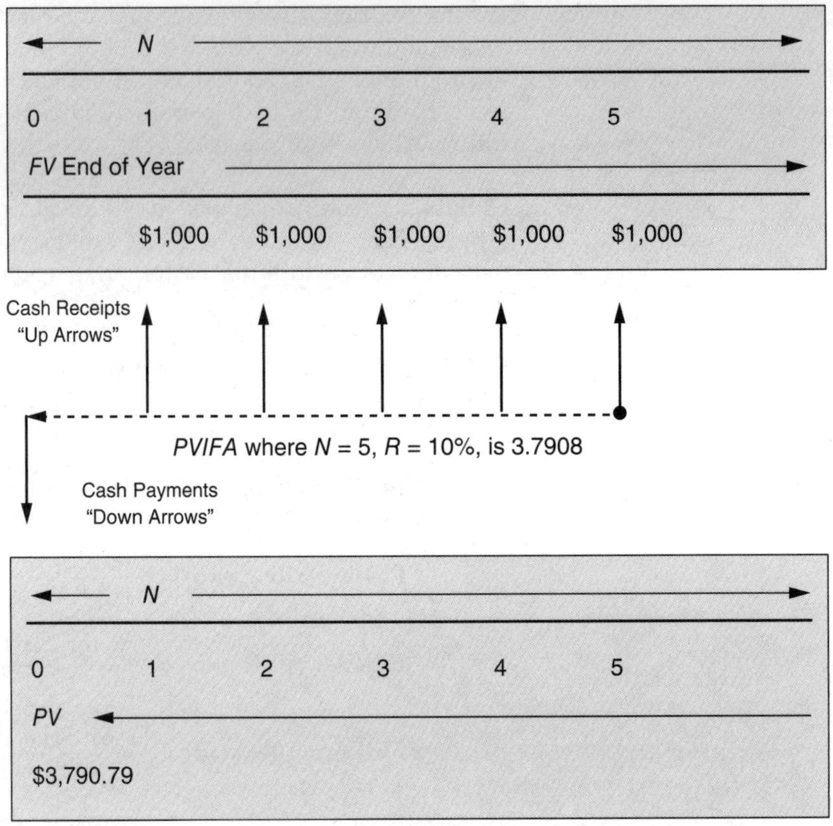


**Figure 3.26**

Present Value Interest Factors of an Annuity

| Period | 1.0% | 2% | 3% | 4% | 5% | 6% | 7% | 8% | 9% | 10% |
|---|---|---|---|---|---|---|---|---|---|---|
| 1 | 0.9901 | 0.9804 | 0.9709 | 0.9615 | 0.9524 | 0.9434 | 0.9346 | 0.9259 | 0.9174 | 0.9091 |
| 2 | 1.9704 | 1.9416 | 1.9135 | 1.8861 | 1.8594 | 1.8334 | 1.8080 | 1.7833 | 1.7591 | 1.7355 |
| 3 | 2.9410 | 2.8839 | 2.8286 | 2.7751 | 2.7232 | 2.6730 | 2.6243 | 2.5771 | 2.5313 | 2.4869 |
| 4 | 3.9020 | 3.8077 | 3.7171 | 3.6299 | 3.5460 | 3.4651 | 3.3872 | 3.3121 | 3.2397 | 3.1699 |
| 5 | 4.8534 | 4.7135 | 4.5797 | 4.4518 | 4.3295 | 4.2124 | 4.1002 | 3.9927 | 3.8897 | 3.7908 |
| 6 | 5.7955 | 5.6014 | 5.4172 | 5.2421 | 5.0757 | 4.9173 | 4.7665 | 4.6229 | 4.4859 | 4.3553 |
| 7 | 6.7282 | 6.4720 | 6.2303 | 6.0021 | 5.7864 | 5.5824 | 5.3893 | 5.2064 | 5.0330 | 4.8684 |
| 8 | 7.6517 | 7.3255 | 7.0197 | 6.7327 | 6.4632 | 6.2098 | 5.9713 | 5.7466 | 5.5348 | 5.3349 |
| 9 | 8.5660 | 8.1622 | 7.7861 | 7.4353 | 7.1078 | 6.8017 | 6.5152 | 6.2469 | 5.9952 | 5.7590 |
| 10 | 9.4713 | 8.9826 | 8.5302 | 8.1109 | 7.7217 | 7.3601 | 7.0236 | 6.7101 | 6.4177 | 6.1446 |
| 11 | 10.3676 | 9.7868 | 9.2526 | 8.7605 | 8.3064 | 7.8869 | 7.4987 | 7.1390 | 6.8052 | 6.4951 |
| 12 | 11.2551 | 10.5753 | 9.9540 | 9.3851 | 8.8633 | 8.3838 | 7.9427 | 7.5361 | 7.1607 | 6.8137 |
| 13 | 12.1337 | 11.3484 | 10.6350 | 9.9856 | 9.3936 | 8.8527 | 8.3577 | 7.9038 | 7.4869 | 7.1034 |
| 14 | 13.0037 | 12.1062 | 11.2961 | 10.5631 | 9.8986 | 9.2950 | 8.7455 | 8.2442 | 7.7862 | 7.3667 |
| 15 | 13.8651 | 12.8493 | 11.9379 | 11.1184 | 10.3797 | 9.7122 | 9.1079 | 8.5595 | 8.0607 | 7.6061 |

In other words, the present value of an annuity of $1,000 per year for five years, discounted at 10 percent per year and compounded annually for five years, is $3,790.79. Figure 3.25 shows a cash-flow diagram for this present value of an annuity investment.

However, because all the payments are equal and for the same amounts, we could determine the present value of the annuity by employing an annuity factor that considers the term and interest rate of the investment. Figure 3.26 contains the present value interest factors of an annuity (PVIFA) for interest rates ranging from 1 percent to 10 percent and for periods of 0 (present value) to 15 years.

Using these present value interest factors of an annuity, we can "cut to the chase" and determine the present value of an amount simply by knowing the length of the investment period and the rate of interest. For example, if we wanted to know the present value of $1,000 deposited each year for five years at 10 percent, we would use the factor of 3.7908 and multiply it against the deposited amount, as follows:

$$\$1{,}000 \times 3.7908 = \$3{,}790.80$$

The formula for any PVIFA is as follows:

$$\text{PVIFA}(r,n) = 1 - \left[ \frac{\frac{1}{(1+r)^n}}{r} \right]$$

Where: r = the interest rate
n = the number of periods (how many times the formula is multiplied against itself)

For example, the PVIFA for the previous five-year annuity of $1,000 payments at a 10 percent yield rate would be calculated as follows:

$$\text{PVIFA}(r=10\%, n=5) = \frac{1 - \{[(\frac{1}{(1+0.10)^5]}}{0.10\ \}}$$

$$\text{PVIFA}(r=10\%, n=5) = \frac{1 - \{[(\frac{1}{(1.10)^5]}}{0.10\ \}}$$

$$\text{PVIFA}(r=10\%, n=5) = \frac{1 - \{[(\frac{1}{(1.10) \times (1.10) \times (1.10) \times (1.10) \times (1.10)]}}{0.10\ \}}$$

$$\text{PVIFA}(r=10\%, n=5) = \frac{1 - \{[(\frac{1}{1.61051\ ]}}{0.10\ \}}$$

$$\text{PVIFA}(r{=}10\%, n{=}5) = \frac{1 - 0.62092}{0.10}$$

$$\text{PVIFA}(r{=}10\%, n{=}5) = \frac{0.37908}{0.10}$$

$$\text{PVIFA}(r{=}10\%, n{=}5) = 3.7908$$

If our deposits were unequal and for differing amounts, the forecasted cash flows would be unequal payments, and we could not employ a PVIFA. Instead, we would discount each payment separately to arrive at a present worth.

## Relevance of Time Value of Money to Yield Capitalization

Most real estate investment properties are characterized by uneven annuities, which become the basis of a property's forecasted cash flows.

As we have been discussing, yield capitalization concepts are dependent upon an understanding of time value of money concepts. We may come across many different types of forecasted cash flows, including level annuities, increasing annuities, and decreasing annuities. However, most real estate investment properties are characterized by uneven annuities, which become the basis of a property's forecasted cash flows.

### *Price/Value of the Ten-Unit Rental Annuity*

Let's say that we are interested in acquiring the ten-unit rental apartment property presented in Figure 3.3. We expect to hold the property for five years, then sell the property at the end of the fifth year. So we are acquiring the "financial architecture," the forecasted cash flows, as the basis for a five-year uneven annuity.

We know that investors are demanding somewhere around a 13.5 percent yield rate on reasonably similar investments. What price should we pay today to obtain this return? That price would be the present value of the five individual payments, discounted at 13.5 percent per year. Based on the PVIFs for each year, our annuity would have a present value of $597,000, as calculated in Figure 3.27.

**Figure 3.27**

PV/Price of Ten-Unit Property at a 13.5 Percent Yield

| N/Period | "FV" Payment | Multiplied By | PVIF @ (13.5%,n) | Discounted PV |
|---|---|---|---|---|
| 1 | $57,822 | × | 0.881057269 | $50,944.49 |
| 2 | $63,742 | × | 0.776261911 | $49,480.49 |
| 3 | $66,541 | × | 0.683931199 | $45,509.47 |
| 4 | $69,397 | × | 0.602582554 | $41,817.42 |
| 5 | $770,202 | × | 0.530909739 | $408,907.74 |
| Price to Pay Today/Summation of Discounted PV | | | | $596,659.61 |
| Discounted PV—Rounded | | | | $597,000.00 |

**Figure 3.28**

Cash-Flow Diagram—
Price of Ten-Unit Property
at a 13.5 Percent Yield

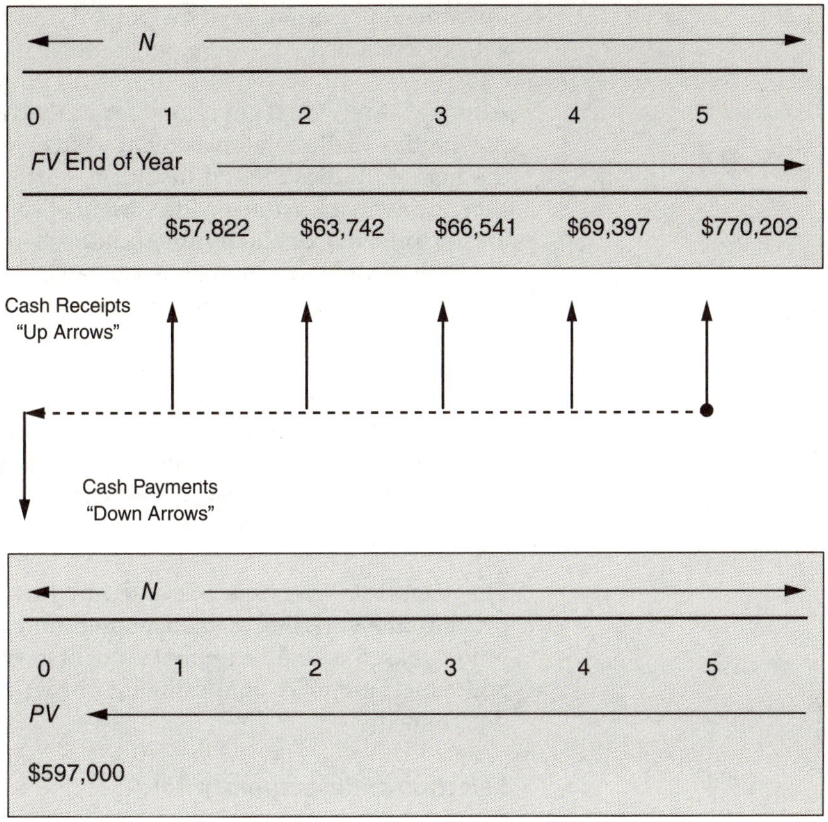


In other words, the present value of this uneven five-year annuity when discounted at 13.5 percent per year is $597,000.

Figure 3.28 shows a cash-flow diagram for the present value of this annuity investment.

### *Selection of Yield Rates*

Combining the return of capital and the return on capital produces the investment's rate of return on capital. The rate of return on capital is measured in terms of an interest rate. Each year of the investment, it is expected to generate a certain rate of interest. However, because its income may fluctuate from one year to the next, so will the rate of interest. The rate of return that the investment generates over the entire investment period is called a yield rate.

The true yield of a real estate investment cannot be determined until the termination of the investment upon the sale of the property. However, a prudent/prospective investor should establish a desired yield rate attributable to the forecasted cash flows/periodic income prior to purchasing the property. Establishing a yield rate addresses the purchaser's investment sentiment. *Investment sentiment* is our disposition or attitude toward investing, which is influenced by financial logic and economic facts, as well as our personal emotions about such factors as safety, risk, and income. So our investment sentiment represents a distillation of both facts and feelings. Investment sentiment can be measured by such indicators as risk tolerance, the forecasted investment performance of the property, and the purchaser's forecast of market expectations.

Although individual investors set individual investment objectives, their prospective real estate investment yields are overwhelmingly influenced by the market. Indications of historical, current, and projected yield expectations are available from a wide variety of sources, including appraisers, lenders, brokers, owners, and buyers and sellers of investment real estate. Also, a wealth of yield information is available from real estate trade publications, newspapers, magazines, and Internet-based sources.

Additionally, published real estate investor surveys are available; these provide overviews of the national and regional economies, capital market reports, and real estate market reports by class and quality of property type and location. These surveys also present detailed information on direct capitalization rates, reversionary capitalization rates, yield capitalization rates, revenue and expense-growth rate expectations, and holding periods.

The composite overview presented by this information provides an appropriate framework from which an investor can further fine-tune yield expectations, based on the additional input of local and regional market conditions and expectations. A final estimate of the investor's yield rate can then be determined.

### *Selection of Reversionary Rates*

Reversion is usually a significant part of the overall income to be derived from a real estate investment. Its relative percentage is important in determining both reversionary rates and yield rates. In an ideal but unlikely situation, the present value of a property's reversion would be the same percentage as the present value of the periodic cash flows, so the relationship of cash flow to reversion would be 50–50.

If most of a real estate investment's capital is forecast to be recaptured through periodic cash flows (say 75 percent) and only a small percentage through capital reversion (say 25 percent), the investment carried greater risk than in a more balanced distribution (50–50). We would want to know why there is such a disparity between the two components.

For example, we might consider buying an apartment property leased to tenants at contract rents, which are equal to market rents. So the property has no real upside from rental increases. Then we become aware of new apartment supply that is rumored to be coming to the market before our holding period ends. We might conclude that the additional supply will result in downward pressure on the property's future unit rent. The lower future revenues would lower our future NOI, which would be capitalized into a lower future reversionary value. This would result in most of the present value of the investment coming from the cash flows (e.g., 75 percent), and a smaller percentage recaptured through future capital reversion (e.g., 25 percent).

Alternatively, if most of the real estate investment's capital is forecast to be recaptured through reversion (say 75 percent) and only a small percentage through periodic cash flows (say 25 percent), the investment holds more risk than if the distribution was more balanced, (say 50–50). We would want to know why there is such a disparity between the two components.

For example, once again, we might consider buying an apartment property leased to tenants at contract rents, which are equal to market rents. So the property has no initial upside from rental increases. Then we become aware that not only is demand increasing for units in this market, but there is also no land available for new construction. Thus forecasted demand will result in upward pressure on the property's future unit rent. The higher future revenues would increase our future NOI, which would be capitalized into a higher future reversionary value. This would result in most of the present value of the investment coming from the future capital reversion (e.g., 75 percent), and smaller percentage recaptured through periodic cash flows (e.g., 25 percent).

How does forecasted value dispersion impact reversion? Because reversion occurs in the future, it is subject to risk. If most of the return on capital and return of capital occurs at reversion, risk moves to the latter part of the investment. Therefore, the investment would warrant a higher yield (risk) rate and higher reversionary rate. The underlying forecasted cash flows provide key information as to the direction, quality, and quantity of income at the termination of the investment.

Market intelligence is an important factor in the selection of a reversion rate. It can work in the following ways:

- If our market intelligence supports a forecast of increasing demand for our prospective purchase, we may conclude that reversionary capitalization rates will be declining during our holding period.
- If our market intelligence supports a forecast of decreasing demand for our prospective purchase, we may conclude that reversionary capitalization rates will be rising during our holding period.
- If our market intelligence supports a forecast of comparable demand for our prospective purchase, we may conclude that reversionary capitalization rates will be relatively stable during our holding period.

Generally, but not always, the reversionary rate should be somewhat higher, as measured in **basis points,** than the going-in rate or OAR to reflect the additional age of the property and perceived risk in the future cash flow. A *basis point* is one one-hundredth of one percentage point (0.01%). Basis points are sometimes referred to in real estate jargon as "beeps."

### *Net Sales Proceeds from Reversionary Value*

Once an NOI has been capitalized into value via the reversionary rate, the forecasted gross sales transaction price must be adjusted for the costs of sales associated with that transaction to arrive at the net sales proceeds. These costs of sales, known as *transaction costs*, are often expressed as a percent and may include:

- Brokerage commissions and other sales and marketing expenses
- Seller's expenses associated with property transfer and other taxes
- Attorney's fees, consultant's fees, and intracompany-related charges
- Costs associated with debt prepayment penalties

## Case Study: Yield Capitalization

Based upon our review of the most credible information about a property, we conclude that yield rates for apartment buildings in our property's class and quality, which would be acceptable to us as a purchaser range from 13 percent to 14 percent. Furthermore, reversionary rates for apartment buildings in our property's class and quality, which would be acceptable to us as a purchaser, range from 10 percent to 10.5 percent. These figures are supported by market information.

We then consider three scenarios:

1. We would accept a 13 percent yield (i.e., a lower yield implying lower risk) if more disposition risk were mitigated by employing a 10.5 percent reversionary rate (i.e., a higher yield implying higher risk). However, we believe that this scenario is not the most probable of the three possible scenarios.

**Figure 3.29**

DCFA Yield of 13 Percent and Reversion of 10.5 Percent

| Forecast Year | Status | NOI | PVIF @ 13.00% | Discounted Cash Flows |
|---|---|---|---|---|
| 2005 | Holding | $57,822 | 0.884955750 | $51,170 |
| 2006 | Holding | $63,742 | 0.783146680 | $49,919 |
| 2007 | Holding | $66,541 | 0.693050160 | $46,116 |
| 2008 | Holding | $69,397 | 0.613318730 | $42,562 |
| 2009 | Holding | $72,500 | 0.542759940 | $39,350 |
| | | | subtotal | $229,118 |
| | | | Percent Total Value | 38.26% |
| *add:* | | | | |
| 2010 | Reversion | $681,089 | 0.542759940 | $369,668 |
| *equals:* | | | Percent Total Value | 61.74% |
| **Discounted NOI and Reversion** | | | | $598,786 |
| *rounded to:* | | | | $599,000 |
| Total | | | | $599,000 |
| Per Unit | | | | $59,900 |

| Reversion Calculation | |
|---|---|
| 6th Year NOI | $75,278 |
| *divided by:* | |
| Reversionary Rate | 10.50% |
| *equals:* | |
| Gross Sales Proceeds | $716,936 |
| *less:* | |
| Transaction Costs @ 5% | $35,847 |
| *equals:* | |
| Net Sales Proceeds/Reversion | $681,089 |

2. We would accept a 13.5 percent yield (i.e., a higher yield implying higher risk) if less disposition risk were mitigated by employing a 10.25 percent reversionary rate (i.e., a lower yield implying lower risk). We believe that this scenario is the most probable of the three possible scenarios.
3. We would accept a 14 percent yield (i.e., a higher yield implying higher risk) if very little reversionary risk was mitigated by employing a 10 percent reversionary rate (i.e., a lower yield implying more risk). We believe that this scenario, like scenario #1, is not the most probable of the three possible scenarios.

Why consider different possible combinations of yield rate and reversionary rate?

The true yield of a real estate investment cannot be determined until its termination at the time of the sale of the property. However, a prudent prospective investor should establish a desired yield rate, or rates, attributable to

**Figure 3.30**

DCFA Yield of 13.5 Percent and Reversion of 10.25 Percent

| Forecast Year | Status | NOI | PVIF @ 13.50% | Discounted Cash Flows |
|---|---|---|---|---|
| 2005 | Holding | $57,822 | 0.881057270 | $50,944 |
| 2006 | Holding | $63,742 | 0.776261910 | $49,480 |
| 2007 | Holding | $66,541 | 0.683931200 | $45,509 |
| 2008 | Holding | $69,397 | 0.602582550 | $41,817 |
| 2009 | Holding | $72,500 | 0.530909740 | $38,491 |
| | | | subtotal | $226,243 |
| | | | Percent Total Value | 37.92% |
| *add:* | | | | |
| 2010 | Reversion | $697,701 | 0.530909740 | $370,416 |
| *equals:* | | | Percent Total Value | 62.08% |
| **Discounted NOI and Reversion** | | | | $596,659 |
| *rounded to:* | | | | $597,000 |
| Total | | | | $597,000 |
| Per Unit | | | | $59,700 |

| Reversion Calculation | |
|---|---|
| 6th Year NOI | $75,278 |
| *divided by:* | |
| Reversionary Rate | 10.25% |
| *equals:* | |
| Gross Sales Proceeds | $734,423 |
| *less:* | |
| Transaction Costs @ 5% | $36,721 |
| *equals:* | |
| Net Sales Proceeds/Reversion | $697,701 |

**Figure 3.31**

DCFA Yield of 14 Percent and Reversion of 10 Percent

| Forecast Year | Status | NOI | PVIF @ 13.00% | Discounted Cash Flows |
|---|---|---|---|---|
| 2005 | Holding | $57,822 | 0.877192980 | $50,721 |
| 2006 | Holding | $63,742 | 0.769467530 | $49,047 |
| 2007 | Holding | $66,541 | 0.674971520 | $44,913 |
| 2008 | Holding | $69,397 | 0.592080280 | $41,088 |
| 2009 | Holding | $72,500 | 0.519368660 | $37,654 |
| | | | subtotal | $223,424 |
| | | | Percent Total Value | 37.56% |
| *add:* | | | | |
| 2010 | Reversion | $715,144 | 0.519368660 | $371,423 |
| *equals:* | | | Percent Total Value | 62.44% |
| **Discounted NOI and Reversion** | | | | $594,848 |
| *rounded to:* | | | | $595,000 |
| Total | | | | $595,000 |
| Per Unit | | | | $59,500 |

| Reversion Calculation | |
|---|---|
| 6th Year NOI | $75,278 |
| *divided by:* | |
| Reversionary Rate | 10.00% |
| *equals:* | |
| Gross Sales Proceeds | $752,783 |
| *less:* | |
| Transaction Costs @ 5% | $37,639 |
| *equals:* | |
| Net Sales Proceeds/Reversion | $715,144 |

the forecasted cash flows/periodic income prior to purchasing the property. Establishing a yield rate, or rates, addresses the investor's sentiment, which is influenced by risk tolerance, the forecasted investment performance of the property, and the forecasted market expectations.

Figures 3.29–3.31 lay out three scenarios for the discounted cash flow of our forecasted income and expenses analysis first presented in Figure 3.3.

When considering the purchase of the ten-unit rental property, using a combination of a yield rate of 13 percent and a reversionary rate of 10.5 percent results in a discounted present value of $599,000. A total of $229,118, or 38 percent, of the present value is attributable to discounted cash flows, and $369,668, or 62 percent, is attributable to the discounted reversion.

**Figure 3.32**

Yield Capitalization Valuation Matrix

| Yield Rate | Reversion Rate | Present Value Cash Flows | Present Value Reversion | Present Value Total | % Cash Flows | % Reversion | % Total |
|---|---|---|---|---|---|---|---|
| 13.00% | 10.50% | $229,118 | $369,668 | $599,000 | 38.26% | 61.74% | 100.00% |
| 13.50% | 10.25% | $226,243 | $370,416 | $597,000 | 37.92% | 62.08% | 100.00% |
| 14.00% | 10.00% | $223,424 | $371,423 | $595,000 | 37.56% | 62.44% | 100.00% |

Using a combination of a yield rate of 13.5 percent and a reversionary rate of 10.25 percent results in a discounted present value of $597,000. A total of $226,243, or 38 percent, of the present value is attributable to discounted cash flows, and $370,416, or 62 percent, of the present value is attributable to the discounted reversion.

Using a combination of a yield rate of 14 percent and a reversionary rate of 10 percent results in a discounted present value of $595,000. A total of $223,424, or 38 percent, of the present value is attributable to discounted cash flows, and $371,423, or 62 percent, of the present value is attributable to the discounted reversion.

### *Analysis*

Based upon our review of the most credible information available, we concluded that

- yield rates for apartment buildings of our class and quality ranged from 13 percent to 14 percent; and
- reversionary rates for apartment buildings of our class and quality ranged from 10 percent to 10.5 percent.

We used these investment criteria along with our forecasted income and expense analysis to prepare three scenarios of the discounted cash flows. These DCFA results are summarized in Figure 3.32.

## Reconciling Direct Capitalization with Yield Capitalization

Consider the following investment scenario:

- From our yield capitalization analysis, we conclude that the most probable valuation scenario would result in a combination of a 13.50 percent yield rate and a 10.25 percent reversion rate, resulting in a discounted present value of $597,000 for the ten-unit rental property.
- Based on our direct capitalization analysis, we conclude that the most probable scenario would result in a direct cap rate of 10 percent, resulting in a capitalized value of $578,000.
- We make an offer based on a direct cap price of $578,000. The offer is accepted, and we contract to acquire the property for $578,000.

- Separately, a third-party real estate appraisal firm appraises the property using yield capitalization analysis. It concludes that the market value of the ten-unit rental is indeed $597,000.

What if we acquired the ten-unit rental property for a purchase price of $578,000(rd) and wanted to discount the future cash flows at a yield rate that would make their present value equivalent to the purchase price? That yield rate would be 14.36600565 percent, which when rounded would come to 14.37 percent. This scenario is presented in Figure 3.33.

The difference between the $578,000 acquisition price and the $597,000 discounted present value of this investment is $19,000. This $19,000 represents the net present value of the investment. The **net present value (NPV)** of an investment is the measured difference between the discounted present value of the investment, evaluated at a yield rate considered reasonable and appropriate, and the initial acquisition cost of the investment.

**Figure 3.33**

DCFA Yield of 14.37 Percent (rd) and Reversion of 10.25 Percent

| Forecast Year | Status | NOI | PVIF @ 13.00% | Discounted Cash Flows |
|---|---|---|---|---|
| 2005 | Holding | $57,822 | 0.874385701 | $50,559 |
| 2006 | Holding | $63,742 | 0.764550354 | $48,734 |
| 2007 | Holding | $66,541 | 0.668511897 | $44,483 |
| 2008 | Holding | $69,397 | 0.584537243 | $40,565 |
| 2009 | Holding | $72,500 | 0.511111007 | $37,056 |
| | | | subtotal | $221,397 |
| | | | Percent Total Value | 38.30% |
| *add:* | | | | |
| 2010 | Reversion | $697,701 | 0.511111007 | $356,603 |
| *equals:* | | | Percent Total Value | 61.70% |
| **Discounted NOI and Reversion** | | | | $577,999 |
| *rounded to:* | | | | $578,000 |
| Total | | | | $578,000 |
| Per Unit | | | | $57,800 |

| Reversion Calculation | |
|---|---|
| 6th Year NOI | $75,278 |
| *divided by:* | |
| Reversionary Rate | 10.25% |
| *equals:* | |
| Gross Sales Proceeds | $734,423 |
| *less:* | |
| Transaction Costs @ 5% | $36,721 |
| *equals:* | |
| Net Sales Proceeds/Reversion | $697,701 |

**Figure 3.34**

Comparison of Yield Capitalization Based on a Yield Rate of 13.5 Percent and IRR of 14.37 Percent

| Yield Capitalization and NPV | | | |
|---|---|---|---|
| N/Period | Cash Flows | Yield Rate @13.50% | Discounted Cash Flows |
| 1 | $57,822 | 0.881057269 | $50,944 |
| 2 | $63,742 | 0.776261911 | $49,480 |
| 3 | $66,541 | 0.683931199 | $45,509 |
| 4 | $69,397 | 0.602582554 | $41,817 |
| 5 | $770,202 | 0.530909739 | $408,908 |
| PV of Discounted Cash Flows (rounded) | | | $597,000 |
| *less:* | | | |
| Acquisition Costs | | | $578,000 |
| *equals:* | | | |
| Net Present Value of Acquisition | | | $19,000 |

| IRR and NPV | | | |
|---|---|---|---|
| N/Period | Cash Flows | IRR Rate @14.37% | Discounted Cash Flows |
| 1 | $57,822 | 0.874385701 | $50,559 |
| 2 | $63,742 | 0.764550354 | $48,734 |
| 3 | $66,541 | 0.668511897 | $44,483 |
| 4 | $69,397 | 0.584537243 | $40,565 |
| 5 | $770,202 | 0.511111007 | $393,659 |
| PV of Discounted Cash Flows (rounded) | | | $578,000 |
| *less:* | | | |
| Acquisition Costs | | | $578,000 |
| *equals:* | | | |
| Net Present Value of Acquisition | | | $- |

We also found that we would have to discount the future cash flows at a yield rate of exactly 14.36600565 percent (which rounded comes to 14.37 percent) to derive the present value that is exactly equal to the initial investment. That yield rate represents the internal rate of return of the investment. The **internal rate of return (IRR)** of an investment is the rate of return that discounts the future benefits of the investment to a present value that is *exactly* equal to the initial investment. When a property is purchased at its IRR, its NPV is zero. Stated differently, the IRR is the rate of return that puts the present value of the periodic cash flows and reversion equal to the initial investment.

Figure 3.34 shows a side-by-side comparison of yield capitalization based on a yield rate of 13.5 percent and the exact IRR of 14.37 percent.

## Summary

Capitalization is the conversion of income into value. Whereas direct capitalization converts one year's income into an estimate of value, yield capitalization converts all of the income associated with the investment into an estimate of value. Yield capitalization converts a property's future income into a value today. The present value represents a discounted value of the total of all the anticipated future income streams associated with the investment during the anticipated investment period.

Yield capitalization brings together different and complementary disciplines and techniques, which are used in conjunction with one another to create a sophisticated form of real estate investment analysis. As such, it is significantly more involved than direct capitalization.

Yield capitalization consists of four broad areas of consideration:

1. A projection period
2. A reconstruction of the current year's and forecast of future years' revenues, expenses, and operating income, consistent with the projection period
3. The selection of a yield rate, consistent with the type of capitalization, either investor specific or market oriented
4. The capitalization of future income into a present value

In a multiple-year forecast, yield capitalization is referred to as discounted cash flow analysis or DCFA.

Real estate investors expect the recovery of all their invested capital, called return of capital, as well as a payment for the use of the capital, called return on capital. The rate of return on invested capital is equivalent to the yield rate. The total of the return on capital plus return of capital equals the rate of return on capital. The rate of return on capital is equivalent to the interest rate earned on the investment. For real estate investments, this interest rate is known as a yield rate.

Real estate is physical, consisting of the physical land and all structures and other improvements attached to the land. However, real estate does not consider any of the rights associated with ownership. Real property rights, referred to as the bundle of rights, are intangible. The bundle of rights is a concept that compares property ownership rights to a bundle of sticks, where each stick represents a distinct and separate right, interest, and benefit of ownership, including the right to sell, use, buy, mortgage, pledge, trade, or lease the property and the right not to exercise any of these rights.

Generally speaking, there are two aspects of a real estate investment: its physical aspects and its financial aspects. The physical architecture of real estate consists of its tangible qualities, such as the concrete, steel, and glass required to create the physical property. The financial architecture of real estate consists of its bundle of rights, such as the leases, revenues, expenses, income, mortgage and other debt service and cash flow, and return on investment and return of investment, that are required to create the financial annuity.

An annuity is a schedule of cash payments where the payments occur at regular, fixed intervals. An example of a real estate annuity would be a pro forma forecast of net operating income or cash flows. The physical architecture of real estate can be seen in the physical world and is used for various commercial purposes. The financial architecture of real estate exists in cyberspace, within computer spreadsheets, forecast pro formas, and discounted cash-flow-yield analysis models and is used for various ownership and investment purposes.

Time value of money concepts are often represented utilizing cash-flow dia grams. Cash-flow diagrams are widely used visual tools that present a picture of financial problems. Often, drawing a cash-flow diagram is the first step in solving complex financial problems. Once the diagram is set up, we would identify what is known and unknown about the investment. A horizontal line represents time. Money invested is considered cash payments or outflows and represented as negative, with a down arrow. Money returned is considered cash received or inflows and is represented as positive, with an up arrow.

The time value of money is an economic principal that states that a dollar received today is worth more than a dollar received in the future. The reasoning is that a dollar received today can be invested and earn interest (a rate of return), thereby growing into a larger future amount than the same noninvested dollar. The concept of time value of money provides the foundation for all discounted cash-flow analysis. Discounted cash-flow analysis is also known as yield capitalization. Yield capitalization concepts include the future value of a dollar, the present value of a dollar, the future value of an annuity, and the present value of an annuity.

A future value can be converted into an equivalent present amount through the use of discount rates, also known as discount factors. A discount rate is a special type of interest rate known as a yield rate. Discount rates are used to convert a future value into a present value. A discount rate is also known as a present value interest factor (PVIF). A PVIF is based on a formula and is used in a mathematical process called discounting.

A present value can be converted into an equivalent future amount through the use of compound rates, also known as compound factors. A compound rate is a special type of interest rate, known as a yield rate or a future value interest factor (FVIF). A FVIF is based on a formula and is used as part of a mathematical process called compounding.

Future value concepts and present value concepts can also be applied to annuities. There are many different types of forecasted cash flows, including level annuities, increasing annuities, and decreasing annuities. However, most real estate investment properties are characterized by uneven annuities; these become the basis of a property's forecasted cash flows.

The difference between the acquisition price of a property and its discounted present value represents the net present value of the investment. The yield rate required to discount future cash flows to be exactly equal to the initial investment is the internal rate of return of the investment. The internal rate of return of the investment discounts the future benefits of the investment to a present value that is exactly equal to the initial investment itself. At such an IRR, the net present value of the investment is zero.

## Review Questions

1. Yield capitalization
   a. converts one year's income to value.
   b. is also referred to as "direct cap."
   c. converts future benefits into a present value.
   d. does all of the above.

2. Yield capitalization consists of four areas of consideration, which may be stated as
   a. income, rate, value, and risk factor.
   b. projection period, forecast, yield rate selection, and direct capitalization.
   c. projection period, forecast, yield rate selection, capitalization.
   d. all of the above.

3. A projection period
   a. considers the investor's anticipated ownership period.
   b. may also be referred to as the holding period.
   c. is usually more than one year.
   d. does all of the above.

4. Reversion
   a. is a premature exit from the investment.
   b. is a negotiating tactic of making a counteroffer.
   c. is a lump-sum benefit of the return of capital.
   d. is an alternate investment selection, also known as "opportunity cost."

5. The future value of a dollar concept
   a. employs the time value of money concept.
   b. holds that a dollar acquired today is worth less than a dollar acquired in the future.
   c. holds that the lower the risk, the greater the OAR necessary to induce investment.
   d. does all of the above.

6. The present value of a dollar concept
   a. employs the time value of money concept.
   b. holds that a dollar acquired today is worth less than a dollar acquired in the future.
   c. holds that the lower the risk, the greater the OAR necessary to induce investment.
   d. does all of the above.

7. FVIFA stands for
   a. forecasted variable income factor of availability.
   b. future variable interest factor of annuity.
   c. future value interest factor of availability.
   d. future value interest factor of annuity.

8. An annuity
   a. has the feature of predictability of income and regularity of payment.
   b. is a cash flow consisting only of level payment income streams.
   c. is a new cash flow that has the feature of predictability of future payment.
   d. is a cash flow consisting only of uneven payment income streams.

9. PVIFA stands for
   a. prospective variable income factor of availability.
   b. present variable interest factor of annuity.
   c. prospective value interest factor of availability.
   d. present value interest factor of annuity.

10. The true yield rate of a real estate investment
    a. cannot be determined until the termination of the investment.
    b. should be estimated prior to acquiring the property.
    c. should consider an investor's sentiment.
    d. does all of the above.

11. You are considering the acquisition of a 20-unit rental apartment property on a direct capitalization basis. The projected current year net operating income is $182,690, and you are comfortable that this is a solid projection. Based upon your individual investor sentiment, tempered by market support, you conclude that the property should be acquired on an 8.5 percent direct capitalization basis. If the seller accepts your offer, what is your purchase price?
    a. $167,161.35
    b. $198,218.65
    c. $2,150,000
    d. The purchase price cannot be determined until the termination of the investment.

12. You are considering acquiring the same 20-unit rental apartment property, this time on a yield capitalization basis. The projected current year's net operating income is $182,690, and you are comfortable that this is a solid projection. You expect to hold the property for five years. You will establish your future sales price based upon the sixth year's NOI. You anticipate NOI will grow at an annual rate of 5 percent. You project your reversionary capitalization rate to be 9 percent. Transaction costs are estimated at 5 percent of gross sales proceeds. Using this information, prepare a summary analysis of the total cash flows from all sources, for each year of the projection.

13. Using the summary cash-flow analysis you derived in question 12, prepare a discounted cash-flow analysis based on a 10 percent yield rate. What is the present value of the discounted cash flows, rounded?
    a. $2,065,500
    b. $2,200,500
    c. $2,000,500
    d. $2,265,500

14. Using your answers to questions 12 and 13, what is the net present value of this investment?
    a. $163,500
    b. $136,500
    c. $631,500
    d. $361,500

15. If this investment was evaluated at approximately an 11.59 percent yield rate, what would the net present value be, and is this yield rate the IRR?
    a. The NPV would be $50,000, and the 11.59 percent yield rate would not be the IRR.
    b. The NPV would be $50,000, and the 11.59 percent yield rate would be the IRR.
    c. The NPV would be $0, and the 11.59 percent yield rate would not be the IRR.
    d. The NPV would be $0, and the 11.59 percent yield rate would be the IRR.

c h a p t e r   f o u r

# FINANCING COMMERCIAL REAL ESTATE AND MEASURING INVESTMENT PERFORMANCE

## Key Terminology

- Amortized Loan
- Correspondent Lender
- Equity Dividend
- Equity Overall Rate
- Exit Strategy
- Internal Rate of Return (IRR)
- Lender's Overall Rate (Debt Overall Rate)
- Leverage
- Loan Constant
- Loan-to-Value Ratio
- Mortgage
- Mortgage Banker
- Mortgate Broker
- Mortgage Note
- Negative Leverage
- Positive Leverage
- Rate of Return

## Overview

In this chapter, the use of debt for the acquisition of real estate is discussed, with an emphasis on the importance of financing as a credible method of property acquisition. The allocation of NOI to the various interests in the NOI, namely debt and equity, is described. The concepts of rates of return to the debt component, to the equity component, and to the overall property cash flow are introduced. The differences between equity dividend rate, equity yield rate, debt dividend rate, and debt yield rate and the internal rate of return are explained. Variations of the IRV formula and its applications are presented in great detail. The concepts of employing someone else's money to buy property to achieve investment goals are discussed.

As we explore the differences between an unleveraged and a leveraged property acquisition, numerous new terms are introduced and the importance of applying advanced financial and investment analysis skills becomes apparent. Multistep calculations for measuring the performance of the investment are introduced. The ability to employ various combinations of yield and reversion rates to a discounted cash-flow analysis is emphasized as fundamental to the decision-making process.

## Learning Objectives

After completing this chapter, you should be able to accomplish the following:

- Discuss the reasons for financing
- Define amortization
- List the four broad areas of consideration of yield capitalization
- Discuss rates of return
- Explain the difference between positive leverage and negative leverage
- Discuss the relationship between equity dividend rates and equity yield rates
- Explain the concept of exit
- Describe the concept of internal rate of return
- Discuss the difference between a mortgage and a note
- Explain LTV

## Reasons for Financing

Commercial investment property may be acquired entirely with cash. However, the majority of commercial investment property acquisitions involve a combination of equity (the investor's cash) and debt (a lender's financing). In fact, it has been estimated that approximately 90 percent of all real estate transactions occurring within the United States involve some sort of financing.

Many valid reasons exist to employ financing in the acquisition of real estate. However, all these reasons have a central point in common: they allow a purchaser to acquire and become the owner of the property without actually owning the capital used to acquire it. Essentially, the purchaser borrows someone else's money to buy the property and to achieve their own goals.

Because approximately 90 percent of all U.S. real estate transactions involve some sort of financing, transaction-based financing will likely be required for your investments. Regardless of who provides these financing services, having a working knowledge of the essentials of real estate financing benefits all parties involved.

There are four compelling reasons for the use of financing in a real estate transaction:

1. Commercial real estate is capital intensive.
2. Financing increases the capital amount available for a purchase.
3. Financing a property acquisition affects investment returns and leverage.
4. Acquisition financing is repaid by the property's income.

## Commercial Real Estate Is Capital Intensive

From a transaction perspective, commercial real estate is capital intensive, meaning that it requires a significant amount of money for purchase. Few investors have the financial capability of buying entirely with cash. Even if a buyer could purchase a property for cash, there are other considerations. For example, financing allows a purchaser to become the owner of real estate without actually owning the capital used to acquire that property. Essentially, the investor borrows someone else's money to acquire the property and achieve investment goals.

## Financing Increases the Capital Amount Available for a Purchase

Using financing in a real estate purchase has the effect of increasing the capital amount available for the purchase, based on loan-to-value ratios. A **loan-to-value ratio (LTV)** is a basic yet important ratio that expresses the relationship of borrowed funds to the value of the property. From a lender's perspective, the LTV is usually the lesser of the acquisition price or the appraised value of the property. Accordingly, LTVs are an important risk measure for lenders, because the property is usually pledged as security for the loan. The formula for determining the loan-to-value ratio is:

$$\text{Loan} \div \text{Value} = \text{LTV Ratio}$$

For example, let's say an investor is considering buying a ten-unit apartment building for $578,000. The investor has cash equity of $144,500, which represents only 25 percent of the purchase price. The investors must find the balance of the money to purchase the property from somewhere. The investor considers using a first (senior) loan. The property could be acquired with a combination of the investor's cash, called equity, and borrowed funds from a lender, called debt. If a lender provides the debt based upon a 75 percent LTV, the lender would provide $433,500, as noted in Figure 4.1.

The $144,500 of owner's equity and $433,500 of lender's debt together equal the $578,000 of capital necessary for the purchase. *Capital* is the total amount of money from all sources that is available for an acquisition. Using financing increases the capital available for this purchase from $144,500 to $578,000, based on a 75 percent loan-to-value ratio.

## Financing a Property Acquisition Affects Investment Returns and Leverage

Borrowing money to finance a property has an effect on investment returns. This effect is called **leverage**. Leverage may increase or decrease the investor's return that otherwise would be received on an all-cash basis. Usually,

**Figure 4.1**

Components of Capital

| | Capital Available = | Lender Debt + | Owner Equity |
|---|---|---|---|
| Acquisition Price | $578,000 = | $433,500 + | $144,500 |
| Percent of Price | 100% = | 75% + | 25% |

**Figure 4.2**

Pro Rata Allocation of Property Investment Return to Debt and Equity

| | Capital Available = | Lender Debt + | Owner Equity |
|---|---|---|---|
| Acquisition Price | $578,000 = | $433,500 + | $144,500 |
| Percent of Price | 100% = | 75% + | 25% |
| Pro Rata Return $ | $57,800 = | $43,350 + | $14,450 |
| Pro Rata Return % | 10% | 10% | 10% |

investors borrow money for purchases with the expectation that the investment's financial returns will increase. **Positive leverage** occurs when the rate of return that an investment generates is greater than the interest rate charged by a lender for funds used to acquire that investment.

### *Positive Leverage*

For example, let's say that that an investor acquires a ten-unit rental for $578,000. The investor anticipates an all-cash NOI of $57,800, a 10 percent rate of return. Furthermore, the $578,000 property was acquired with a combination of $144,500 of owner's equity and $433,500 of lender's debt. If we allocated the 10 percent return to its component parts, the pro rata return on equity is also 10 percent, or $14,450; the pro rata return on debt is also 10 percent, or $43,350. These returns are shown in Figure 4.2.

However, if a lender provides a loan commitment based on an interest rate of 6.5 percent and a loan amortization period of 25 years, then the total annual debt service is only $35,124, resulting in positive leverage as noted in Figure 4.3.

Positive leverage occurs because the 10 percent rate of return that this investment generates is greater than the 6.5 percent interest rate charged by the lender. In this case, the rate of return that the investment generates on an all-cash basis is 10 percent, which is greater than the 8.1 percent total return due the lender (i.e., 6.5 percent interest rate charged by a lender for borrowed funds plus return of principal). Accordingly, the investor expects to make a $8,226 profit on the borrowed funds (i.e., $43,350 minus $35,124 equals $8,226 profit). This $8,226 is added to the investor's return of $14,450, increasing the return on the investor's cash portion of the investment from $14,450 to $22,676. It also has the effect of increasing the rate of return on the investor's cash portion of the investment from 10 percent to 15.69 percent.

**Figure 4.3**

Leveraged Allocation of Property Investment Return to Debt and Equity

| | Capital Available = | Lender Debt + | Owner Equity |
|---|---|---|---|
| Acquisition Price | $578,000 = | $433,500 + | $144,500 |
| Percent of Price | 100% = | 75% + | 25% |
| Leveraged Return $ | $57,800 = | $35,124 + | $22,676 |
| Unweighted Return % | 10% | 8.10% | 15.69% |

**Figure 4.4**

Lender's Return of Interest and Principal from Amortizing a 6.5 Percent Loan

| | |
|---|---|
| Interest Paid | $27,966.76 |
| Principal Reduction | $7,157.48 |
| Total Annual Debt Service | $35,124.00 (rounded) |
| Original Principal Amount Borrowed | $433,500.00 |
| Total Debt Service as % Original Principal | 8.1% |

The lender receives a 6.5 percent rate of interest on the outstanding balance in addition to a return of a portion of the original loan amount. For example, during the first year of this loan, the lender receives total interest of $27,966.76 plus total principal reduction of $7,157.48, resulting in total interest and principal payments of $35,124.24 (rounds to $35,124) as shown in Figure 4.4.

Positive leverage occurs when the rate of return that an investment generates is greater than the interest rate charged for the funds borrowed to acquire that investment.

The rate of return to the owner's equity position of 15.7 percent and the rate of return to the lender's debt of 8.1 percent originate from the same rate of return that the investment generates on an all-cash basis of 10 percent. However, these rates of return to equity and debt must be adjusted by their relative percentage of capital, as noted in Figure 4.5.

### *Negative Leverage*

When leverage decreases the return to the investor, it is called negative leverage. **Negative leverage** occurs when the interest rate charged by a lender for borrowed funds is greater than the rate of return that an investment generates on those borrowed funds. The investor's loss is deducted from the investor's return, reducing the rate of return on the investor's cash portion of the investment. For example, let's say that that the investor acquires a ten-unit rental for $578,000. The investor anticipates a 10 percent rate of return on the investment, which would come to $57,800. Furthermore, the $578,000 property was acquired with a combination of $144,500 of owner's equity and $433,500 of lender's debt. If we allocate the 10 percent return to its component parts, the pro rata return on equity is also 10 percent or $14,500; the pro rata return on debt is 10 percent or $43,350. These returns are shown in Figure 4.6.

**Figure 4.5**

Allocation of Available Capital to the Weighted Cost of Capital

| | Capital Available = | Lender Debt + | Owner Equity |
|---|---|---|---|
| Acquisition Price | $578,000 = | $433,500 + | $144,500 |
| Percent of Price | 100% = | 75% + | 25% |
| Unleveraged Return $ | $57,800 = | $35,124 + | $22,676 |
| Unweighted Return % | 10% | 8.10% | 15.69% |
| *multiplied by:* | | | |
| Percent of Return | 100% = | 75% + | 25% |
| *equals:* | | | |
| Weighted Return % | 10% = | 6.08% + | 3.92% |

**Figure 4.6**

Pro Rata Allocation of Property Investment Return to Debt and Equity

| | Capital Available = | Lender Debt + | Owner Equity |
|---|---|---|---|
| Acquisition Price | $578,000 = | $433,500 + | $144,500 |
| Percent of Price | 100% = | 75% + | 25% |
| Pro Rata Return $ | $57,800 = | $43,350 + | $14,450 |
| Pro Rata Return % | 10% | 10% | 10% |

However, if a lender provides a preliminary loan commitment based on an interest rate of 12 percent and loan amortization period of 25 years, then the total annual debt service is $54,789, which would result in negative leverage as shown in Figure 4.7.

Negative leverage occurs, because the 12 percent interest rate charged by the lender is greater than then 10 percent rate of return that the investment generates. In this case, the rate of return that the investment generates on an all-cash basis is 10 percent, which is less than the 12.64 percent total return due the lender (i.e., 12 percent interest rate charged by a lender for borrowed funds plus return of principal). Accordingly, the investor incurs a loss of $10,885 on the borrowed funds (i.e., $43,350 minus $54,789 equals a $11,439 loss). The $11,439 is deducted from the investor's return of $14,450, reducing the rate of return on the investor's cash portion of the investment to $3,011, or only 2.08 percent.

Negative leverage occurs when the interest rate charged for borrowed funds used to acquire an investment is greater than the rate of return that the investment generates.

The lender receives a 12 percent rate of interest on the outstanding balance in addition to a return of a portion of the original loan amount. For example, during the first year of this loan, the lender receives total interest of $51,862.52 plus principal reduction of $2,926.24, resulting in total interest and principal payments of $54,788.76 (rounded to $54,789), as shown in Figure 4.8.

The rate of return to the owner's equity of 2.08 percent and the rate of return to the lender's debt of 12.64 percent originate from the same rate of return that the investment generates on an all-cash basis of 10 percent. However, these rates of return to equity and debt must be adjusted by their relative percentage of capital, as shown in Figure 4.9.

## Acquisition Financing Is Repaid by the Property's Income

While the investor borrows money to finance a property, the lender looks primarily to the property itself, and not the investor-borrower, for repayment of debt. The source of the repayment of debt is the property's operating income.

**Figure 4.7**

Leveraged Allocation of Property Investment Return to Debt and Equity

| | Capital Available = | Lender Debt + | Owner Equity |
|---|---|---|---|
| Acquisition Price | $578,000 = | $433,500 + | $144,500 |
| Percent of Price | 100% = | 75% + | 25% |
| Pro Forma Return $ | $57,800 = | $54,789 + | $3,011 |
| Unweighted Return % | 10% | 12.64% | 2.08% |

**Figure 4.8**

Lender's Return of Interest and Principal from Amortizing a 12 Percent Loan

| | |
|---|---|
| Interest Paid | $51,862.52 |
| Principal Reduction | $2,926.24 |
| Total Annual Debt Service | $54,789.00 (rounded) |
| Original Principal Amount Borrowed | $433,500.00 |
| Total Debt Service as % of Original Principal | 12.64% |

From a lender's point of view, the greater the annual operating income available to pay back the annual debt service, the greater the probability the debt will actually be repaid.

The relationship between annual operating income and annual debt service is expressed by a debt coverage ratio. A *debt coverage ratio* is a basic yet important ratio that expresses the relationship of the annual net operating income to the annual debt service of the property. The term is also known as the DCR. From a lender's perspective, the larger the DCR, the more of the property's operating income is available to pay annual debt service. Accordingly, DCRs are an important risk measure for lenders, because the property is the primary source of income available for repayment of the loan. The formula for determining the debt coverage ratio of a property is:

$$\text{Annual Operating Income} \div \text{Annual Debt Service} = \text{DCR}$$

For example, let's say an investor is considering the acquisition of a ten-unit apartment building for $578,000. The investor has cash equity of $144,500, only 25 percent of the purchase price. The investor considers using a first (senior) loan based upon a 75 percent LTV, which would be $433,500 of debt. The investor finds a lender, who provides a preliminary loan commitment based on an interest rate of 6.5 percent and a loan amortization period of 25 years, contingent upon a DCR of at least 1.2. Based upon initial underwriting, the lender calculates that the DCR for this loan would be 1.57, as shown in Figure 4.10.

**Figure 4.9**

Allocation of Available Capital to the Weighted Cost of Capital

| | Capital Available = | Lender Debt + | Owner Equity |
|---|---|---|---|
| Acquisition Price | $578,000 = | $433,500 + | $144,500 |
| Percent of Price | 100% = | 75% + | 25% |
| Pro Forma Return $ | $57,800 = | $ 54,789 + | $3,011 |
| Unweighted Return % | 10% | 12.64% | 2.08% |
| *multiplied by:* | | | |
| Percent of Return | 100% = | 75% + | 25% |
| *equals:* | | | |
| Weighted Return % | 10% = | 9.48% + | 0.52% |

**Figure 4.10**

Ten-Unit Apartment—First Year's Projected NOI and DCR

| | |
|---|---|
| Annual Effective Apartment Revenues | $95,000 |
| *less:* | |
| Annual Operating Expenses | $40,000 |
| *equals:* | |
| Annual Operating Income | $55,000 |
| *divided by:* | |
| Annual Debt Service | $35,124 |
| *equals:* | |
| Debt Coverage Ratio (DCR) | 1.57 |

Because the DCR is greater than 1.2, the lender continued the underwriting process.

## Sources of Financing

The commercial mortgage brokerage business can implement financing services on behalf of a client-borrower in three primary ways: as a mortgage broker, a mortgage banker, or a correspondent lender. These three sources of financing play an important role in providing mortgage funds to borrowers on a regional and national level.

### *Mortgage Brokers*

A **mortgage broker** brings a borrower of funds and a lender of funds together for the purpose of providing financing. So mortgage brokers are intermediaries. The mortgage broker's compensation is usually contingent upon "a success performance basis," meaning that the broker is paid a percentage of the financing amount if and when financing is accomplished. As part of the service, the broker might also negotiate with the lender to find the best possible financing deal for the borrower. However, the mortgage broker does not originate, close, or service the loan. The actual financing is accomplished through the lender's loan origination process.

Loans that are originated based on a mortgage broker's efforts are usually closed in the lender's name and are usually serviced by the lender. A mortgage broker may accept an application for a mortgage loan, solicit a mortgage loan on behalf of a borrower, negotiate the sale of an existing mortgage loan on behalf of a lender, or negotiate the sale of an existing mortgage loan to an investor in the secondary mortgage market.

### *Mortgage Bankers*

A mortgage broker may expand its services further by acting as a mortgage banker. A **mortgage banker** may originate, close, and service a loan. Mortgage bankers can provide short-term, interim financing and long-term financing. Mortgage bankers use their own funds, or they may borrow funds from other commercial sources for the mortgage financing. In the latter case, mortgage bankers are not the ultimate lender in the transaction.

**Figure 4.11**

Mortgage Brokers, Mortgage Bankers, and Correspondent Lenders

| Mortgage Brokers | Mortgage Bankers | Correspondent Lenders |
|---|---|---|
| Intermediary | Intermediary | Intermediary |
| Does not originate, close, or service loans | Can originate, close, or service loans | Can originate, close, or service loans |
| Financed through lender's loan origination process | Financed through mortgage banker's or lender's loan origination process | Financed through correspondent on behalf of a lender |
| Loan closed in lender's name | Loan closed in lender's name | Loan closed in lender's name |
| Loan serviced by lender | Loan serviced by mortgage banker or lender | Loan serviced by correspondent lender or lender |
| Can sell mortgages in the secondary market | Can sell mortgages in the secondary market | Can sell mortgages in the secondary market |

Usually, a mortgage banker will sell the mortgage in the secondary mortgage market, where existing mortgages and mortgage-backed securities are bought and sold. Loans are sold in the secondary market based on specific criteria required by specific investors. Loans may be sold individually or may be sold as "bundles" or "pools" of like-kind loans. In real estate jargon, selling the loan on the secondary market is referred to as "selling the paper" or "turning the paper." However, the mortgage banker may service the underlying mortgage, including collecting monthly payments, disbursing the funds to pay taxes and property insurance, supervising the loan, preventing delinquencies, and taking appropriate action in the event of a default.

### Correspondent Lenders

Some mortgage banking firms expand their services still further by acting in the capacity of a correspondent lender. A **correspondent lender** provides lending services on behalf of other lenders who desire to provide financing within a certain area but do not have a physical presence in that area. Also known as *loan correspondents*, they essentially negotiate a loan on behalf of another lender. Sources of financing for the correspondent lender include banks located in "money center" markets such as New York and Chicago as well as insurance companies, pension funds, and other commercial banks. The correspondent lender originates loans on behalf of another lender through a process or system known as a *correspondence system*. Often, the correspondent will continue to service the loan for the lender and act as a collecting agent.

Figure 4.11 summarizes the characteristics of these three financing sources.

### Financial Intermediaries—The Traditional Lenders

A discussion pertaining to real estate financing would not be complete without at least a review of the traditional real estate lenders. Financial institutions have money to lend for real estate endeavors. A *financial institution* is an organization in the business of holding cash and other assets on behalf of others. Examples of financial institutions include commercial banks, savings associations, credit unions, insurance companies, pension funds, and investment companies. These financial institutions also act as fiduciaries on behalf of their depositors and investors. What makes these financial institutions distinctive is that they also act as financial intermediaries within the real estate markets.

*Financial intermediaries* are financial institutions that act as middlemen between depositors and borrowers. *Intermediation* is a process in which middlemen accumulate, combine, and consolidate a number of smaller, individual equity accounts for the purpose of either lending or investing in real estate properties. Due to their size and vast deposit base, these intermediaries can provide financing or investment funds for larger, more complex, more management- and capital-intensive real estate properties. However, if a state or federal charter regulates these institutions, they operate with significantly less risk tolerance and are more conservative than mortgage brokers, mortgage bankers, and correspondent lenders.

If a financial institution is operating under a federal charter, it is considered a federally chartered financial institution. Any real estate transaction undertaken by such a financial institution is considered a federally related transaction. The Financial Institutions Reform, Recovery, and Enforcement Act (FIRREA) defines a federally related transaction as any real estate-related financial transaction in which any federal financial institution is involved. FIRREA was enacted in response to the savings and loan (S&L) crisis of the 1980s and restructured the S&L industry.

### Market Niches

A link exists between traditional lenders and mortgage brokers, mortgage bankers, and correspondent lenders. All three provide lending opportunities for the traditional lenders, which have money to lend but are located in other parts of the country. Other sources of funds include insurance companies, pension funds, and private sources that actively seek out broker and correspondent relationships. Accordingly, mortgage brokers, mortgage bankers, and correspondent lenders serve as "virtual branch offices" for these sources of equity and debt. As such, they bring additional vibrancy to the equity and debt markets, adding a new competitive element, which encourages the creation of new capital and loan products for commercial real estate investments of all types.

Often mortgage brokers, mortgage bankers, and correspondent lenders serve niche markets that provide a vital need in the financing arena. They can be more aggressive, more flexible, and more creative than traditional lenders, which are closely regulated. For example, consider lending limits. A traditional lender can generally provide a loan-to-value ratio of, say, 70 percent to 75 percent. However, mortgage brokers can structure financing packages with a higher loan-to-value ratio, say, 80 percent. Moreover, by using sophisticated capital structuring techniques such as equity or "mezzanine" financing, they can provide even more capital for a transaction. *Mezzanine equity*, also referred to as *mezzanine financing*, provides capital to fill the gap between the senior first mortgage loan and the owner's equity investment in a property acquisition. Because equity is not debt, the equity does not impact the loan-to-value ratio. For example, consider the lender who can provide both interest-only loans and mezzanine financing for a transaction. Very creative indeed!

Because of their flexibility, mortgage brokers can also provide financing for a wider variety of real estate deals, differentiated within the industry as "prime" and "subprime" real estate. Based on a combination of a competitive environment and the growth of the commercial mortgage-backed securities (CMBS) market, their loan underwriting criteria for mortgages is often less stringent than that of other lenders, making them more flexible. *CMBS loans* are commercial real estate loans that are pooled together and transferred to a trust, which then issues securities based on the strength of the underlying mortgages. The results are more aggressive loans with higher loan-to-value ratios and lower debt coverage ratios. At the more risky end of the lending spectrum, mortgage brokers can provide negative amortizing loans and other creative loan structures designed to "make a deal happen."

### *Historical Perspective*

The 1980s saw a high interest rate environment, which lead to lax lending practices and ultimately resulted in a significant rate of loan default. These defaults, combined with the crisis and ultimate failure of the savings and loan industry, gave rise to the largest bailout of the U.S. banking system in history and the formation of the Resolution Trust Corporation (RTC). Congress formed the RTC in 1989 to replace the Federal Savings and Loan Insurance Corporation and respond to the insolvencies of about 750 savings and loan associations. As receiver, it sold assets of failed S&Ls and paid insured depositors. In 1995, its duties, including the insurance of deposits in thrift institutions, were transferred to the Savings Association Insurance Fund.

Today, lenders are even more aggressive than they were in the 1980s. However, they are also subject to more stringent underwriting standards than in the 1980s. Figure 4.12 summarizes the primary sources of financing a real estate transaction.

## Costs of Financing: Mortgage Brokerage Fees, Origination Fees, and Servicing Fees

A mortgage broker's compensation is generally computed as a percentage of the face value of the brokered loan. For example, let's say that the mortgage broker was going to charge a *point*, which is real estate jargon for a fee of 1 percent of the face value of the loan. If the loan amount were $433,500, then the compensation due the mortgage broker would be $4,335. This 1 percent fee, or point, is the broker's compensation, not an origination fee.

**Figure 4.12**

Sources of Financing a Transaction

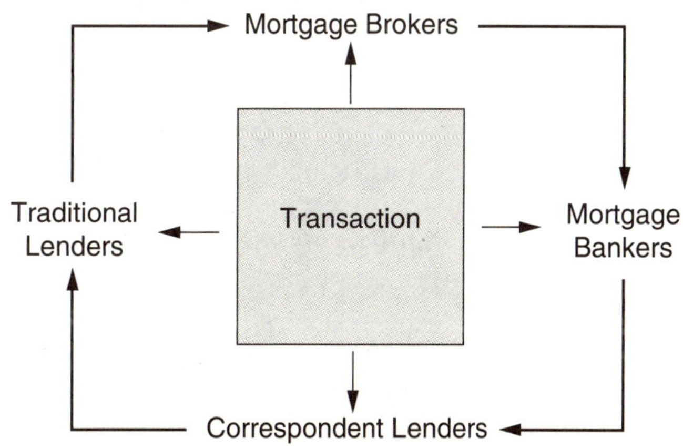

An *origination fee* is charged by a lender for making a loan. Origination fees may be all-inclusive or net of lender costs. An all-inclusive origination fee covers such costs as the lender's up-front costs, including general and administrative costs, preparation of documents, recording costs, property inspections, environmental reports, and appraisals. For example, if the loan amount were $433,500 and the lender charged two points that covered all fees and expenses, then the total origination fees due the lender would be $8,670. Alternatively, if the lender's origination fee was net of lender costs and the lender charged one point plus costs associated with the preparation of documents, recordating costs, property inspections, environmental reports, and appraisals, then the total origination fees due the lender would be $4,335, and all other loan costs would be either prepaid or billed directly to the borrower. As a matter of business practice, mortgage brokerage fees, loan origination fees, and loan origination costs may be imposed on a borrower in the same financing transaction.

A mortgage banker may have an agreement with a lender to service a loan. *Servicing a loan* includes collecting payments such as interest, principal, insurance, and taxes in accordance with the terms of the note. Servicing also includes accounting, bookkeeping, preparation of insurance and tax records, loan payment follow-up, and delinquency follow-up and loan analysis. A servicing agreement is usually written and includes the obligations of both parties. Servicing fees vary widely, ranging from one quarter of 1 percent (0.025 percent) to one half of 1 percent (0.5 percent) per year of the outstanding loan balance. Some lenders place a maximum on annual income from servicing any one mortgage.

Those that service loans are interested in building a volume of loans to service, because as the number of loans increases, so do the servicing fees. For example, if the loan amount were $433,500 and the service agreement called for a one quarter of 1 percent (0.025 percent) servicing fee, then the total servicing fees would be approximately $1,083.75 for the year, or an average of $90.31 per month. If, however, there were 1,000 such loans to service, then the total servicing fees would be approximately $1,083,750 for the year, or an average of $90,313 per month. Many loan servicing businesses take advantage of this potentially significant income stream, and they actively compete for such opportunities. As a matter of business practice, a mortgage banker can earn mortgage brokerage fees and loan-servicing fees in the same financing transaction.

## Case Study: Unleveraged Property Acquisition

Figure 4.13 is an analysis of the unleveraged cash flows of the ten-unit apartment we are considering acquiring on the direct capitalization purchase price basis of $578,000 derived in Chapter 2 and analyzed on a DCFA yield capitalization basis derived in Chapter 3.

### *Analysis of Unleveraged Property Acquisition*

Figure 4.13 presents an expanded version of the forecasted income and expense analysis for the period 2005 through 2010 first presented in Figure 3.3. However, in this presentation, the analysis template has been enhanced to include two sections.

The first section contains the revenues, expenses, and operating income for the property. This section is similar to earlier presentations and represents the property's profit and loss statement.

The second section contains four important areas of consideration, as follows:

1. *Allocation of NOI to interests.* This section addresses the allocation of NOI to the interests in the NOI, namely the debt and equity positions that make up the capital structure of the property.
2. *Rates of return.* This section addresses the rates of return to the debt and equity positions.
3. *Exit.* This section addresses the future expected sale of the property, then allocates the sales proceeds to the debt and equity positions.
4. *DCFA.* This section addresses the yield/discount rate used to discount the expected future cash flow and sales proceeds into today's present value.

Together, these two sections of the template represent the financial architecture of the real estate. This financial architecture contains the revenues, expenses, income, mortgage debt service and cash flow, and return on investment and return of investment that are required to determine the financial annuity.

### Allocation of NOI to Interests

**Net operating income (NOI)** results from a property's operations. It is the amount that remains after all operating expenses have been deducted from effective gross income. Net operating income can be calculated on the basis of a property's actual or projected operations. It is also the amount that is used to determine the value or price of the property by capitalizing the NOI by either direct capitalization or yield capitalization. NOI represents the income available to satisfy the interests in the real estate: namely the equity investor and the lender of debt, as appropriate. NOI does not consider payments for mortgage debt service and cash flow; rather, NOI represents the amount of money *available* to pay the mortgage debt service and the cash flow.

Net Operating Income – Debt Service = Cash Flow

In Figure 4.14, net operating income is presented as the money available to pay debt service, as appropriate. Although line items are presented for debt service (e.g., mortgage interest expense and principal reduction), a mortgage is not considered, because this is an all-cash acquisition. Accordingly, pretax cash flow is the same amount as operating income (NOI). However, although NOI and PTCF are the same amount, they do not represent the same concept. NOI represents income before debt consideration, while PTCF represents income after debt consideration.

### Income Refers to Net Operating Income, Not Cash Flow

Cash Flow + Debt Service = Net Operating Income

*Cash flow* is the income that remains after the cost of financing, or debt service, is deducted from NOI. But what if there is no financing to consider and the investor is evaluating the property before any tax considerations? Then pretax cash flow would be numerically equal to net operating income. However, PTCF is not the same financial concept as NOI.

**Figure 4.13**

Unleveraged Property Acquisition

**Ten-Unit Apartment Building—Forecasted Income and Expense Analysis**

Units 10
Living Area Square Feet 10,500

For the Period 2005–2010

| Period | Forecast 2005 | | Forecast 2006 | | Forecast 2007 | | Forecast 2008 | | Forecast 2009 | | Forecast 2010 | |
|---|---|---|---|---|---|---|---|---|---|---|---|---|
| | Holding Year 1 | | Holding Year 2 | | Holding Year 3 | | Holding Year 4 | | Holding Year 5 | | Reversion | |
| **REVENUES** | | | | | | | | | | | | |
| Category | Amount | Amount per Unit | Amount | Amount per Unit | Amount | Amount per Unit | Amount | Amount per Unit | Amount | Amount per Unit | Amount | Amount per Unit |
| Scheduled Base Rent | $102,382 | $10,238 | $107,245 | $10,725 | $110,462 | $11,046 | $113,776 | $11,378 | $117,190 | $11,719 | $120,705 | $12,071 |
| **Market Rent for Vacant Units** | $- | $- | $- | $- | $- | $- | $- | $- | $- | $- | $- | $- |
| ***Subtotal: Adjusted Base Rent*** | $102,382 | $10,238 | $107,245 | $10,725 | $110,462 | $11,046 | $113,776 | $11,378 | $117,190 | $11,719 | $120,705 | $12,071 |
| **Other Income** | | | | | | | | | | | | |
| Laundry | $630 | $63 | $690 | $69 | $759 | $76 | $835 | $83 | $918 | $92 | $1,010 | $101 |
| ***Subtotal: Other Income*** | $630 | $63 | $690 | $69 | $759 | $76 | $835 | $83 | $918 | $92 | $1,010 | $101 |
| **Potential Gross Income @ 100% Occupancy** | $103,012 | $10,301 | $107,935 | $10,793 | $111,221 | $11,122 | $114,611 | $11,461 | $118,108 | $11,811 | $121,715 | $12,172 |
| **Vacancy and Collection Loss @ 5%** | $5,151 | $515 | $5,397 | $540 | $5,283 | $528 | $5,157 | $516 | $4,724 | $472 | $4,869 | $487 |
| **Effective Gross Income** | $97,861 | $9,786 | $102,538 | $10,254 | $105,938 | $10,594 | $109,454 | $10,945 | $113,384 | $11,338 | $116,847 | $11,685 |
| **EXPENSES** | | | | | | | | | | | | |
| **Operating Expenses** | | | | | | | | | | | | |
| *Fixed* | Amount | Amount per Unit | Amount | Amount per Unit | Amount | Amount per Unit | Amount | Amount per Unit | Amount | Amount per Unit | Amount | Amount per Unit |
| Real Estate Taxes | $11,000 | $1,100 | $11,165 | $1,117 | $11,165 | $1,117 | $11,165 | $1,117 | $11,332 | $1,133 | $11,332 | $1,133 |
| Insurance | $1,750 | $175 | $1,500 | $150 | $1,500 | $150 | $1,500 | $150 | $1,500 | $150 | $1,500 | $150 |
| ***Subtotal Fixed*** | $12,750 | 1,275 | $12,665 | 1,267 | $12,665 | 1,267 | $12,665 | 1,267 | $12,832 | 1,283 | $12,832 | 1,283 |
| *Variable* | | | | | | | | | | | | |
| Management Fee @ 4% | $3,914 | $391 | $4,102 | $410 | $4,238 | $424 | $4,378 | $438 | $4,535 | $454 | $4,674 | $467 |
| Advertising and Promotion | $800 | $80 | $700 | $70 | $721 | $72 | $743 | $74 | $765 | $76 | $788 | $79 |
| Telephone | $900 | $90 | $800 | $80 | $824 | $82 | $849 | $85 | $874 | $87 | $900 | $90 |
| Utilities (Water, Sewer, Electric) | $1,600 | $160 | $1,575 | $158 | $1,607 | $161 | $1,639 | $164 | $1,671 | $167 | $1,705 | $170 |
| Trash Removal | $1,000 | $100 | $1,030 | $103 | $1,030 | $103 | $1,060 | $106 | $1,060 | $106 | $1,092 | $109 |
| Repairs, Maintenance, and Supplies | $11,000 | $1,100 | $10,000 | $1,000 | $10,300 | $1,030 | $10,609 | $1,061 | $10,927 | $1,093 | $11,255 | $1,126 |
| Unit Interior Redecorating | $1,425 | $143 | $1,275 | $128 | $1,313 | $131 | $1,353 | $135 | $1,393 | $139 | $1,435 | $144 |
| Landscape, Lawn, and Grounds | $1,200 | $120 | $1,250 | $125 | $1,300 | $130 | $1,350 | $135 | $1,400 | $140 | $1,450 | $145 |
| Pest Control | $450 | $45 | $400 | $40 | $400 | $40 | $412 | $41 | $424 | $42 | $437 | $44 |
| ***Subtotal Variable*** | $22,289 | $2,229 | $21,132 | $2,113 | $21,732 | $2,173 | $22,392 | $2,239 | $23,051 | $2,305 | $23,736 | $2,374 |
| Replacement Allowances | | | | | | | | | | | | |
| ***Subtotal Replacement Allowances*** | $5,000 | $500 | $5,000 | $500 | $5,000 | $500 | $5,000 | $500 | $5,000 | $500 | $5,000 | $500 |
| **Total Operating Expenses** | $40,039 | $4,004 | $38,797 | $3,880 | $39,397 | $3,940 | $40,057 | $4,006 | $40,883 | $4,088 | $41,568 | $4,157 |
| **OPERATING INCOME** | | | | | | | | | | | | |
| **Net Operating Income** | $57,822 | $5,782 | $63,742 | $6,374 | $66,541 | $6,654 | $69,397 | $6,940 | $72,500 | $7,250 | $75,278 | $7,528 |

**Figure 4.13 (continued)**

Unleveraged Property Acquisition

| Period | Forecast 2005<br>Holding Year 1 | Forecast 2006<br>Holding Year 2 | Forecast 2007<br>Holding Year 3 | Forecast 2008<br>Holding Year 4 | Forecast 2009<br>Holding Year 5 | Forecast 2010<br>Reversion |
|---|---|---|---|---|---|---|
| **Allocation of NOI to Interests** | | | | | | |
| Category | Amount | Amount | Amount | Amount | Amount | Amount |
| **Net Operating Income** | $57,882 | $63,742 | $66,541 | $69,397 | $72,500 | $75,278 |
| *less:* | | | | | | |
| **Mortgage Loans** | | | | | | |
| **First (Senior) Loan** | | | | | | |
| Interest Expense | $- | $- | $- | $- | $- | $- |
| Principal Reduction | $- | $- | $- | $- | $- | $- |
| **Total Debt Service First (Senior) Loan** | $- | $- | $- | $- | $- | $- |
| *equals:* | | | | | | |
| **Pre Tax Cash Flow (CF to Equity)** | $57,882 | $63,742 | $66,541 | $69,397 | $72,500 | |
| | | | | | | |
| **Rates of Return** | | | | | | |
| **Mortgage Loans** | | | | | | |
| **First (Senior) Loan—Loan Reduction** | Amount | Amount | Amount | Amount | Amount | Amount |
| Amount Outstanding BOP | $- | $- | $- | $- | $- | $- |
| Principal Reduction | $- | $- | $- | $- | $- | $- |
| Amount Outstanding EOP | $- | $- | $- | $- | $- | $- |
| **First (Senior) Loan—Rate of Return** | | | | | | |
| Debt Service | $- | $- | $- | $- | $- | $- |
| Original Amount Borrowed | $- | $- | $- | $- | $- | $- |
| Rate of Return First (Senior) Loan | | | | | | |
| **Cash Flow to Equity** | | | | | | |
| CF to Equity | $57,822 | $63,742 | $66,541 | $69,397 | $72,500 | |
| Original Amount Invested | $578,000 | $578,000 | $578,000 | $578,000 | $578,000 | |
| Rate of Return to Equity | 10.00% | 11.03% | 11.51% | 12.01% | 12.54% | |
| | | | | | | |
| **Exit** | | | | | | |
| Cash Flow to Equity | $57,822 | $63,742 | $66,541 | $69,397 | $72,500 | |
| *add:* | | | | | | |
| Reversion: Yr 6 NOI Exit Cap Rate @ 10.25% | | | | | | $734,423 |
| *less:* | | | | | | |
| Reversion Disposition Costs @ 5% | | | | | | $36,721 |
| *equals:* | | | | | | |
| Net Sales Proceeds EOY 5 | $- | $- | $- | $- | $697,701 | |
| *equals:* | | | | | | |
| CF and Net Sales Proceeds | $57,822 | $63,742 | $66,541 | $69,397 | $770,202 | |
| | | | | | | |
| **DCFA** | | | | | | |
| Yield Rate @ 13.50% | 0.881057 | 0.776262 | 0.683931 | 0.602583 | 0.530910 | |
| *equals:* | | | | | | |
| Discounted CF and Net Sales Proceeds | $50,944 | $49,480 | $45,509 | $41,817 | $408,908 | |
| *equals:* | | | | | | |
| Present Value | $596,659 | | | | | |
| Rounded to: | $597,000 | | | | | |
| OAR | 9.69% | | | | | |
| IRR | 14.37% | | | | | |

**Figure 4.14**

Allocations of NOI to Debt and Equity Interests

| Period | Forecast 2005 Holding Year 1 | Forecast 2006 Holding Year 2 | Forecast 2007 Holding Year 3 | Forecast 2008 Holding Year 4 | Forecast 2009 Holding Year 5 | Forecast 2010 Reversion |
|---|---|---|---|---|---|---|
| Allocation of NOI to Interests | | | | | | |
| Category | Amount | Amount | Amount | Amount | Amount | Amount |
| Net Operating Income | $57,822 | $63,742 | $66,541 | $69,397 | $72,500 | $75,278 |
| *less:* | | | | | | |
| Total Debt Service | $- | $- | $- | $- | $- | $- |
| *equals:* | | | | | | |
| Pre-Tax Cash Flow to Equity | $57,822 | $63,742 | $66,541 | $69,397 | $72,500 | Reversion Calc |

### *Rates of Return*

In an unleveraged property acquisition, all of the cash flows to the equity position. Stated differently, all net operating income returns to the equity position. So what is a rate of return and how is it calculated? A **rate of return** is the ratio of income to the original investment. A rate of return is a percentage, calculated as the ratio of the current net income generated from property operation to the initial capital investment, as shown in Figure 4.15.

### *Rate of Return to Equity*

Each year of the investment, the property generates cash flow to the equity position, also known as an equity dividend. An **equity dividend** is the cash flow that remains after debt service but before income taxes are considered. Stated differently, the rate of return to the equity position is known as the equity dividend. In our analysis of the unleveraged property, the equity dividend rate is ascertained by dividing the cash flow by the original investment; it is the ratio of income to the initial investment. For our unleveraged property, the formula looks like this:

$$10\% = \$57{,}822 \div \$578{,}000$$

**Figure 4.15**

Equity Dividend Rates

| Period | Forecast 2005 Holding Year 1 | Forecast 2006 Holding Year 2 | Forecast 2007 Holding Year 3 | Forecast 2008 Holding Year 4 | Forecast 2009 Holding Year 5 | Forecast 2010 Reversion |
|---|---|---|---|---|---|---|
| Equity Dividend Rate | | | | | | |
| Category | Amount | Amount | Amount | Amount | Amount | Amount |
| Cash Flow to Equity | $57,822 | $63,742 | $66,541 | $69,397 | $72,500 | N/A |
| *divided by:* | | | | | | |
| Original Amount Invested | $578,000 | $578,000 | $578,000 | $578,000 | $578,000 | N/A |
| *equals:* | | | | | | |
| Rate of Return to Equity | 10.00% | 11.03% | 11.51% | 12.01% | 12.54% | N/A |

Equity Dividend Rate = Annual Cash Flow ÷ Original Investment

Using this formula, we can calculate the equity dividend rate (EDR) for our unleveraged property for each year of the holding period. Some investors consider each year's equity dividend rate to provide insight into the investment performance of the property. However, other investors only consider the first year's equity dividend rate to be significant. Because we are dividing income by value to obtain a rate, we are employing the IRV formula to determine the equity dividend rate. The equity dividend rate is also referred to as the *cash on cash rate.*

### *Exit*

The term *exit* is real estate jargon for an exit strategy. An **exit strategy** concerns itself with the eventual sale, or disposition, of a real estate asset. It addresses the investor's objective for the real estate investment by providing a viable scenario, or alternative scenarios, through which an orderly sale of the property will occur. For example, will the ten-unit rental property be sold as the existing ten-unit rental, or will it be converted to a condominium with ten individual units for sale? In other words, an exit strategy concerns itself with reversion.

Figure 4.16 is a restatement of that part of Figure 3.30. The difference is that the reversion section has now been integrated into our overall larger template of analysis for the property. We employed our "most probable scenario" combination of a 10.25 percent reversionary capitalization rate and a cost of sales of 5 percent of gross sales proceeds to obtain net sales proceeds from the property's exit of $697,701.

### *DCFA*

In Figure 4.17, we discount the future forecasted cash flows to a present worth by using a discount rate of 13.5 percent. Stated differently, we are evaluating the prospective purchase to yield 13.5 percent. The present worth of those future monetary benefits, evaluated at 13.5 percent, is $597,000(rd).

**Figure 4.16**

Cash Flows and Net Sales Proceeds

| Period | Forecast 2005<br>Holding Year 1 | Forecast 2006<br>Holding Year 2 | Forecast 2007<br>Holding Year 3 | Forecast 2008<br>Holding Year 4 | Forecast 2009<br>Holding Year 5 | Forecast 2010<br>Reversion |
|---|---|---|---|---|---|---|
| Exit | | | | | | |
| Category | Amount | Amount | Amount | Amount | Amount | Amount |
| Cash Flow | $57,822 | $63,742 | $66,541 | $69,397 | $72,500 | $75,278 |
| *add:* | | | | | | |
| Sale: Y-6 NOI Cap @ 10.25% | | | | | | $734,423 |
| *less:* | | | | | | |
| Disposition Costs @ 5% | | | | | | $(36,721) |
| *equals:* | | | | | | |
| Net Sales Proceeds EOY 5 | $- | $- | $- | $- | $697,701 | $697,701 |
| *equals:* | | | | | | |
| Cash Flow and Sales Proceeds | $57,822 | $63,742 | $66,541 | $69,397 | $770,202 | |

**Figure 4.17**

Discounted Cash-Flow Analysis

| Period | Forecast 2005 | Forecast 2006 | Forecast 2007 | Forecast 2008 | Forecast 2009 | Forecast 2010 |
|---|---|---|---|---|---|---|
| | Holding Year 1 | Holding Year 2 | Holding Year 3 | Holding Year 4 | Holding Year 5 | Reversion |
| DCFA | | | | | | |
| Category | Amount | Amount | Amount | Amount | Amount | Amount |
| Cash Flow and Sales Proceeds | $57,822 | $63,742 | $66,541 | $69,397 | $770,202 | |
| *multiplied by:* | | | | | | |
| PVIF @ 13.50% | 0.881057 | 0.776262 | 0.683931 | 0.602583 | 0.530910 | |
| *equals:* | | | | | | |
| Discounted Cash Flows | $50,945 | $49,480 | $45,509 | $41,817 | $408,908 | |
| Present Value OF DCFA | $596,659 | | | | | |
| *Rounded to:* | $597,000 | | | | | |

### *Cap Rate/OAR*

If we purchased the property for $578,000 with a forecasted 2005 NOI of $57,822, we would acquire the property at an overall cap rate (OAR) of 10 percent, calculated as follows:

$$\text{OAR (R)} = \frac{\text{NOI (I)}}{\text{Value or Price (V)}}$$

$$\text{OAR} = 10.00\% = \frac{\$57{,}822}{578{,}220}$$

Refer to Chapter 2 for an in-depth discussion of the IRV formula.

Why then is the OAR indicated to be 9.69 percent? Because if we purchase the property for $578,000(rd), yet evaluate that same property at a 13.5 percent yield, and the present value of those future benefits are $597,000, then the overall rate for a property with a 2005 NOI of $57,822 and a prospective value of $597,000 would come to 9.69 percent, calculated as follows:

$$\text{OAR (R)} = \frac{\text{NOI (I)}}{\text{Value or Price (V)}}$$

$$9.69\% = \frac{\$57{,}822}{597{,}000}$$

As we discussed at length in Chapter 2, given an income stream, when the OAR goes up the value goes down, and when the OAR goes down, the value goes up.

### Net Present Value

The difference between the $578,000 acquisition price and the $597,000 discounted present value of this investment is $19,000. This $19,000 represents the net present value of the investment. Remember that the *net present value (NPV)* of an investment is the difference between the discounted present value of the investment ($597,000) evaluated at a yield rate (13.5 percent) and its initial acquisition cost ($578,000).

We would have to discount the future cash flows at a yield rate of exactly 14.36600565 percent (14.37 percent rounded) to derive a present value amount ($578,000) that is exactly equal to the initial investment ($587,000). That yield rate represents the internal rate of return of the investment. Remember that the **internal rate of return (IRR)** of an investment is the rate of return that discounts the future benefits of the investment to a present value that is exactly equal to the initial investment. In such a case, the NPV of the investment is zero. Stated differently, the IRR is the rate of return that makes the present value of the periodic cash flows and reversion equal to the initial investment.

Figure 4.18 shows a side-by-side comparison of the discounted present value of the ten-unit rental property based on a yield rate of 13.5 percent and the exact IRR of 14.37 percent.

Both net present value and internal rate of return are widely used to measure the performance of a real estate investment. After all of the complexities associated with assumptions, forecasting, and the profit and loss statement,

**Figure 4.18**

Comparison of Yield Capitalization Based on a Yield Rate of 13.5 Percent and an IRR of 14.37 Percent

**DCFA Using 13.5 Percent Investor Yield Rate**

| N/Period | Cash Flows | Yield Rate @13.50% | Discounted Cash Flows |
|---|---|---|---|
| 1 | $57,822 | 0.881057269 | $50,944 |
| 2 | $63,742 | 0.776261911 | $49,480 |
| 3 | $66,541 | 0.683931199 | $45,509 |
| 4 | $69,397 | 0.602582554 | $41,817 |
| 5 | $770,202 | 0.530909739 | $408,908 |
| PV of Discounted Cash Flows (rounded) | | | $597,000 |
| *less:* | | | |
| Acquisition Costs | | | $578,000 |
| *equals:* | | | |
| Net Present Value of Acquisition | | | $19,000 |

**DCFA Using 14.37 Percent IRR Yield Rate**

| N/Period | Cash Flows | IRR @ 14.37% | Discounted Cash Flows |
|---|---|---|---|
| 1 | $57,822 | 0.874385701 | $50,559 |
| 2 | $63,742 | 0.764550354 | $48,734 |
| 3 | $66,541 | 0.668511897 | $44,483 |
| 4 | $69,397 | 0.584537243 | $40,565 |
| 5 | $770,202 | 0.511111007 | $393,659 |
| PV of Discounted Cash Flows (rounded) | | | $578,000 |
| *less:* | | | |
| Acquisition Costs | | | $578,000 |
| *equals:* | | | |
| Net Present Value of Acquisition | | | $- |

the NPV and IRR allow for straightforward tests to determine if the property meets, exceeds, or falls short of the investor's objectives. However, to realize the full potential of these powerful measurement tools, they should be used to compare one investment to another.

## Case Study: Leveraged Property Acquisition

What would happen to the investment performance of our property if we considered acquiring it with a combination of equity and debt? What would be the impact on the cash flows and the reversion? What would be the impact on the rates of return? Figure 4.18 shows an analysis of the leveraged cash flows of the ten-unit apartment we are considering acquiring on a direct capitalization purchase price basis of $578,000 (derived in Chapter 2), analyzed on the DCFA yield capitalization basis (derived in Chapter 3).

## Analysis of Leveraged Property Acquisition

Figure 4.21 presents an expanded version of the forecasted income and expense analysis for the period 2005 through 2010 that was first presented in Figure 3.3. However, in this presentation, the analysis template has been enhanced to include two sections.

The first section contains the revenues, expenses, and operating income for the property. This section is similar to earlier presentations and represents the property's profit and loss statement.

The second section contains the following four important areas of consideration:

1. *Allocation of NOI to interests.* This section addresses the allocation of NOI to the interests in the NOI, namely the debt and equity positions that make up the capital structure of the property.
2. *Rates of return.* This section addresses the rates of return to the debt and equity positions.
3. *Exit.* This section addresses the future expected sale of the property, then allocates the sales proceeds to the debt and equity positions.
4. *DCFA.* This section addresses the yield/discount rate used to discount the expected future cash flow and sales proceeds and arrive at a discounted value—today's present value.

Together, these two sections of the template represent the financial architecture of the real estate. This financial architecture contains the revenues, expenses, income, mortgage debt service and cash flow, and return on investment and return of investment that are required to create the financial annuity.

### *Allocation of NOI to Interests*

Net Operating Income – Debt Service = Cash Flow

Figure 4.19 illustrates how a property's NOI is allocated to the debt and equity interests. The NOI does not consider payments for mortgage debt service and cash flow; rather, NOI represents the amount of money *available* to pay the mortgage debt service and cash flow.

As Figure 4.20 illustrates, we can allocate the components of NOI to the debt and equity components of our capital stack.

**Figure 4.19**

Allocations of NOI to Debt and Equity Interests

| Period | Forecast 2005 Holding Year 1 | Forecast 2006 Holding Year 2 | Forecast 2007 Holding Year 3 | Forecast 2008 Holding Year 4 | Forecast 2009 Holding Year 5 | Forecast 2010 Reversion |
|---|---|---|---|---|---|---|
| Allocation of NOI to Interests | | | | | | |
| Category | Amount | Amount | Amount | Amount | Amount | Amount |
| Net Operating Income | $57,822 | $63,742 | $66,541 | $69,397 | $72,500 | $75,278 |
| *less:* | | | | | | |
| Total Debt Service | $35,124 | $35,124 | $35,124 | $35,124 | $35,124 | $- |
| *equals:* | | | | | | |
| Pre-Tax Cash Flow to Equity | $22,698 | $28,618 | $31,417 | $34,273 | $37,376 | Reversion Calc |

Note the following rates of return shown in Figure 4.20:

- The total debt service of $35,124 is allocated to the $433,500 debt portion of the capital stack. The debt service generates an 8.1 percent rate of return to *debt*.
- The total pretax cash flow of $22,698 is allocated to the $144,500 equity portion of the capital stack. The cash flow generates a 15.71 percent rate of return to *equity*.
- The total NOI of $57,822 can be allocated to the total capital stack of $578,000. The NOI generates a 10 percent rate of return to *capital*.
- The weighted returns to debt and equity result in the *weighted return to capital*, also 10 percent.

Cash Flow + Debt Service = Net Operating Income

**Figure 4.20**

Return to Debt and Equity Positions

| Components of Income | Allocation | / | Interests | Capital Stack | = | Return | × | % Capital | = | | Weighted Return |
|---|---|---|---|---|---|---|---|---|---|---|---|
| Debt Service | $35,124 | / | Debt | $433,500 | = | 8.10% | × | 75% | = | 6.08% | Weighted Return to Debt |
| *add:* | | | | | | | | | | | |
| Cash Flow | $22,698 | / | Equity | $144,500 | = | 15.71% | × | 25% | = | 3.93% | Weighted Return to Equity |
| *equals:* | | | | | | | | | | | |
| Net Op. Income | $57,822 | / | Capital | $578,000 | = | 10.00% | × | 100% | = | 10.00% | Weighted Return to Capital |

**Figure 4.21**

Case Study: Leveraged Property Acquisition

**Ten-Unit Apartment Building—Forecasted Income and Expense Analysis**

Units 10
Living Area Square Feet 10,500

For the Period 2005–2010

| Period | Forecast 2005 | | Forecast 2006 | | Forecast 2007 | | Forecast 2008 | | Forecast 2009 | | Forecast 2010 | |
|---|---|---|---|---|---|---|---|---|---|---|---|---|
| | Holding Year 1 | | Holding Year 2 | | Holding Year 3 | | Holding Year 4 | | Holding Year 5 | | Reversion | |
| **REVENUES** | | | | | | | | | | | | |
| Category | Amount | Amount per Unit | Amount | Amount per Unit | Amount | Amount per Unit | Amount | Amount per Unit | Amount | Amount per Unit | Amount | Amount per Unit |
| Scheduled Base Rent | $102,382 | $10,238 | $107,245 | $10,725 | $110,462 | $11,046 | $113,776 | $11,378 | $117,190 | $11,719 | $120,705 | $12,071 |
| **Market Rent for Vacant Units** | $- | $- | $- | $- | $- | $- | $- | $- | $- | $- | $- | $- |
| ***Subtotal: Adjusted Base Rent*** | $102,382 | $10,238 | $107,245 | $10,725 | $110,462 | $11,046 | $113,776 | $11,378 | $117,190 | $11,719 | $120,705 | $12,071 |
| **Other Income** | | | | | | | | | | | | |
| Laundry | $630 | $63 | $690 | $69 | $759 | $76 | $835 | $83 | $918 | $92 | $1,010 | $101 |
| ***Subtotal: Other Income*** | $630 | $63 | $690 | $69 | $759 | $76 | $835 | $83 | $918 | $92 | $1,010 | $101 |
| **Potential Gross Income @ 100% Occupancy** | $103,012 | $10,301 | $107,935 | $10,793 | $111,221 | $11,122 | $114,611 | $11,461 | $118,108 | $11,811 | $121,715 | $12,172 |
| **Vacancy and Collection Loss @ 5%** | $5,151 | $515 | $5,397 | $540 | $5,283 | $528 | $5,157 | $516 | $4,724 | $472 | $4,869 | $487 |
| **Effective Gross Income** | $97,861 | $9,786 | $102,538 | $10,254 | $105,938 | $10,594 | $109,454 | $10,945 | $113,384 | $11,338 | $116,847 | $11,685 |
| **EXPENSES** | | | | | | | | | | | | |
| **Operating Expenses** | | | | | | | | | | | | |
| *Fixed* | Amount | Amount per Unit | Amount | Amount per Unit | Amount | Amount per Unit | Amount | Amount per Unit | Amount | Amount per Unit | Amount | Amount per Unit |
| Real Estate Taxes | $11,000 | $1,100 | $11,165 | $1,117 | $11,165 | $1,117 | $11,165 | $1,117 | $11,332 | $1,133 | $11,332 | $1,133 |
| Insurance | $1,750 | $175 | $1,500 | $150 | $1,500 | $150 | $1,500 | $150 | $1,500 | $150 | $1,500 | $150 |
| ***Subtotal Fixed*** | $12,750 | 1,275 | $12,665 | 1,267 | $12,665 | 1,267 | $12,665 | 1,267 | $12,832 | 1,283 | $12,832 | 1,283 |
| *Variable* | | | | | | | | | | | | |
| Management Fee @ 4% | $3,914 | $391 | $4,102 | $410 | $4,238 | $424 | $4,378 | $438 | $4,535 | $454 | $4,674 | $467 |
| Advertising and Promotion | $800 | $80 | $700 | $70 | $721 | $72 | $743 | $74 | $765 | $76 | $788 | $79 |
| Telephone | $900 | $90 | $800 | $80 | $824 | $82 | $849 | $85 | $874 | $87 | $900 | $90 |
| Utilities (Water, Sewer, Electric | $1,600 | $160 | $1,575 | $158 | $1,607 | $161 | $1,639 | $164 | $1,671 | $167 | $1,705 | $170 |
| Trash Removal | $1,000 | $100 | $1,030 | $103 | $1,030 | $103 | $1,060 | $106 | $1,060 | $106 | $1,092 | $109 |
| Repairs, Maintenance, and Supplies | $11,000 | $1,100 | $10,000 | $1,000 | $10,300 | $1,030 | $10,609 | $1,061 | $10,927 | $1,093 | $11,255 | $1,126 |
| Unit Interior Redecorating | $1,425 | $143 | $1,275 | $128 | $1,313 | $131 | $1,353 | $135 | $1,393 | $139 | $1,435 | $144 |
| Landscape, Lawn, and Grounds | $1,200 | $120 | $1,250 | $125 | $1,300 | $130 | $1,350 | $135 | $1,400 | $140 | $1,450 | $145 |
| Pest Control | $450 | $45 | $400 | $40 | $400 | $40 | $412 | $41 | $424 | $42 | $437 | $44 |
| ***Subtotal Variable*** | $22,289 | $2,229 | $21,132 | $2,113 | $21,732 | $2,173 | $22,392 | $2,239 | $23,051 | $2,305 | $23,736 | $2,374 |
| Replacement Allowances | | | | | | | | | | | | |
| ***Subtotal Replacement Allowances*** | $5,000 | $500 | $5,000 | $500 | $5,000 | $500 | $5,000 | $500 | $5,000 | $500 | $5,000 | $500 |
| **Total Operating Expenses** | $40,039 | $4,004 | $38,797 | $3,880 | $39,397 | $3,940 | $40,057 | $4,006 | $40,883 | $4,088 | $41,568 | $4,157 |
| **OPERATING INCOME** | | | | | | | | | | | | |
| **Net Operating Income** | $57,822 | $5,782 | $63,742 | $6,374 | $66,541 | $6,654 | $69,397 | $6,940 | $72,500 | $7,250 | $75,278 | $7,528 |

**Figure 4.21 (continued)**

Case Study: Leveraged Property Acquisition

| Period | Forecast 2005 Holding Year 1 | Forecast 2006 Holding Year 2 | Forecast 2007 Holding Year 3 | Forecast 2008 Holding Year 4 | Forecast 2009 Holding Year 5 | Forecast 2010 Reversion |
|---|---|---|---|---|---|---|
| **Allocation of NOI to Interests** | | | | | | |
| Category | Amount | Amount | Amount | Amount | Amount | Amount |
| **Net Operating Income** | $57,882 | $63,742 | $66,541 | $69,397 | $72,500 | $75,278 |
| *less:* | | | | | | |
| **Mortgage Loans** | | | | | | |
| **First (Senior) Loan** | | | | | | |
| Interest Expense | $29,967 | $27,487 | $26,976 | $26,430 | $25,848 | $- |
| Principal Reduction | $7,157 | $7,637 | $8,148 | $8,694 | $9,276 | $- |
| **Total Debt Service First (Senior) Loan** | $35,124 | $35,124 | $35,124 | $35,124 | $35,124 | $- |
| *equals:* | | | | | | |
| **Pre Tax Cash Flow (CF to Equity)** | $22,698 | $28,617 | $31,417 | $34,273 | $37,376 | |
| | | | | | | |
| **Rates of Return** | | | | | | |
| **Mortgage Loans** | | | | | | |
| **First (Senior) Loan—Loan Reduction** | Amount | Amount | Amount | Amount | Amount | Amount |
| Amount Outstanding BOP | $433,500 | $426,343 | $418,706 | $410,557 | $401,863 | $- |
| Principal Reduction | $7,157 | $7,637 | $8,148 | $8,694 | $9,276 | $- |
| Amount Outstanding EOP | $426,343 | $418,706 | $410,557 | $401,863 | $392,587 | $- |
| **First (Senior) Loan—Rate of Return** | | | | | | |
| Debt Service | $35,124 | $35,124 | $35,124 | $35,124 | $35,124 | $- |
| Original Amount Borrowed | $433,500 | $433,500 | $433,500 | $433,500 | $433,500 | $- |
| Rate of Return First (Senior) Loan | 8.10% | 8.10% | 8.10% | 8.10% | 8.10% | |
| **Cash Flow to Equity** | | | | | | |
| CF to Equity | $22,698 | $28,617 | $31,417 | $34,273 | $37,376 | $- |
| Original Amount Invested | $144,500 | $144,500 | $144,500 | $144,500 | $144,500 | $- |
| Rate of Return to Equity | 15.71% | 19.80% | 21.74% | 23.72% | 25.87% | |
| | | | | | | |
| **Exit** | | | | | | |
| Cash Flow to Equity | $22,698 | $28,617 | $31,417 | $34,273 | $37,376 | |
| *add:* | | | | | | |
| Reversion: Yr 6 NOI Exit Cap Rate @ 10.25% | | | | | | $734,423 |
| *less:* | | | | | | |
| Reversion Disposition Costs @ 5% | | | | | | $36,721 |
| *equals:* | | | | | | |
| Net Sales Proceeds EOY 5 | $- | $- | $- | $- | $697,701 | |
| *less:* | | | | | | |
| First (Senior) Loan Outstanding | | | | | $392,587 | |
| *equals:* | | | | | | |
| CF and Net Sales Proceeds | $22,698 | $28,617 | $31,417 | $34,273 | $342,490 | |
| | | | | | | |
| **DCFA** | | | | | | |
| Yield Rate @ 13.50% | 0.758205 | 0.574875 | 0.435873 | 0.330482 | 0.250573 | |
| *equals:* | | | | | | |
| Discounted CF and Net Sales Proceeds | $17,210 | $16,451 | $13,694 | $11,326 | $85,819 | |
| *equals:* | | | | | | |
| Present Value | $144,500 | | | | | |
| Rounded to: | $144,500 | | | | | |
| Equity Overall Rate | 15.71% | | | | | |
| Equity IRR | 31.89% | | | | | |
| | | | | | | |
| Debt Yield Rate @ 6.50% | | | | | Present Value Total Equity Position | $144,500 |
| Present Value of Senior Loan Position | $433,500 | | | | Present Value of Senior Loan Position | $433,500 |
| Debt Overall Rate | 8.10% | | | | Present Value of Investment | $578,000 |
| Debt IRR | 6.50% | | | | | |

### Rates of Return

As summarized in Figure 4.22, in the leveraged property acquisition, the net operating income is allocated to the debt and equity positions. The NOI is the source to pay back both the debt service to the lender and cash flow to the equity investor. This debt service represents the lender's return on their loan position. Because the lender is paid back first, the lender's position is considered to have lower risk than the equity investor's position. Therefore, the rate of return to the lender is usually lower than the rate of return to the equity investor. Being paid after the lender, the equity position is always considered "at risk" and, accordingly, is entitled to a higher return.

### Rate of Return to Debt

Each year of the investment, the property generates income for the debt position. The relationship of the first year's debt service to the original loan amount is also known as the loan constant. The **loan constant** is the capitalization rate for debt. It is expressed as $Rm$.

$$\text{Debt Capitalization Rate } (Rm) = \text{Annual Debt Service} \div \text{Original Loan}$$
$$8.1\% = \$35{,}124 \div \$433{,}500$$

**Figure 4.22**

Debt and Equity Dividend Rates

| Period | Forecast 2005 Holding Year 1 | Forecast 2006 Holding Year 2 | Forecast 2007 Holding Year 3 | Forecast 2008 Holding Year 4 | Forecast 2009 Holding Year 5 | Forecast 2010 Reversion |
|---|---|---|---|---|---|---|
| Rates of Return | | | | | | |
| Category | Amount | Amount | Amount | Amount | Amount | Amount |
| Income to Debt | $35,124 | $35,124 | $35,124 | $35,124 | $35,124 | N/A |
| *divided by:* | | | | | | |
| Original Amount Borrowed | $433,500 | $433,500 | $433,500 | $433,500 | $433,500 | N/A |
| *equals:* | | | | | | |
| Rate of Return to Debt | 8.10% | 8.10% | 8.10% | 8.10% | 8.10% | N/A |
| Cash Flow to Equity | $22,698 | $28,618 | $31,417 | $34,273 | $37,376 | N/A |
| *divided by:* | | | | | | |
| Original Amount Invested | $144,500 | $144,500 | $144,500 | $144,500 | $144,500 | N/A |
| *equals:* | | | | | | |
| Rate of Return to Equity | 15.71% | 19.80% | 21.74% | 23.72% | 25.87% | N/A |

**Figure 4.23**

DDRs

| Year | DDR |
|---|---|
| 1 | 8.10% |
| 2 | 8.10% |
| 3 | 8.10% |
| 4 | 8.10% |
| 5 | 8.10% |

As summarized in Figure 4.24, using this formula, we can calculate the debt dividend rate (DDR) for our leveraged property for each year of the holding period.

Why is the DDR (or the debt capitalization rate) 8.1 percent? After all, we are borrowing the money at a 6.5 percent rate of interest. The reason is that the loan is amortizing, with each payment containing not only the 6.5 percent interest on the amount outstanding but a principal component as well that goes toward retiring (or amortizing) the loan. Because the debt is a level payment amortizing mortgage, the DDR remains unchanged during the holding period. Also, because we are dividing income by value to obtain a rate, we are using the IRV formula to determine the debt capitalization rate.

### *Rate of Return to Equity*

Each year of the investment, the property generates cash flow to the equity position, also known as an equity dividend. The *equity dividend* is the cash flow that remains after debt service but before income taxes are considered. It is also known as pretax cash flow (PTCF). In our analysis of the leveraged property, the equity dividend rate is determined by dividing the cash flow by the original equity investment, as follows:

Equity Dividend Rate = Annual Cash Flow ÷ Original Investment
15.71% = $22,698 ÷ $144,500

As summarized in Figure 4.24, using this formula, we can calculate the equity dividend rate (EDR) for our leveraged property for each year of the holding period.

Some investors consider each year's equity dividend rate to provide insight into the investment performance of the property. However, other investors consider only the first year's equity dividend rate to be significant. Because we are dividing income by value to obtain a rate, we are employing the IRV formula to determine the equity capitalization rate. Lastly, note that the EDR is also known as the *cash-on-cash rate.*

**Figure 4.24**

EDRs

| Year | EDR |
|---|---|
| 1 | 15.7% |
| 2 | 19.8% |
| 3 | 21.7% |
| 4 | 23.7% |
| 5 | 25.9% |

As the EDRs in Figure 4.24 indicate, the annual equity dividend rates range from 15.7 percent to 25.9 percent. It is important to point out that we are considering the acquisition of the property on the basis of a 10 percent OAR. Also, there are significant differences in the leveraged EDRs over and above the unleveraged EDRs, as summarized in Figure 4.25.

The comparison between the leveraged and unleveraged EDRs provides a compelling argument for the use of borrowed funds.

### *Mortgage Loans*

We are considering a leveraged purchase employing a first (senior) loan at a purchase price of $578,000. The property will be acquired with a combination of our (owner's) cash, known as equity, and borrowed funds from a lender, known as debt. Financing in the amount of $433,500 equals 75 percent of the purchase price, and that 75 percent also represents the loan-to-value ratio.

The annual debt service for principal and interest totals $35,124. The pretax cash flow from this property after debt service but before taxes is $22,698 during the first year of the holding period. Real estate investors are interested in a property's calculated pretax cash flow, as it provides a simple, yet fundamental, measure of the investment's capability to do the following:

1. Pay debt service without "coming out of pocket." The ability of a property to service its debt is sometimes referred as the property's ability "to carry itself."
2. Provide a positive return on capital and a return of capital to the investor. The ability of a property to generate cash flow to the equity position is sometimes referred to as "cash throw off."

The loan is based upon a mortgage and a mortgage note. The borrower is required to sign a mortgage note for the amount borrowed and to execute a mortgage to secure the debt, which is evidenced by the note.

**Figure 4.25**

Comparison of Leveraged and Unleveraged EDRs

| Year | 1 | 2 | 3 | 4 | 5 |
|---|---|---|---|---|---|
| Leveraged EDRs | 15.70% | 19.80% | 21.70% | 23.70% | 25.90% |
| Unleveraged EDRs | 10.00% | 11.03% | 11.51% | 12.01% | 12.54% |

A **mortgage note** is both a written acknowledgment of a debt and a promise to repay a debt, which is secured by a mortgage. The purpose of the mortgage note is to create a personal liability for payment on the part of the borrower. The mortgate note states the terms of repayment of the debt, including the loan amount, duration, interest rate, time, and method of payment. A mortgage note is a promissory note secured by a mortgage.

A **mortgage** is a pledge or conveyance of an interest in real property. The purpose of the mortgage is to create a lien on the mortgaged property as security for the debt. The mortgage provides that the lender can take possession of the property if the borrower defaults.

A reduction in the amount outstanding of the mortgage note occurs periodically, and the investor uses the property's income stream to pay both the mortgage interest expense and the mortgage principal reduction. This process is called *amortizing the loan.*

An **amortized loan** is a loan requiring periodic payments that include both interest and partial repayment of principal. As the loan amortizes, the loan balance declines. Also as the loan amortizes, the interest portion of each periodic payment declines, and the principal portion of each periodic payment increases. This process is shown in Figure 4.26. Because the total purchase price remains unchanged while the debt component is declining, the equity component is increasing in relation to the purchase price.

The particular loan we are taking out to purchase our property is a *partially amortizing loan*, with a 25-year term and a 10-year call, payable monthly, at an interest rate of 6.5 percent per year. Partially amortized mortgages offer benefits to us as a borrower. Most significantly, they allow us to borrow a larger amount of money at a lower monthly payment than if we desired or required the same amount of money for a shorter term.

The ten-year term call offers us greater flexibility in our holding period. For example, we have forecasted a holding period of only five years, but what if ...? For example, what if we actually wind up holding the property for seven years for whatever reason? Having a loan that gives us the opportunity, but not the obligation, to prepay within a five-year to ten-year "window" gives us added flexibility without cost. So if we needed the loan for, say, another two years, it would be of no consequence to either the lender or us.

**Figure 4.26**

Amortization of Level Payment Amortizing Mortgage

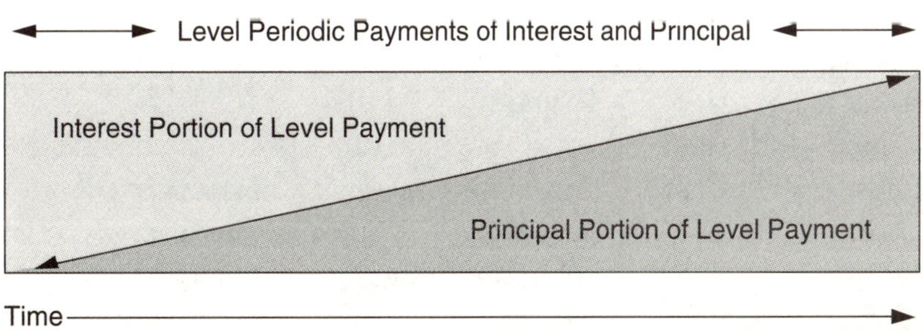

**Figure 4.27**

Loan Amortization

| Month | Beginning Principal | Interest for Period | Total Outstanding | Payment | Ending Principal | Interest | Principal | Amortization | Year |
|---|---|---|---|---|---|---|---|---|---|
| 1 | $433,500.00 | $2,348.13 | $435,848.13 | $2,927.02 | $432,921.11 | | | | |
| 2 | $432,921.11 | $2,344.99 | $435,266.09 | $2,927.02 | $432,339.07 | | | | |
| 3 | $432,339.07 | $2,341.84 | $434,680.91 | $2,927.02 | $431,753.89 | | | | |
| 4 | $431,753.89 | $2,338.67 | $434,092.56 | $2,927.02 | $431,165.54 | | | | |
| 5 | $431,165.54 | $2,335.48 | $433,501.02 | $2,927.02 | $430,574.00 | | | | |
| 6 | $430,574.00 | $2,332.28 | $432,906.27 | $2,927.02 | $429,979.25 | | | | |
| 7 | $429,979.25 | $2,329.05 | $432,308.31 | $2,927.02 | $429,381.29 | | | | |
| 8 | $429,381.29 | $2,325.82 | $431,707.10 | $2,927.02 | $428,780.08 | | | | |
| 9 | $428,780.08 | $2,322.56 | $431,102.64 | $2,927.02 | $428,175.60 | | | | |
| 10 | $428,175.62 | $2,319.28 | $430,494.91 | $2,927.02 | $427,567.89 | | | | |
| 11 | $427,657.89 | $2,315.99 | $429,883.88 | $2,927.02 | $426,956.86 | | | | |
| 12 | $426,956.86 | $2,312.68 | $429,269.54 | $2,927.02 | $426,342.52 | $27,966.76 | $7,157.48 | $35,124.24 | 1 |
| 13 | $426,342.52 | $2,309.36 | $428,651.88 | $2,927.02 | $425,724.86 | | | | |
| 14 | $425,724.86 | $2,306.01 | $428,030.87 | $2,927.02 | $425,103.85 | | | | |
| 15 | $425,103.85 | $2,302.65 | $427,406.49 | $2,927.02 | $424,479.47 | | | | |
| 16 | $424,479.47 | $2,299.26 | $426,778.74 | $2,927.02 | $423,851.72 | | | | |
| 17 | $423,851.72 | $2,295.86 | $426,147.58 | $2,927.02 | $423,220.56 | | | | |
| 18 | $423,220.56 | $2,292.44 | $425,513.01 | $2,927.02 | $422,585.99 | | | | |
| 19 | $422,585.99 | $2,289.01 | $424,874.99 | $2,927.02 | $421,947.97 | | | | |
| 20 | $421,947.97 | $2,285.55 | $424,233.52 | $2,927.02 | $421,306.50 | | | | |
| 21 | $421,306.50 | $2,282.08 | $423,588.58 | $2,927.02 | $420,661.56 | | | | |
| 22 | $420,661.56 | $2,278.58 | $422,940.14 | $2,927.02 | $420,013.12 | | | | |
| 23 | $420,013.12 | $2,275.07 | $422,288.20 | $2,927.02 | $419,361.18 | | | | |
| 24 | $419,361.18 | $2,271.54 | $421,632.72 | $2,927.02 | $418,705.70 | $27,487.41 | $7,636.83 | $35,124.24 | 2 |
| 25 | $418,705.70 | $2,267.99 | $420,973.68 | $2,927.02 | $418,046.66 | | | | |
| 26 | $418,046.66 | $2,264.42 | $420,311.08 | $2,927.02 | $417,384.06 | | | | |
| 27 | $417,384.06 | $2,260.83 | $419,644.89 | $2,927.02 | $416,717.87 | | | | |
| 28 | $416,717.87 | $2,257.22 | $418,975.10 | $2,927.02 | $416,048.08 | | | | |
| 29 | $416,048.08 | $2,253.59 | $418,301.67 | $2,927.02 | $415,374.65 | | | | |
| 30 | $415,374.65 | $2,249.95 | $417,624.60 | $2,927.02 | $414,697.58 | | | | |
| 31 | $414,697.58 | $2,246.28 | $416,943.85 | $2,927.02 | $414,016.83 | | | | |
| 32 | $414,016.83 | $2,242.59 | $416,259.43 | $2,927.02 | $413,332.41 | | | | |
| 33 | $413,332.41 | $2,238.88 | $415,571.29 | $2,927.02 | $412,644.27 | | | | |
| 34 | $412,644.27 | $2,235.16 | $414,879.43 | $2,927.02 | $411,952.41 | | | | |
| 35 | $411,952.41 | $2,231.41 | $414,183.81 | $2,927.02 | $411,256.79 | | | | |
| 36 | $411,256.79 | $2,227.64 | $413,484.44 | $2,927.02 | $410,557.42 | $26,975.96 | $8,148.28 | $35,124.24 | 3 |
| 37 | $410,557.42 | $2,223.85 | $412,781.27 | $2,927.02 | $409,854.25 | | | | |
| 38 | $409,854.25 | $2,220.04 | $412,074.29 | $2,927.02 | $409,147.27 | | | | |
| 39 | $409,147.27 | $2,216.21 | $411,363.49 | $2,927.02 | $408,436.47 | | | | |
| 40 | $408,436.47 | $2,212.36 | $410,648.83 | $2,927.02 | $407,721.81 | | | | |

**Figure 4.27 (continued)**

Loan Amortization

| Month | Beginning Principal | Interest for Period | Total Outstanding | Payment | Ending Principal | Interest | Principal | Amortization | Year |
|---|---|---|---|---|---|---|---|---|---|
| 41 | $407,721.81 | $2,208.49 | $409,930.30 | $2,927.02 | $407,003.28 | | | | |
| 42 | $407,003.28 | $2,204.60 | $409,207.89 | $2,927.02 | $406,280.87 | | | | |
| 43 | $406,280.87 | $2,200.69 | $408,481.55 | $2,927.02 | $405,554.53 | | | | |
| 44 | $405,554.53 | $2,196.75 | $407,751.29 | $2,927.02 | $404,824.27 | | | | |
| 45 | $404,824.27 | $2,192.80 | $407,017.06 | $2,927.02 | $404,090.04 | | | | |
| 46 | $404,090.04 | $2,188.82 | $406,278.87 | $2,927.02 | $403,351.85 | | | | |
| 47 | $403,351.85 | $2,184.82 | $405,536.67 | $2,927.02 | $402,609.65 | | | | |
| 48 | $402,609.65 | $2,180.80 | $404,790.45 | $2,927.02 | $401,863.43 | $26,430.26 | $8,693.98 | $35,124.24 | 4 |
| 49 | $401,863.43 | $2,176.76 | $404,040.19 | $2,927.02 | $401,113.17 | | | | |
| 50 | $401,113.17 | $2,172.70 | $403,285.87 | $2,927.02 | $400,358.85 | | | | |
| 51 | $400,358.85 | $2,168.61 | $402,527.46 | $2,927.02 | $399,600.44 | | | | |
| 52 | $399,600.44 | $2,164.50 | $401,764.94 | $2,927.02 | $398,837.92 | | | | |
| 53 | $398,837.92 | $2,160.37 | $400,998.29 | $2,927.02 | $398,071.27 | | | | |
| 54 | $398,071.27 | $2,156.22 | $400,227.49 | $2,927.02 | $397,300.47 | | | | |
| 55 | $397,300.47 | $2,152.04 | $399,452.52 | $2,927.02 | $396,525.50 | | | | |
| 56 | $396,525.50 | $2,147.85 | $398,673.34 | $2,927.02 | $395,746.32 | | | | |
| 57 | $395,746.32 | $2,143.63 | $397,889.95 | $2,927.02 | $394,962.93 | | | | |
| 58 | $394,962.93 | $2,139.38 | $397,102.31 | $2,927.02 | $394,175.29 | | | | |
| 59 | $394,175.29 | $2,135.12 | $396,310.41 | $2,927.02 | $393,383.39 | | | | |
| 60 | $393,383.39 | $2,130.83 | $395,514.21 | $2,927.02 | $392,587.19 | $25,848.00 | $9,276.24 | $35,124.24 | 5 |

Figure 4.27 shows the loan amortization schedule for the contemplated loan. Payments are made monthly and accounted for annually in this presentation. The amortization schedule is based on a loan term of 25 years, payable monthly, in 300 monthly payments. The note will be "called" (due and payable in full) at the end of the ten years. However, as planned, we will only require the funds through the end of the fifth year, when we will exit the property. Because the loan will not have fully amortized, an unpaid balance will be outstanding and due, resulting in a "balloon" payment.

The annual interest, principal, and debt service payments during each year of the five-year forecast presented in Figure 4.19 come from Figure 4.27, the loan amortization schedule for this loan amount. The principal amount outstanding at the beginning and end of each year also comes from this table.

### *Mortgage Loan Cash-Flow Diagram*

The amortizing mortgage loan used to acquire the ten-unit rental property on a leveraged basis is an annuity. The cash-flow diagram in Figure 4.28 presents a picture of the mortgage loan's cash flow.

**Figure 4.28**

Mortgage Loan Cash-Flow Diagram

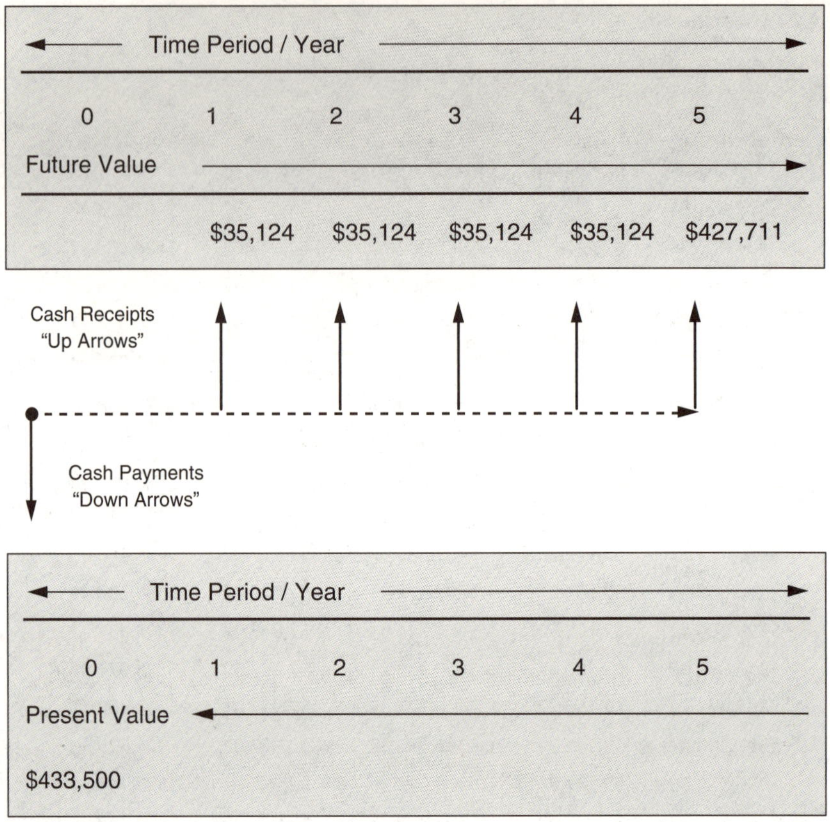


As Figure 4.28 illustrates, the loan amount is the present value, and the debt service payments plus reversion of the outstanding loan balance at the end of the fifth year are the periodic future cash flows.

### *Exit*

The exit for our property, based on the same combination of a 10.25 percent reversionary capitalization rate and a cost of sales of 5 percent of gross sales proceeds, obtains net sales from the exit of $697,701, as shown in Figure 4.29. However, in this leveraged scenario, the lender must also exit out of the real estate investment at the time of sale. Specifically, the outstanding loan balance of $392,587 must be repaid in full from the net sales proceeds. Accordingly, the net proceeds that will revert back to us after the lender is repaid is $342,490.

### *DCFA and Value of the Equity Position*

Because we are using debt and equity and have already evaluated the debt position, we are now evaluating the equity position. The present worth of the future equity monetary benefits, evaluated at 13.5 percent, is $266,200(rd), as shown in Figure 4.30. This amount is more than the $144,500 equity investment. The difference between the $144,500 equity contribution and the $266,200 discounted present value of this equity investment is $121,700. This $121,700 is the net present value of the equity investment.

*Net present value (NPV)* is the difference between the discounted present value of the equity investment ($266,200) evaluated at a yield rate (13.5 percent)

**Figure 4.29**

Cash Flows and Net Sales Proceeds

| Period | Forecast 2005 Holding Year 1 | Forecast 2006 Holding Year 2 | Forecast 2007 Holding Year 3 | Forecast 2008 Holding Year 4 | Forecast 2009 Holding Year 5 | Forecast 2010 Reversion |
|---|---|---|---|---|---|---|
| Exit | | | | | | |
| Category | Amount | Amount | Amount | Amount | Amount | Amount |
| Cash Flow | $22,698 | $28,618 | $31,417 | $34,273 | $37,376 | $75,278 |
| *add:* | | | | | | |
| Sale: Y-6 NOI Cap @ 10.25% | | | | | | $734,423 |
| *less:* | | | | | | |
| Disposition Costs @ 5% | | | | | | $(36,721) |
| *equals:* | | | | | | |
| Net Sales Proceeds EOY 5 | $- | $- | $- | $- | $697,701 | $697,701 |
| *less:* | | | | | | |
| First (Senior) Loan Outstanding | | | | | $392,587 | |
| *equals:* | | | | | | |
| Cash Flow and Sales Proceeds | $22,698 | $28,618 | $31,417 | $34,273 | $342,490 | |

and the initial equity contribution ($144,500). We would have to discount the future cash flows at a yield rate of exactly 31.89055484 percent (which rounds to 31.89 percent) to derive a present value amount ($144,500) exactly equal to the initial equity investment ($144,500). That yield rate represents the internal rate of return of the investment.

The *internal rate of return (IRR)* is the rate of return that discounts the future benefits of an investment to a present value that is exactly equal to the initial

**Figure 4.30**

Equity Discounted Cash-Flow Analysis with Yield Rate of 13.5 Percent

| Period | Forecast 2005 Holding Year 1 | Forecast 2006 Holding Year 2 | Forecast 2007 Holding Year 3 | Forecast 2008 Holding Year 4 | Forecast 2009 Holding Year 5 | Forecast 2010 Reversion |
|---|---|---|---|---|---|---|
| DCFA | | | | | | |
| Category | Amount | Amount | Amount | Amount | Amount | Amount |
| Cash Flow and Sales Proceeds | $22,698 | $28,618 | $31,417 | $34,273 | $342,490 | |
| *multiplied by:* | | | | | | |
| PVIF @ Investor 13.50% | 0.881057 | 0.776262 | 0.683931 | 0.602583 | 0.530910 | |
| *equals:* | | | | | | |
| Discounted Cash Flows | $19,998 | $22,215 | $21,487 | $20,652 | $181,831 | |
| Present Value of DCFA | $266,184 | | | | | |
| Rounded to | $266,200 | | | | | |

**Figure 4.31**

Discounted Cash-Flow Analysis with IRR of 31.89 Percent

| Period | Forecast 2005 Holding Year 1 | Forecast 2006 Holding Year 2 | Forecast 2007 Holding Year 3 | Forecast 2008 Holding Year 4 | Forecast 2009 Holding Year 5 | Forecast 2010 Reversion |
|---|---|---|---|---|---|---|
| IRR- DCFA | | | | | | |
| Category | Amount | Amount | Amount | Amount | Amount | Amount |
| Cash Flow and Sales Proceeds | $22,698 | $28,618 | $31,417 | $34,273 | $342,490 | |
| *multiplied by:* | | | | | | |
| PVIF @ IRR 31.89% | 0.758204 | 0.574874 | 0.435872 | 0.330480 | 0.250571 | |
| *equals:* | | | | | | |
| Discounted Cash Flows | $17,210 | $16,452 | $13,694 | $11,327 | $85,818 | |
| Present Value of DCFA | $144,500 | | | | | |
| Rounded to | $144,500 | | | | | |

investment. In this case, the NPV of the investment is zero. Stated differently, the IRR is the rate of return that makes the present value of the periodic cash flows and reversion equal to the initial investment itself.

Within the DCFA section, we allocate the overall value of the investment to its equity and debt components, which in turn make up the total capital stack of the investment. For the equity component, the cash flows and the net sales proceeds after debt are discounted at a rate of 31.89 percent, the IRR for the equity component, as shown in Figure 4.31. By employing the IRR discount rate, the present worth of the future benefits equals the initial investment. As such, our yield to equity for this contemplated investment is 31.89 percent.

Figure 4.32 shows a side-by-side comparison of the discounted present value of the ten-unit apartment property, based on our yield rate of 13.5 percent and the exact IRR of 31.89 percent.

### *Equity Cash-Flow Diagram*

The equity used to acquire the ten-unit rental property on a leveraged basis is an annuity. We can create a cash-flow diagram to present a picture of the equity's cash flow, as shown in Figure 4.33.

As Figure 4.33 illustrates, the equity investment is the present value, and the cash flow plus reversion of the equity sales proceeds at the end of the fifth year are the periodic future cash flows.

**Figure 4.32**

Comparison of Equity Value Based on Yield Rate of 13.5 Percent and IRR of 31.89 Percent

**Equity DCFA Using 13.50% Yield Rate**

| N/Period | Cash Flows | Yield Rate @13.50% | Discounted Cash Flows |
|---|---|---|---|
| 1 | $22,698 | 0.881057269 | $19,998 |
| 2 | $28,618 | 0.776261911 | $22,215 |
| 3 | $31,417 | 0.683931199 | $21,487 |
| 4 | $34,273 | 0.602582554 | $20,652 |
| 5 | $342,490 | 0.530909739 | $181,831 |
| PV of Discounted Cash Flows (rounded) | | | $266,200 |
| *less:* | | | |
| Acquisition Costs | | | $144,500 |
| *equals:* | | | |
| Net Present Value of Acquisition | | | $121,700 |

**Equity DCFA Using 31.89% IRR Yield Rate**

| N/Period | Cash Flows | IRR @ 31.89% | Discounted Cash Flows |
|---|---|---|---|
| 1 | $22,698 | 0.758204408 | $17,210 |
| 2 | $28,618 | 0.574873924 | $16,452 |
| 3 | $31,417 | 0.435871943 | $13,694 |
| 4 | $34,273 | 0.330480028 | $11,327 |
| 5 | $342,490 | 0.250571414 | $85,818 |
| PV of Discounted Cash Flows (rounded) | | | $144,500 |
| *less:* | | | |
| Acquisition Costs | | | $144,500 |
| *equals:* | | | |
| Net Present Value of Acquisition | | | $- |

**Figure 4.33**

Equity Cash-Flow Diagram

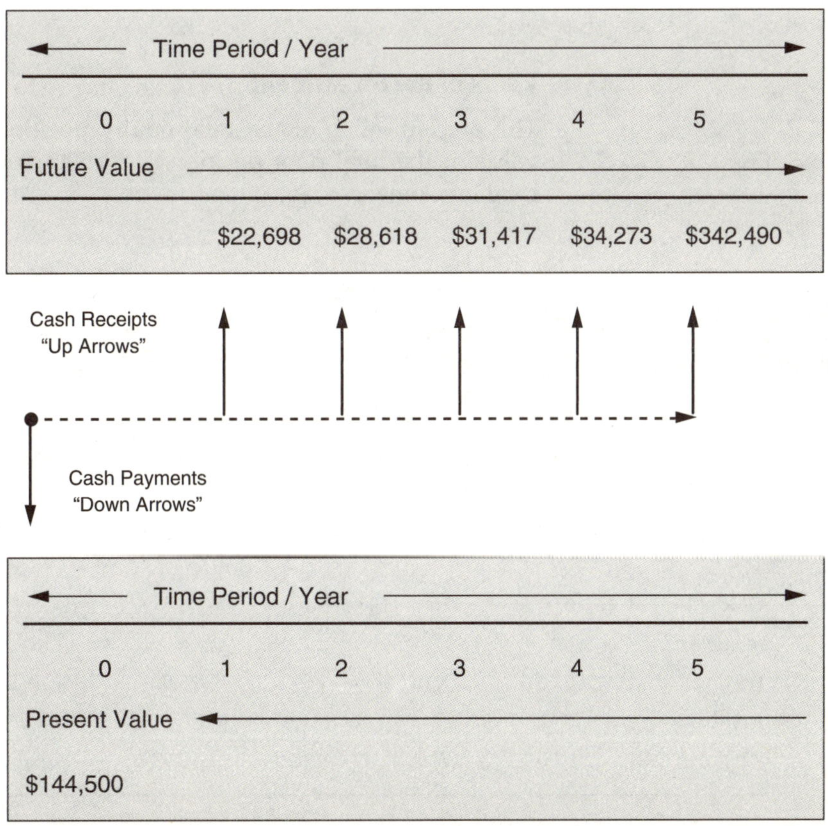

### *Equity Overall Rate*

Based upon our initial investment of $144,500, our **equity overall rate**, symbolized as Re, is 15.71 percent, calculated as follows:

$$\text{Equity Overall Rate } (Re) = \frac{\text{Year-1 CF (I)}}{\text{Equity Investment (V)}}$$

$$15.71\% = \frac{\$22{,}698}{144{,}500}$$

### *Value of the Debt Position*

The present value of the debt position is the original loan amount, $433,500. The IRR on the debt component is the interest rate on the debt. As such, the yield to debt for this contemplated investment is about 6.5 percent.

### *Debt Overall Rate*

Based upon our initial investment of $433,500, the **lender's overall rate** (*Rm*) is 8.1 percent, calculated as follows:

$$\text{Debt Overall Rate } (Rm) = \frac{\text{Loan Amort (I))}}{\text{Debt Investment (V)}}$$

$$8.10\% = \frac{\$35{,}124}{433{,}500}$$

### *Value of the Investment*

The present value of the total equity position ($144,500) plus the present value of the total debt position ($433,500) equals the present value of the total investment ($578,000).

**Figure 4.34**

Weighted OARs

| | | | | | | | |
|---|---|---|---|---|---|---|---|
| NOI | $57,822 | = | Cash Flow Yr 1 | $22,698 | + | Loan Amount Yr 1 | $35,124 |
| Capital | $578,000 | = | Equity Investment | $144,500 | + | Debt Principal | $433,500 |
| OAR | 10.00% | | Equity Dividend | 15.71% | | Debt Dividend | 8.10% |
| *multiplied by:* | | | | | | | |
| Weight | 100.00% | | % of Capital | 25.00% | | % of Capital | 75.00% |
| *equals:* | | | | | | | |
| Weighted OAR | 10.00% | = | Weighted Dividend | 3.93% | + | Weighted Dividend | 6.08% |

**Figure 4.35**

NPV Comparison of All-Cash and Leveraged $578,000 Acquisition

| All-Cash DCFA Using 13.5% Yield Rate | | | |
|---|---|---|---|
| N/Period | Cash Flows | Yield Rate @13.50% | Discounted Cash Flows |
| 1 | $57,822 | 0.881057269 | $50,944 |
| 2 | $63,742 | 0.776261911 | $49,480 |
| 3 | $66,541 | 0.683931199 | $45,509 |
| 4 | $69,397 | 0.602582554 | $41,817 |
| 5 | $770,202 | 0.530909739 | $408,908 |
| PV of Discounted Cash Flows (rounded) | | | $597,000 |
| *less:* | | | |
| Acquisition Costs | | | $578,000 |
| *equals:* | | | |
| Net Present Value of Acquisition | | | $19,000 |

| Leveraged DCFA Using 13.5% Yield Rate | | | |
|---|---|---|---|
| N/Period | Cash Flows | Yield Rate @13.50% | Discounted Cash Flows |
| 1 | $22,698 | 0.88105727 | $19,998 |
| 2 | $28,618 | 0.77626191 | $22,215 |
| 3 | $31,417 | 0.6839312 | $21,487 |
| 4 | $34,273 | 0.60258255 | $20,652 |
| 5 | $342,490 | 0.53090974 | $181,831 |
| PV of Discounted Cash Flows (rounded) | | | $266,200 |
| *less:* | | | |
| Acquisition Costs | | | $144,500 |
| *equals:* | | | |
| Net Present Value of Acquisition | | | $121,700 |

### *Investment Overall Rate*

If the equity overall rate is 15.71 percent and the debt overall rate is 8.1 percent, how can the investment's overall rate be 10 percent? By applying the respective components allocated weighted positions, as summarized in Figure 4.34.

## Measuring Investment Performance

It is easy to get so involved in the details of financial and investment analysis that we "can't see the forest for the trees," meaning that we lose the perspective to look at the situation as a whole. To regain focus, we can use two widely used measures of an investment's performance: net present value and internal rate of return. After considering the complexities associated with all of the assumptions, forecasting, and the profit and loss statement, the NPV and IRR allow for straightforward tests to determine if the property meets, exceeds, or falls short of the investor's objectives. And the purchaser's investment objectives actually are the point of investing, aren't they? For these these powerful measurement tools to fulfill their potential, they should be used to compare one investment to another.

### *Net Present Value*

The NPV of an investment measures the difference between the discounted present worth of the investment, evaluated at a yield rate considered appropriate for the investment, and the initial cost of the investment. Based on either NPV model, the net present value of both the investments shown in Figure 4.35 exceeds the investor's initial expectation of 13.5 percent.

The unleveraged NPV model indicates that, while the investor is paying $578,000 for a property based on a 13.5 percent yield, it has a positive NPV of $19,000, suggesting that the property is yielding more than the 13.5 percent. That's because the investor is paying $578,000, which is $19,000 less than the $597,000 price the 13.5 percent yield would indicate in the marketplace.

The leveraged NPV model indicates that, while the investor is paying $144,500 for the equity position in the property based on a 13.5 percent yield, the investment has a positive NPV of $121,700, suggesting that the equity position in the property is yielding significantly more than the 13.5 percent. That's because the investor is paying $144,500, which is $121,700 less for the equity position than the $266,200 price the 13.5 percent yield would indicate in the marketplace.

An investor should expect to receive a greater yield on a leveraged basis than on an unleveraged basis, because the leveraged equity is perceived by the marketplace to be at risk. It is subordinated to the debt position, which has a priority claim against the net operating income of the property. In conclusion, the leveraged acquisition not only requires less equity but also provides significantly more return than the unleveraged acquisition.

### *Internal Rate of Return*

The IRR of an investment is the rate of return that discounts the future benefits of the investment to a present worth exactly equal to the initial investment. In that case, the NPV of the investment is zero. Stated differently, the IRR is the rate of return that makes the present worth of the periodic cash flows and reversion equal to the equity position. Based on either IRR model, as shown in Figure 4.36, the rate of return exceeds the 13.5 percent that represented the investor's initial expectations.

**Figure 4.36**

IRR Comparison of All-Cash and Leveraged $578,000 Acquisition

| IRR of All-Cash DCFA | | | | IRR of Leveraged DCFA | | | |
|---|---|---|---|---|---|---|---|
| N/Period | Cash Flows | IRR @ 14.37% | Discounted Cash Flows | N/Period | Cash Flows | IRR @ 31.89%% | Discounted Cash Flows |
| 1 | $57,822 | 0.874385701 | $50,559 | 1 | $22,698 | 0.75820441 | $17,210 |
| 2 | $63,742 | 0.764550354 | $48,734 | 2 | $28,618 | 0.57487392 | $16,452 |
| 3 | $66,541 | 0.668511897 | $44,483 | 3 | $31,417 | 0.43587194 | $13,694 |
| 4 | $69,397 | 0.584537243 | $40,565 | 4 | $34,273 | 0.33048003 | $11,327 |
| 5 | $770,202 | 0.511111007 | $393,659 | 5 | $342,490 | 0.25057141 | $85,818 |
| PV of Discounted Cash Flows (rounded) | | | $578,000 | PV of Discounted Cash Flows (rounded) | | | $144,500 |
| *less:* | | | | *less:* | | | |
| Acquisition Costs | | | $578,000 | Acquisition Costs | | | $144,500 |
| *equals:* | | | | *equals:* | | | |
| Net Present Value of Acquisition | | | $- | Net Present Value of Acquisition | | | $- |

The unleveraged IRR model indicates that, while paying $578,000 for the property based on a 13.5 percent yield, the investor is actually acquiring the property based on an anticipated 14.37 percent yield, which is the IRR. Accordingly, when the 14.37 percent IRR yield rate is used to discount the cash flows, the present value of those discounted cash flows exactly equals the initial investment. That's because the investor is paying $578,000, $19,000 less than the $597,000 price the 13.5 percent yield would indicate. So a higher discount rate is required to further reduce the equivalent amount to a present value, and that discount rate is the IRR.

The leveraged IRR model indicates that, while paying $144,500 for the equity position in the property based on a 13.5 percent yield, the investor is actually acquiring the equity position based on an anticipated 31.89 percent yield, which is the IRR. Accordingly, when the 31.89 percent yield rate is used to discount the cash flows, the present value of those discounted cash flows exactly equals the initial investment. That's because the investor is paying $144,500 for the equity position, $121,700 less than the $266,200 price the 13.5 percent yield would indicate. So a higher discount rate is required to further reduce the equivalent amount to a present value. In conclusion, the leveraged acquisition not only requires less equity but also provides significantly more return than the unleveraged acquisition.

## Summary

Commercial investment property may be acquired entirely with cash. However, the majority of commercial investment property acquisitions involve a combination of equity, which is the investor's cash, and debt, which is the lender's financing. There are many valid, even compelling, reasons to employ financing in the acquisition of real estate. However, all these reasons have a central point in common; they allow a purchaser to become the owner without actually owning the capital used to acquire the property. Essentially, the investor is borrowing someone else's money to achieve his or her own goals.

From a transaction perspective, commercial real estate is capital intensive, requiring a significant amount of money for purchase. Using financing increases the capital amount available for the purchase, based on loan-to-value ratios. Borrowing money to finance a property acquisition also affects investment returns. Leverage is the effect of borrowed funds on real estate purchases; it may increase or decrease the return that would be received on all-cash equity.

The lender looks primarily to the property itself, not the investor-borrower, for repayment of debt. The source of the repayment of debt is the property's operating income. To determine the risk associated with a loan, lenders look at two basic, yet important, ratios: the loan-to-value ratio and the debt coverage ratio. A loan-to-value ratio expresses the relationship of borrowed funds as a percentage of the value of the property. A debt coverage ratio expresses the relationship of the annual net operating income to the annual debt service.

Amortized loans are based upon a mortgage and a mortgage note. A mortgage note is a written promise to pay a sum of money at a stated interest rate over a specified term. It is secured by a mortgage. A mortgage is a conveyance of an interest in real property given as security for the payment of a debt. A reduction in the outstanding amount of the mortgage note occurs periodically, and the investor uses the property's income stream to pay both the mortgage interest expense and the mortgage principal reduction. This process is called amortizing the loan. An amortized loan requires periodic payments that include both interest and partial repayments of principal. As the loan amortizes, the loan balance declines. Because the total purchase price remains unchanged while the debt component declines, the equity component increases in relation to the purchase price.

There are three primary ways that the commercial mortgage brokerage industry can implement financing services on behalf of a client-borrower: as a mortgage broker, a mortgage banker, or a correspondent lender. These three sources of financing play an important role in providing mortgage funds to borrowers on a regional and national level. Often mortgage brokers, mortgage bankers, and correspondent lenders serve niche markets that provide a vital need in the financing arena. These lenders can also be more aggressive, more flexible, and more creative than traditional lenders, which are closely regulated.

Net operating income (NOI) is the actual or anticipated net income that remains after all operating expenses are deducted from effective gross income but before mortgage debt service and depreciation are deducted. NOI is used to determine the value or price of the property through capitalizing the NOI, using either direct capitalization or yield capitalization. NOI represents the income available to satisfy the interests in the real estate, namely the equity investor and the lender of debt, as appropriate. NOI does not consider payments for mortgage debt service and cash flow; rather, NOI is the amount of money available to pay the mortgage debt service and the cash flow.

A rate of return is the ratio of income to the original investment. It is a percentage calculated as the ratio of the current net income generated from property operation to the initial capital investment. Each year of the investment, the property generates net operating income, which is allocated to debt service and cash flow. If a property is acquired with all cash, the rate of return to equity is called an equity dividend rate. If both equity and debt positions are in property, the rate of return to equity is called the equity dividend rate, and the rate of return to debt is called the debt dividend rate or loan constant. Because we are dividing income by value to obtain a rate, we are employing the IRV formula.

The term *exit* is real estate jargon meaning "exit strategy." An exit strategy concerns the eventual sale, or disposition, of a real estate asset. It is an operating framework that addresses the investor's objective of the real estate investment by providing a viable scenario, or alternative scenarios, through which an orderly sale of the property will occur. As such, an exit strategy concerns itself with reversion.

It is easy to get so involved in the details of financial and investment analysis that we "can't see the forest for the trees," meaning that we lose the perspective to see the situation as a whole. Two widely used measures of an investment's performance can help us regain focus: net present value and internal rate of return. After considering the complexities associated with all of the assumptions, forecasting, and the profit and loss statement, the NPV and IRR allow for straightforward tests to determine if the property meets, exceeds, or falls short of the investor's objectives. And the purchaser's investment objectives actually are the point of investing. For these powerful measurement tools to fulfill their potential, they should be used to compare one investment to another.

The net present value (NPV) of an investment is the difference between the discounted present value of the investment, evaluated at a yield rate considered reasonable and appropriate, and the initial acquisition cost of the investment. The internal rate of return (IRR) of an investment is the rate of return that discounts the future benefits of the investment to a present value exactly equal to the initial investment. In that case, the NPV of the investment is zero. Stated differently, the IRR is the rate of return that makes the present value of the periodic cash flows and reversion equal to the initial investment.

## Review Questions

1. Leverage is the effect of
   a. free and clear equity on real estate purchases.
   b. borrowed funds on real estate purchases.
   c. equity funds on real estate purchases.
   d. free and clear equity on yield rates.

2. Positive leverage
   a. is the increase in financial losses that result from borrowing.
   b. is the increase in financial profits that result from borrowing.
   c. converts future benefits into a present value.
   d. does all of the above.

3. Negative leverage
   a. is the increase in financial losses that result from borrowing.
   b. is the increase in financial profits that result from borrowing.
   c. converts future benefits into a present value.
   d. does all of the above.

4. Rate of return
   a. is the ratio of income or yield to the original investment.
   b. discounts the future benefits of an investment to a present worth equal to the initial investment.
   c. is the relationship of borrowed funds as a percentage of the value of the property.
   d. is the inverse of annuity capitalization.

5. An equity dividend
   a. measures the relationship between income, value, and risk.
   b. is the cash flow that remains after debt service but before income taxes are considered.
   c. is the cash flow that remains before debt services but after income taxes are considered.
   d. is determined by dividing the original investment by the cash flow.

6. The term *exit* refers to
   a. the eventual sale, or disposition, of a real estate asset.
   b. the investor's objective for the real estate investment.
   c. reversion.
   d. all of the above.

7. IRR
   a. measures the lump-sum benefit of the return of capital.
   b. is an alternate investment matrix that factors opportunity cost.
   c. is the rate of return that discounts future benefits to a present worth exactly equal to the initial investment.
   d. does all of the above.

8. LTV
   a. is the ratio of income or yield to the original investment.
   b. discounts the future benefits of an investment to a present worth equal to the initial investment.
   c. is the relationship of borrowed funds as a percentage of the value of the property.
   d. is the inverse of annuity capitalization.

9. A mortgage note
   a. employs the time value of money concept.
   b. is a conveyance of an interest in real property given as security for the payment of a debt.
   c. is a written promise to pay a sum of money at a stated interest rate over a specified term.
   d. has the feature of predictability of income and regularity of payment.

10. A mortgage
    a. employs the time value of money concept.
    b. is a conveyance of an interest in real property given as security for the payment of a debt.
    c. is a written promise to pay a sum of money at a stated interest rate over a specified term.
    d. has the feature of predictability of income and regularity of payment.

11. It is January 1 of the current year. You are considering the acquisition of a 20-unit rental apartment property on a yield capitalization basis. The projected current year's net operating income is $110,000, and you are comfortable that this is a solid projection. You anticipate NOI to grow at an annual rate of 5 percent. You are considering acquiring this property on the basis of a 10 percent direct capitalization rate. If the seller accepts your offer, what is your purchase price?
    a. $1,100,000
    b. $1,155,000
    c. $2,200,000
    d. $2,420,000

12. You are considering the use of debt in your property acquisition. If a lender will provide the debt based upon a 75 percent loan-to-value ratio, how much debt could the lender provide?
    a. $825,000
    b. $866,250
    c. $1,650,000
    d. $1,815,000

13. The lender in question 12 offers to provide a mortgage loan with a 25-year term and a 10-year call, payable monthly, at an interest rate of 7.25 percent per year. If the loan constant for this loan is 0.08670, what is the annual amount of debt service?
    a. $59,812.50
    b. $62,803.13
    c. $71,527.50
    d. $75,103.88

14. Based on the loan offered in question 13, what is the DCR? If the lender requires a minimum DCR of 1.35, does this loan meet these criteria?
    a. The DCR is 1.54. The loan meets the lender's criteria.
    b. The DCR is 1.44. The loan meets the lender's criteria.
    c. The DCR is 1.34. The loan does not meet the lender's criteria.
    d. The DCR is 1.24. The loan does not meet the lender's criteria.

15. What cash flow to equity and equity dividend rate (EDR) can be expected by using this acquisition scenario?
    a. Cash flow is $59,812.50, and the EDR is 21.75%.
    b. Cash flow is $47,196.87, and the EDR is 17.16%.
    c. Cash flow is $38,472.50, and the EDR is 13.99%.
    d. Cash flow is $34,896.12, and the EDR is 12.69%.

# ANSWER KEY

## Chapter 1

### *Multiple-Choice Questions*

1. D  2. D  3. A  4. B  5. C  6. A  7. C  8. A  9. D  10. B

### *Application Questions*

11. A

The current year's effective gross income is $154,752 in total and $7,738 per unit.

| | | Total | Per Unit |
|---|---|---|---|
| Base Rents/Potential Gross Income | | $253,920 | $12,696 |
| *less:* | | | |
| Vacancy & Collection Loss @ | 25% | $(63,480) | $(3,174) |
| *equals:* | | | |
| Subtotal | | $190,440 | $9,522 |
| *less:* | | | |
| Rental Concessions @ | 20% | $(38,088) | $(1,904) |
| *equals:* | | | |
| Subtotal | | $152,352 | $7,618 |
| *add:* | | | |
| Other Income | | $2,400 | $120 |
| *equals:* | | | |
| Effective Gross Income | | $154,752 | $7,738 |

The base rents are reported to be $253,920. Due to the "upgrade and beautification" project, the property has a 25 percent vacancy and collection loss factor, which reduces the base rents by the same percentage to an adjusted amount of $190,440. Additionally, the owner has put in place a temporary rental concession program, discounting in-place rents by 20 percent until the project is completed. This concession further reduces base rents by $38,088 to an adjusted base rent amount of $152,352 per year. The owner receives $200 per month or $2,400 per year from a service company for the operation of washers, dryers, and vending machines at the property. This amount is added to the adjusted base rents to arrive at the current year's expected effective gross income of $154,752 per year or $7,738 per unit.

12. C

The current year's fixed expenses are $26,000 in total and $1,300 per unit.

| Fixed Expenses | Benchmark | Total | Per Unit |
|---|---|---|---|
| Real Estate Taxes As Amount Per Unit | $1,100.00 | $22,000 | $1,100 |
| *add:* | | | |
| Insurance As Amount PSF | $0.20 | $4,000 | $200 |
| *equals:* | | | |
| Total Fixed Expenses | | $26,000 | $1,300 |

The fixed expenses were provided in the case study but used differing units of measure, as follows:

- The real estate taxes expense was quoted on the basis of $1,100 per unit. Given that there are 20 units in the building, tax expense would be $22,000 in total.
- The property insurance was quoted on the basis of $0.20 per square foot. Given that there are 20,000 square feet of rentable area in the building, the insurance expense would be $4,000 in total, $200 per unit.
- Adding both of the fixed operating expenses gives $26,000 in total, $1,300 per unit.

13. B

The current year's variable expenses are $34,810 in total, $1,741 per unit.

| Variable Expenses | Benchmark | Total | Per Unit |
|---|---|---|---|
| Management Fees as % of EGI | 4.00% | $6,190 | $310 |
| Advertising & Promo as Amount PSF | $0.07 | $1,400 | $70 |
| Telephone as Amount per Unit | $75.00 | $1,500 | $75 |
| Utilities as % of EGI | 1.50% | 2,320 | $116 |
| Trash as Amount PSF | $0.10 | $2,000 | $100 |
| Repairs and Maintenance | $0.80 | $16,000 | $800 |
| Int. Redecorating as Amount per Unit | $100 | $2,000 | $100 |
| Landscape as Amount per Annum | $2,400 | $2,400 | $120 |
| Pest Control as Amount PSF | $0.05 | $1,000 | $50 |
| *equals:* | | | |
| Total Variable Expenses | | $34,810 | $1,741 |

The variable expenses were provided in the case study but used differing units of measure, as follows:

- The management fees expense was quoted on the basis of 4 percent of effective gross income. Given that the EGI was previously estimated as $154,752, the management fee expense would be $6,190 in total, $310 per unit.
- The advertising and promotional expense was quoted on the basis of $0.07 per square foot. Given that there are 20,000 square feet of rentable area in the building, the advertising and promotional expense would be $1,400 in total, $70 per unit.
- The telephone expenses were quoted on the basis of $75 per unit. Given that there are 20 units, the telephone expense would be $1,500 in total, $75 per unit.
- The utilities expenses were quoted on the basis of 1.5 percent of effective gross income. Given that the EGI was previously estimated as $154,752, the utilities expense would be $2,320 in total, $116 per unit.
- The trash expense was quoted on the basis of $0.10 per square foot. Given that there are 20,000 square feet of rentable area in the building, the trash expense would be $2,000 in total, $100 per unit.
- The repairs and maintenance expenses were quoted on the basis of $0.80 per square foot. Given that there are 20,000 square feet of rentable area in the building, the trash expense would be $16,000 in total, $800 per unit.
- The unit interior redecorating expenses were quoted on the basis of $100 per unit. Given that there are 20 units, the unit redecorating expense would be $2,000 in total, $100 per unit.
- The landscape expenses were quoted on the basis of $2,400 per year. Given that there are 20 units, the unit redecorating expense would be $2,400 in total, $120 per unit.
- The pest control expense was quoted on the basis of $0.05 per square foot. Given that there are 20,000 square feet of rentable area in the building, the pest control expense would be $1,000 in total, $50 per unit.
- Adding up the entire variable operating expenses comes to $34,810 in total, $1,741 per unit.

14. D

The replacement reserve expenses were quoted on the basis of $350 per unit. Given that there are 20 units, the replacement reserve expense would be $7,000 in total, $350 per unit.

| Replacement Reserves | Benchmark | Total | Per Unit |
|---|---|---|---|
| Reserves as Amount per Unit | $350 | $7,000 | $350 |

15. C

The current year's net operating income is $86,942 in total, $4,347 per unit.

| | % | Total | Per Unit |
|---|---|---|---|
| Effective Gross Income | 100.00% | $154,752 | $7,738 |
| *less:* | | | |
| Operating Expenses | | | |
| Fixed Expenses | | $(26,000) | $(1,300) |
| Variable Expenses | | $(34,810) | $(1,741) |
| Replacement Reserves | | $(7,000) | $(350) |
| Total Operating Expenses | –43.82% | $(67,810) | $(3,391) |
| *equals:* | | | |
| Net Operating Income | 56.18% | $86,942 | $4,347 |

Following are answers based on the above table:

- Effective gross income was previously estimated at $154,752 in total, $7,738 per unit.
- The three categories of operating expenses were previously estimated. The addition of the fixed, variable, and replacement reserve expenses come to $67,810 in total, $3,391 per unit.
- Subtracting the current year's total operating expenses from the current year's effective gross income results in a current year net operating income of $86,942 in total, $4,347 per unit.

Following is a current year reconstructed operating statement for the case study property:

| Reconstructed Operating Statement | | Total | Per Unit |
|---|---|---|---|
| Base Rents / Potential Gross Income | | $253,920 | $12,696 |
| *less:* | | | |
| Vacancy and Collection Loss @ | 25% | $(63,480) | $(3,174) |
| *equals:* | | | |
| Subtotal | | $190,440 | $9,522 |
| *less:* | | | |
| Rental Concessions @ | 20% | $(38,088) | $(1,904) |
| *equals:* | | | |
| Subtotal | | $152,352 | $7,618 |
| *add:* | | | |
| Other Income | | $2,400 | $120 |
| *equals:* | | | |
| Effective Gross Income | | $154,752 | $7,738 |
| *less:* | | | |
| Total Operating Expenses | | $(67,810) | $(3,391) |
| *equals:* | | | |
| Net Operating Income | | $86,942 | $4,347 |

## Chapter 2

### *Multiple-Choice Questions*

1. C 2. D 3. D 4. D 5. A 6. A 7. D 8. D 9. A 10. A

### *Application Questions*

11. C

Using the IRV formula, the current year's price or value, if income is capitalized at 9 percent, is $966,022.

The current year's "as is" net operating income is $86,942. The selected cap rate is 9 percent. Employing the IRV formula, we can solve for price or value using the direct capitalization of "as is" NOI, as follows:

$$\text{Value} = \text{Income} \div \text{Rate}$$

$$\$966{,}022 \text{ Value (V)} = \frac{\text{Net Operating Income (I) } \$86{,}942}{\text{Overall Capitalization Rate (R) } 0.09}$$

12. C

Using the IRV formula, the current year's price or value, if income is capitalized at 10 percent, is $869,420.

The current year's "as is" net operating income is $86,942. The selected cap rate is 10 percent. Employing the IRV formula, we can solve for price or value by using direct capitalization of "as is" NOI, as follows:

$$\text{Value} = \text{Income} \div \text{Rate}$$

$$\$869{,}420 \text{ Value (V)} = \frac{\text{Net Operating Income (I) } \$86{,}942}{\text{Overall Capitalization Rate (R) } 0.10}$$

13. D

All of the above. Explanations of each choice follow:

a. When the cap rate is increased from 9 percent to 10 percent, an increase of 1 percent, the price or value declines from $966,022 to $869,420, or $96,602, which is 10 percent of $966,022.

b. Given an NOI of $86,942, an increase in the cap rate from 9 percent to 10 percent will result in a decease in price or value from $966,022 to $869,420.

c. Given an NOI of $86,942, a decrease in the cap rate from 10 percent to 9 percent will result in an increase in price or value from $869,420 to $966,022.

14. B

The pro forma NOI is $182,690.

Following is a pro forma operating statement for the property based upon the information contained within the case study.

| Pro Forma Operating Statement | PGI | Total | Per Unit |
|---|---|---|---|
| Base Rents / Potential Gross Income | | $266,616 | $13,331 |
| *less:* | | | |
| Vacancy and Collection Loss @ | 5% | $(13,331) | $(667) |
| *equals:* | | | |
| Subtotal | | $253,285 | $12,664 |
| *less:* | | | |
| Rental Concessions @ | 0% | $- | $- |
| *equals:* | | | |
| Subtotal | | $253,285 | $12,664 |
| *add:* | | | |
| Other Income | | $2,640 | $132 |
| *equals:* | | | |
| Effective Gross Income | EGI | $255,925 | $12,796 |
| *less:* | | | |
| Total Operating Expenses | 29% | $(73,236) | $(3,662) |
| *equals:* | | | |
| Net Operating Income | 71% | $182,690 | $9,135 |

- Potential gross income: Escalating at 5 percent above the prior year
- Vacancy and collection: Stabilizing at 5 percent
- Effective gross income: Estimated at $255,925
- Operating expenses:
  - Fixed expenses: Increasing at 2 percent over the prior year's expenses
  - Variable expenses: Increasing at 3 percent above the prior year's expenses
  - Management fees: 4 percent of current year's EGI
  - Reserves: Remain unchanged from the prior year
- Operating expense detail: Based upon the fixed, variable, management fee, and reserves assumptions, the following table can be prepared:

| Pro Forma Year Op Expense | Total per Annum | Total per Unit/Annum |
|---|---|---|
| ***Fixed Expenses*** | | |
| Real Estate Taxes: | $22,440 | $1,122 |
| Insurance: | $4,080 | $204 |
| ***Variable Expenses*** | | |
| Management Fees: | $10,237 | $512 |
| Advertising and Promotion: | $1,442 | $72 |
| Telephone: | $1,545 | $77 |
| Utilities: | $2,390 | $120 |
| Trash: | $2,060 | $103 |
| Repairs and Maintenance: | $16,480 | $824 |
| Unit Interior Redecorating: | $2,060 | $103 |
| Landscape, Lawn, and Grounds: | $2,472 | $124 |
| Pest Control: | $1,030 | $52 |
| ***Replacement Reserves*** | | |
| Reserves: | $7,000 | $350 |
| **Total Operating Expenses** | **$73,236** | **$3,662** |

The pro forma NOI is $182,690.

15. B

    If the pro forma NOI of $182,690 is capitalized at 8.5 percent, the forecast year price or value is $2,149,295.

    The pro forma year's net operating income is $182,690. The selected cap rate is 8.5 percent. Employing the IRV formula, we can solve for price or value by direct capitalization of pro forma NOI, as follows:

$$\text{Value} = \text{Income} \div \text{Rate}$$

$$\$2{,}149{,}295 \text{ Value (V)} = \frac{\text{Net Operating Income (I) } \$182{,}690}{\text{Overall Capitalization Rate (R) } 0.085}$$

## Chapter 3

### *Multiple-Choice Questions*

1. C 2. D 3. D 4. C 5. A 6. A 7. D 8. A 9. D 10. A

### *Application Questions*

11. C

    If acquired on a direct capitalization basis, the capitalized NOI equates to a purchase price of $2,150,000.

Following is a summary of the direct capitalization process for this investment:

| | |
|---|---|
| Current Year NOI | $182,690 |
| *divided by:* | |
| Direct Cap Rate | 8.50% |
| *equals:* | |
| Value-Direct Cap | $2,149,294 |
| *rounded to:* | |
| Rounded Value | $2,150,000 |

12. Refer to the table for the calculations of the summary analysis of total cash flows.

    We expect to hold this property for five years. The projected current year's net operating income is $182,690. Each year during the holding period, this NOI is anticipated to grow at an annual rate of 5 percent. We expect to sell this property at the end of the fifth year, with the future reversion or exit based upon the six-year NOI capitalized at a 9 percent reversionary rate. From the capitalized NOI, we then deduct estimated transaction costs of 5 percent of gross sales proceeds.

    The total cash flows from all sources, for each year of the projection, are summarized below:

| Period/N | Status | NOI | + | Reversion | = | Total Cash Flows |
|---|---|---|---|---|---|---|
| 1 | Holding | $182,690 | + | $- | = | $182,690 |
| 2 | Holding | $191,825 | + | $- | = | $191,825 |
| 3 | Holding | $201,416 | + | $- | = | $201,416 |
| 4 | Holding | $211,487 | + | $- | = | $211,487 |
| 5 | Holding | $222,061 | + | $2,461,174 | = | $2,683,235 |
| *add:* | | | | | | |
| EOY 5 | Reversion | | | | | |

| Reversionary Calculation | | |
|---|---|---|
| **Period / N** | **Status** | **NOI** |
| 6 | Reversion | $233,164 |
| *divided by:* | | |
| Reversionary Rate of | | 9.00% |
| *equals:* | | |
| Gross Sales Proceeds | | $2,590,710 |
| *less:* | | |
| Transacation Costs @ 5% | | $129,536 |
| *equals:* | | |
| Net Sales Proceeds | | $2,461,174 |

13. D

$2,265,000

Following is a summary of the discounted cash flow analysis for the property, based on a 10 percent yield rate:

| N/Period | Status | Total Cash Flows | × | PVIFr,n | = | Discounted CF |
|---|---|---|---|---|---|---|
| 1 | Holding | $182,690 | × | 0.909090909 | = | $166,082 |
| 2 | Holding | $191,825 | × | 0.826446281 | = | $158,533 |
| 3 | Holding | $201,416 | × | 0.751314801 | = | $151,327 |
| 4 | Holding | $211,487 | × | 0.683013455 | = | $144,448 |
| 5 | Holding | $2,683,235 | × | 0.620921323 | = | $1,666,078 |
| Present Value of Discounted Cash Flows | | | | | | $2,286,467 |
| Rounded to | | | | | | $2,286,500 |

14. B

$136,500

Following is a summary of the net present value analysis for the property, based on a discounted present value of $2,286,500 and a direct capitalization acquisition price of $2,150,000.

| N/Period | Cash Flow | Yield Rate @ 10.00% | Discounted Cash Flows |
|---|---|---|---|
| 1 | $182,690 | 0.909090909 | $166,082 |
| 2 | $191,825 | 0.826446281 | $158,533 |
| 3 | $201,416 | 0.751314801 | $151,327 |
| 4 | $211,487 | 0.683013455 | $144,448 |
| 5 | $2,683,235 | 0.620921323 | $1,666,078 |
| PV of Discounted Cash Flows (rounded) | | | $2,286,500 |
| *less:* | | | |
| Acqusition Costs | | | $2,150,000 |
| *equals:* | | | |
| Net Present Value of Acquisition | | | $136,500 |

15. D

The NPV would be $0, and the 11.59 percent yield rate would be the IRR.

Following is a summary of the net present value analysis for the property, based on a discounted present value basis factoring a yield rate of 11.59 percent:

| N/Period | Cash Flow | Yield Rate @ 11.59% | Discounted Cash Flows |
|---|---|---|---|
| 1 | $182,690 | 0.896155259 | $163,719 |
| 2 | $191,825 | 0.803094249 | $154,053 |
| 3 | $201,416 | 0.719697135 | $144,958 |
| 4 | $211,487 | 0.644960373 | $136,400 |
| 5 | $2,683,235 | 0.57798463 | $1,550,869 |
| PV of Discounted Cash Flows (rounded) | | | $2,150,000 |
| *less:* | | | |
| Acqusition Costs | | | $2,150,000 |
| *equals:* | | | |
| Net Present Value of Acquisition | | | $- |

## Chapter 4

### *Multiple-Choice Questions*

1. B 2. B 3. A 4. A 5. D 6. D 7. C 8. C 9. C 10. B

### *Application Questions*

11. A

If acquired on a direct capitalization basis, the capitalized NOI generates a purchase price of $1,100,000. Because we are evaluating this property as of the beginning of the current year, the projected NOI of $110,000 would not have to be adjusted, as it is already a forecast of the coming year.

Following is a summary of the direct capitalization process for this investment:

| | |
|---|---|
| Current Year NOI | $110,000 |
| *divided by:* | |
| Direct Cap Rate | 10.00% |
| *equals:* | |
| Value-Direct Cap | $1,100,000 |

12. A

Based on a loan-to-value ratio of 75 percent, the lender could provide $825,000 of debt.

Following is a summary of the loan-to-value ratio and debt calculation for this property:

| | |
|---|---|
| Value-Direct Cap | $1,110,000 |
| *multiplied by:* | |
| LTV Ratio | 75.00% |
| *equals:* | |
| Lender Debt | $825,000 |

13. C

Based on a principal amount of debt of $825,000 and a loan constant of 0.08670, the annual amount of debt service is $71,527.50.

Following is a summary of the annual debt service calculation for this investment:

| | |
|---|---|
| Lender Debt | $825,000 |
| *multiplied by:* | |
| Loan Constant | 0.08670 |
| *equals:* | |
| Lender Debt | $71,527.50 |

14. A

Based on an NOI of $110,000 and an annual debt service of $71,527.50, the debt coverage ratio is 1.54. This DCR meets the lender's criteria of a minimum DCR of 1.35.

Following is a summary of the DCR calculation for this investment:

| | |
|---|---|
| Current Year NOI | $110,000 |
| *divided by:* | |
| Lender Debt | $71,527.50 |
| *equals:* | |
| Debt Coverage Ratio | 1.54 |

15. C

Based on this acquisition scenario, the investment's cash flow to equity comes to $38,472.50, and the equity dividend rate is 13.99 percent.

Following is a summary of the cash flow to equity and EDR calculations for this investment:

| | |
|---|---|
| Current Year NOI | $110,000 |
| *less:* | |
| Lender Debt | $71,527.50 |
| *equals:* | |
| Cash Flow to Equity | $38.472.50 |
| *divided by:* | |
| Equity | $275,000 |
| *equals:* | |
| Equity Dividend Rate | 13.99% |

# WEB SITE DIRECTORY

**Appraisal Foundation** *(www.appraisalfoundation.org)*
The Appraisal Foundation, a not-for-profit educational organization dedicated to the advancement of professional valuation, was established by the appraisal profession in the United States in 1987. Since its inception, the foundation has worked to foster professionalism in appraising by establishing, improving, and promoting the Uniform Standards of Professional Appraisal Practice (USPAP); establishing educational and experience qualification criteria for the licensing, certification, and recertification of appraisers; disseminating information on USPAP and the appraiser qualification criteria to the appraisal profession, state and federal government agencies, users of appraisal services, related industries and industry groups, and the general public; and sponsoring appropriate activities relating to standards, qualifications, and issues of importance to appraisers and users of appraisal services.

**Appraisal Institute** *(www.appraisalinstitute.org)*
The Appraisal Institute is an international membership association of professional real estate appraisers with more than 18,000 members and 99 chapters throughout the United States, Canada, and abroad. Its mission is to support and advance its members as the choice for real estate solutions and uphold professional credentials, standards of professional practice, and ethics consistent with the public good. The Appraisal Institute is the acknowledged worldwide leader in residential and commercial real estate appraisal education, research, and publishing, and professional membership designation programs. Its extensive curriculum of courses and specialty seminars provides a well-rounded education in valuation methodology for both the novice and seasoned practitioner. The Appraisal Institute also houses the Lum Library, which provides support for the research needs of members as well as the profession at large.

**Black's Guide** *(www.blacksguide.com)*
Black's Guide delivers actionable data to commercial real estate brokers, owners, developers, property managers, and tenants. Published throughout the year, 55 print directories contain information, statistics, and trends on more than 80,000 properties in 19 major metropolitan markets. With its companion Web site, Black's Guide provides free comprehensive and accurate data

that helps deal makers quickly find and compare properties and then locate the right people to contact. The *Black's Guide* Web site has the largest, most comprehensive and accurate free data on commercial properties. Free to registered users, *Black's Guide* is an incredibly useful research and marketing tool for commercial real estate brokers, owners, developers, and tenants. *Black's Guide* publishes more free commercial real estate data in more markets than any other publication or electronic service.

**Building Owners and Managers Association** *(www.boma.org)*
BOMA International was founded in 1907 as the National Association of Building Owners and Managers. Today, BOMA International represents nearly 100 North American and 9 overseas affiliates. BOMA International is a primary source of information on office building development, leasing, building operating costs, energy consumption patterns, local and national building codes, legislation, occupancy statistics, and technological developments.

The organization publishes *BOMA.org* magazine, the official publication of BOMA International; research documents; and how-to guidebooks, including *Standard Method for Measuring Floor Area in Office Buildings*, recognized as an industry benchmark for over 75 years. BOMA presents The Office Building of the Year (TOBY) and Earth Awards, the most prestigious and coveted awards in the commercial real estate industry. The TOBY honors buildings demonstrating excellence in building management, operational efficiency, tenant retention, emergency planning, and community impact; the Earth Award honors environmentally friendly buildings.

**CCIM Institute** *(www.ccim.com)*
Practitioners holding the CCIM designation are recognized as experts in commercial investment real estate and live up to their distinguished reputation as model business partners for commercial real estate users, owners, and investors. Only 7,500 commercial real estate practitioners nationwide hold the CCIM designation. This statistic reflects the caliber of the program and why it is the most coveted and respected designation in commercial investment real estate.

***Commercial Investment Real Estate* magazine** *(www.ciremagazine.com)*
The online version of the magazine of the CCIM Institute. This member publication of the CCIM Institute reports on market trends and analysis, current developments in the field, and successful business strategies.

**CoStar Group** *(www.costar.com)*
Marketed as the commercial real estate information leader, CoStar offers commercial real estate's premier database of property for sale listings, space for lease listings, and comparable sales listings. CoStar's proprietary databases are widely used by over 70,000 commercial real estate brokers, owners, lenders, and appraisers, offering the power to close more deals, generate more income, and save research time.

**Counselors of Real Estate** *(www.cre.org)*
The Counselors of Real Estate (CRE) is a professional membership organization established exclusively for leading real property advisors. The purpose of the organization is to advance, enhance, and support these leaders by serving as a resource for information, creating opportunities for professional

development, facilitating networking, and providing the benefits of camaraderie. Members are awarded the CRE designation, bestowed by invitation only, in recognition of their achievements in real estate counseling.

**Council of Real Estate Broker Managers** *(www.crb.com)*
The council confers the Certified Real Estate Brokerage Manager (CRB) designation, while continuously providing members with the educational, informational, and networking resources necessary to compete and succeed in the real estate marketplace.

**Council of Residential Specialists** *(www.crs.com)*
The Certified Residential Specialist (CRS) is the highest designation awarded to sales associates in the residential sales field. The CRS designation recognizes professional accomplishments in both experience and education. Since 1977, the Council of Residential Specialists has been conferring the CRS designation on agents who meet its stringent requirements. Currently, there are more than 34,000 active CRS designees.

**Emporis** *(www.emporis.com)*
Emporis leads the world today as the most comprehensive information provider on highrise buildings of 12 floors or more, with the ambition to cover the whole building market in the years to come. Emporis is already one of the world's most respected, widely utilized sources for research, ratings, and analysis on information concerning buildings. The firm publishes research results and commentary that reach millions of Web site users around the globe. Emporis rates and analyzes hundreds of domestic and international real estate markets covering approximately 135,000 buildings, 40,500 companies, 350,000 points of interest, and 8,000 cities within 206 countries. The Emporis Image Database publishes more than 80,000 new building photographs each year. The building data and services of Emporis help customers analyze the building industry. Independent ratings and research also contribute to efficiencies for firms operating in the architectural, construction, financial, insurance, engineering, and supply industries.

**Institute of Real Estate Management** *(www.irem.org)*
The Institute of Real Estate Management (IREM) is an association of property and asset managers who have met strict criteria in the areas of education, experience, and ethics. Founded in 1933, IREM's mission is to educate real estate managers, certify their competence and professionalism, serve as an advocate on issues affecting the real estate management industry, and enhance its members' professional competence so they can better identify and meet the needs of those who use their services

**International Council of Shopping Centers** *(www.icsc.org)*
Founded in 1957, the International Council of Shopping Centers (ICSC) is the global trade association of the shopping center industry. Its 54,000 members in the United States, Canada, and more than 80 other countries include shopping center owners, developers, managers, marketing specialists, investors, lenders, retailers, and other professionals, as well as academics and public officials. As the global industry trade association, ICSC links with more than 25 national and regional shopping center councils throughout the world.

The principal aims of ICSC are to advance the development of the shopping center industry and to establish the individual shopping center as a major institution in the community through promoting the role of shopping centers; establishing codes of fair business ethics and dealings with retailers and consumers and with government and public agencies; encouraging research into the architecture and design of shopping centers and into the development of improved management and maintenance methods; collecting and disseminating information among members pertaining to techniques of profitable operation, which can serve to improve the individual shopping center and the industry; studying economic, marketing, and promotional conditions affecting the shopping center industry; and promoting the prestige and standing of members as reputable specialists in the field of shopping center development and management.

**investorwords.com** *(www.investorwords.com)*
Promoted as the largest and most comprehensive financial glossary online or offline, it offers over 6,000 definitions and 20,000 links between related terms. The Web site has multiple search engines.

**Korpacz Real Estate Investor Survey®** *(www.pwcreval.com/survey/home.asp)*
The *Korpacz Real Estate Investor Survey®* is widely recognized as an authoritative source for capitalization and discount rates, cash-flow assumptions, and actual criteria of active investors, as well as property market information. Each quarterly issue of the *Survey* contains current, prior-quarter, and year-ago rates; cash-flow assumptions and other criteria used to analyze real estate investments; survey results with discussion and analysis vis-à-vis prior quarters for current and long-range perspectives of buyers' strategies; more than 40 tables, including yield comparisons, dividend comparisons, key value indicators by market, marketing time, institutional-grade versus noninstitutional-grade property rates, forecast periods and growth rates, and market characteristics; trends in real estate investment and valuation; economic news; plus separate quarterly reports covering the following markets: retail (three major sectors), office (two national and 14 specific), industrial (flexR&D and warehouse), multifamily, and net lease; and semiannual reports covering the following markets: hotel (four national; first and third quarter issues), development land (second and fourth quarters), and waste management markets (first and third quarter issues).

**LoopNet** *(www.loopnet.com)*
LoopNet, Inc., a leading information services provider to the commercial real estate industry, delivers a comprehensive suite of products and services to meet the national and local needs of commercial real estate firms, organizations, and professionals. LoopNet members can list, search, market, and finance commercial real estate properties over the Internet, reducing their marketing costs, expanding their reach, and accelerating the pace of transactions.

LoopNet operates the largest commercial real estate listing service online, with more than $240 billion of property listed for sale and 2.7 billion square feet of space for lease. With more than 1 million members, LoopNet attracts the largest community of commercial real estate professionals. LoopNet's market-leading LoopLink product powers the Web sites of more than 1,000 commercial real estate organizations and seamlessly integrates their Web sites with LoopNet's listing service (at *www.loopnet.com*).

LoopNet customers include virtually all of the top commercial real estate firms in the United States, including CB Richard Ellis, Century 21 Commercial, Coldwell Banker Commercial, Colliers International, The CORE

Network, Cushman & Wakefield, Grubb & Ellis, Lincoln Property Company, Marcus & Millichap, NAI Global, Prudential CRES, REMAX, RREEF, Sperry Van Ness, The Staubach Company, and Trammell Crow Company.

LoopLender, LoopNet's online financing service, provides direct access and fast loan approval to many of the industry's top lenders.

LoopNet also owns and operates BizBuySell, Inc., the largest and most heavily trafficked online exchange for businesses for sale in North America, with more business listings, users, and search activity than any other Web site. BizBuySell features over 30,000 businesses for sale listings that are searched by more than 400,000 monthly visitors, and has the largest database of sales comparables for recently sold businesses.

**Marshall & Swift** *(www.marshallswift.com)*
Marshall & Swift (M&S) is dedicated to providing the residential and commercial real estate industries with the most current building cost data and valuation software technologies available. M&S has the single most comprehensive building cost database in the marketplace. The M&S data has become the industry benchmark for preliminary budget feasibility and design alternative life-cycle costing; energy audits; estimating and bidding for new construction or partial loss and damage repair; evaluations for lending, assessing, insurance, and rate-setting purposes; real estate listing and market comparable tools; sinking funds and reserve estimates; and valuation.

**Mortgage Bankers Association** *(www.mortgagebankers.org)*
The Mortgage Bankers Association seeks to create an environment that enables its members to invest in communities and achieve their business objectives. The association creates this environment by developing innovative business tools, educating and training industry professionals, providing a gathering place for the sharing of ideas, acting as the industry's voice on legislative and regulatory issues, and developing open and fair standards and practices for the industry.

**Municipal Code Corporation** *(www.municode.com)*
Municipal Code Corporation (MCC) is the leader in the ordinance codification industry. MCC has over 50 years of experience publishing codes of ordinances, land use codes, charters, etc., for local governments. This includes original codification, recodifications, republications, and updating. MCC updates codes in print and electronic format on any schedule from biweekly to annual updates. The Web site contains the codes for more than 1,500 local governments in searchable online databases, and information about many other services and products including custom publishing and document management.

**National Association of REALTORS®** *(www.realtor.org)*
The National Association of REALTORS® is America's largest trade association, representing one million members, including NAR's institutes, societies, and councils involved in all aspects of the residential and commercial real estate industries. NAR membership is composed of residential and commercial REALTORS®, who are brokers, salespeople, property managers, appraisers, counselors, and others engaged in all aspects of the real estate industry. Members belong to one or more of some 1,600 local associations/boards and 54 state and territory associations of REALTORS®. They are pledged to a strict code of ethics and standards of practice.

***National Real Estate Investor*** *(http:nreionline.com)*
*National Real Estate Investor* is the leading authority on commercial real estate trends. The magazine's readers represent a cross-section of disciplines—brokerage, construction, owner/development, finance/investment, property management, corporate real estate, and real estate services. No other publication provides as much independent research on a variety of topics that pertain to the office, industrial, retail, hotel, and multifamily markets as *National Real Estate Investor.*

**National Real Estate Investor Association** *(www.nationalreia.com)*
The National Real Estate Investors Association (NREIA) is a federation made up of local associations or investment clubs throughout the United States. The NREIA is an association of real estate professionals who know firsthand the unique problems and challenges of real estate investing. The NREIA represents local investor associations, property owner associations, apartment associations, and landlord associations on a national scale. Together NREIA represents the interests of over 20,000 members across the United States and is the largest broad-based organization dedicated to the individual investor. The mission of the NREIA is to educate and support the leaders of real estate associations through training, networking, motivation, and provision of benefits to their associations. The NREIA promotes a high standard of business ethics and professionalism.

**National Research Bureau** *(www.nrbonline.com)*
The National Research Bureau is a recognized leader in comprehensive shopping center intelligence offering "everything about retail property." It provides an extensive amount of information, reports, and services, some at no cost. It is a subsidiary of CoStar Group, Inc.

**Real Estate Buyer's Agent Council** *(www.rebc.net)*
Real Estate Buyer's Agent Council (REBAC) is the world's largest association of real estate professionals focusing specifically on representing the real estate buyer. There are more than 42,000 active members of the organization worldwide. The REBAC awards the Accredited Buyer's Representative (ABR) and the Accredited Buyer's Representative Manager (ABRM) designations.

**Real Estate Media Online Newsletters** *(www.remnewsletters.com)*
Real Estate Media Online Newsletters offers access to industry newsletters published by Real Estate Media. The newsletters are published weekly, biweekly, or monthly and include the *Debt and Equity Journal, Industrial Property Journal, Multi-housing Forum, Net Lease Forum, TIC Monthly, GlobeStreet Week*, and *GSR Week*. The Web site offers free trail issues of each publication and a searchable archive database.

**REALTORS® Land Institute** *(www.rliland.com)*
The REALTORS® Land Institute is the only branch of the REALTOR® family focused on land brokerage transactions of five specialized types: (1) farms and ranches, (2) undeveloped tracts of land, (3) transitional and development land, (4) subdivision and wholesaling of lots, and (5) site selection and assemblage of land parcels.

**RealtyRates.com** *(www.realtyrates.com)*
RealtyRates.com is a comprehensive resource of real estate investment and development news, trends, analytics, and market research that supports real estate professionals involved with more than 50 income-producing and sell-out property types throughout the United States. RealtyRates.com is the publisher of the award-winning Investor Survey, Developer Survey, and Market Survey, providing data essential to the appraisal, evaluation, disposition, and marketing of investment and development real estate nationwide.

**Society of Industrial and Office REALTORS®** *(www.sior.com)*
The society certifies its members with the prestigious specialist, industrial, and office real estate (SIOR) designation, a professional symbol of the highest level of knowledge, production, and ethics in the commercial real estate industry. Designees specialize in industrial, office, sales manager, or advisory services categories.

**Urban Land Institute** *(www.uli.org)*
The mission of the Urban Land Institute (ULI) is to provide responsible leadership in the use of land to enhance the total environment. Founded in 1936, the institute now has more than 25,000 members worldwide representing the entire spectrum of land use and real estate development disciplines, working in private enterprise and public service. As the preeminent, multidisciplinary real estate forum, ULI facilitates the open exchange of ideas, information, and experience among local, national, and international industry leaders and policy makers dedicated to creating better places.

The members of the Urban Land Institute are community builders, the people who develop and redevelop neighborhoods, business districts, and communities across the United States. ULI's practice program is interdisciplinary and practical, focusing on trends and the basics of many different parts of the industry including: resort and residential, retail and destination development, office and industrial development, transportation and parking, real estate finance, and capital markets. In local communities, ULI district councils bring together a variety of stakeholders to find solutions and build consensus around land use and development challenges.

# GLOSSARY

**accrual basis** A method of accounting in which income and expenses are recorded on the books in the fiscal period when they are earned or incurred, regardless of when they are actually received or paid.

**after-tax cash flow (ATCF)** The portion of pretax cash flow that remains after all income tax liabilities have been deducted. Cash flow is measured in accounting periods that are typically stated monthly, quarterly, or annually.

**amortized loan** A loan requiring periodic payments that include both interest and partial repayment of principal. As the loan amortizes, the loan balance declines, the interest portion of each periodic payment declines, and the principal portion of each periodic payment increases.

**annuity** A schedule of cash payments where the payments occur at regular, fixed intervals. As it applies to real estate, an example of an annuity would be a pro forma forecast of net operating income or cash flows.

**"as is" cap rate** A rate used to convert existing or "as is" income into an actual or expected price or value of a property. "As is" income may or may not be considered stabilized. "As is" cap rates are also referred to as "going in" or "acquisition" cap rates.

**assets** Any owned property that has value. Assets may be tangible, having a physical dimension, such as real estate, also known as real property. Property other than real property is known as personal property, which includes tangible financial assets such as automobiles, boats, and gold coins. Assets may also be intangible, such as cash, bonds, and mortgage notes receivable. Total assets are calculated by adding the equity claim to the debt claim.

**balance sheet** A financial statement that summarizes the total assets, total liabilities, and net worth of an individual or business entity. An individual may use a balance sheet to qualify for a loan. As it applies to real estate, a business or "entity" that has acquired a real estate asset would use a balance sheet as part of its financial statements. The difference between assets and liabilities is net worth. Net worth is sometimes referred to as equity.

**basis point** One one-hundredth of one percentage point. Basis points, which in real estate jargon are sometimes referred to as "beeps," are used to indicate changes in interest rates and in yields and are expressed as fractions of a percent.

**bundle of rights** A concept that compares property ownership rights to a bundle of sticks where each stick represents a distinct and separate right, interest, and benefit of ownership, including the right to sell, use, buy, mortgage, pledge, trade, lease the property and the right not to exercise any of these rights. The bundle of rights concept addresses the legal rights associated with ownership.

**capitalization** The conversion of income into an estimate of value. Although there are various capitalization methods, processes, and techniques, the most well-known among real estate investors are direct capitalization and yield capitalization.

**capitalization rate** Used to convert income into value. However, because there are different types of income at different periods of time during an investment, there are different types of cap rates.

**capital recapture** The return of equity in an investment as distinguished from the return on equity. Invested capital may be recaptured through annual income, or it may be recaptured all or in part through resale of the property at the conclusion of the investment.

**cash basis** A method of accounting in which income and expenses are recognized when they are actually received or paid out.

**cash flow (CF)** The income that remains after the cost of financing, or debt service, is deducted from net operating income.

**cash-flow diagrams** Widely used visual tools that present a picture of financial problems. Often a cash-flow diagram is the first step in solving complex financial problems. A cash-flow diagram can represent any cash-flow problem. Once the diagram is set up, we would identify what is known and unknown about the investment. A horizontal line represents time. Money invested is considered cash payments or outflows and represented as negative, with a down arrow. Money returned is considered cash received or inflows represented as positive, with an up arrow.

**CMBS loans (commercial mortgage-backed securities)** Commercial real estate loans that are pooled together and transferred to a trust, which then issues securities based on the strength of the underlying mortgages. CMBS loans are considered aggressive loans offering higher loan-to-value ratios and lower debt coverage ratios.

**compound rate** A special type of interest rate, also known as a yield rate. A compound rate is used to convert a present value into a future value. A compound rate is also known as a future value interest factor (FVIF). An FVIF is based on a formula and is used as part of a mathematical process called compounding.

**compounding** The process whereby a principal amount earns interest and that previously earned interest will then be added to the principal amount, creating a larger amount of money, which will then earn additional interest, occurring over successive time periods.

**correspondent lender** Provides lending services on behalf of other lenders who desire to provide financing within a certain area but do not have a physical presence there. Also known as loan correspondents, they essentially negotiate a loan on behalf of another lender. Sources of financing for the correspondent lender include banks located in "money center" markets such as New York and Chicago along with insurance companies, pension funds, and other commercial banks. The correspondent lender originates loans on behalf of another lender through a process or system known as a correspondence system. Often, the correspondent will continue to service the loan for the lender and act as a collecting agent.

**debt coverage ratio** A basic yet important ratio that expresses the relationship of the annual net operating income to the annual debt service of the property. The term is also known as the DCR. From a lender's perspective, the larger the DCR, the more of the property's operating income is available to pay annual debt service. Accordingly, DCRs are an important risk measure for lenders because the property is the primary source of income used for repayment of the loan.

**discounting** Literally discounts, or reduces, future income forecasted to be received into an equivalent present value. Hence, the term *discounted cash-flow analysis*.

**discount rate** A special type of interest rate, also known as a yield rate. Discount rates are used to convert a future value into a present value. A discount rate is also known as a present value interest factor (PVIF). A PVIF is based on a formula and is used as part of a mathematical process called discounting.

**direct capitalization** A method of converting an estimate of a single year's expected income into an indicator of value in one direct step, hence the term *direct capitalization*. Direct capitalization converts income into value, either by dividing the estimated income by a rate (the most widely recognized technique) or by multiplying the estimated income by a factor. These rates and factors are known as capitalization rates. Direct capitalization is often referred to as direct cap, and capitalization rates are often referred to as caps.

**effective gross income** The expected income from all operations of the real property after an allowance is made for vacancy and collection losses. Effective gross income includes lease income from space or units and other income from sources such as parking, washers, dryers, or vending machines. Effective gross income is sometimes referred to as gross operating income (GOI).

**equity** The ownership claim on property. In real estate, equity refers to the net worth of a property obtained by subtracting all liens and other charges against it from its total asset value.

**equity dividend** The cash flow that remains after debt service but before income taxes are considered. Stated differently, the rate of return to the equity position is known as the equity dividend. In unleveraged property, the equity dividend rate is calculated by dividing the cash flow by the original investment. It is the ratio of income to the initial investment. The equity dividend rate is also referred to as the cash-on-cash rate.

**financial institution** An organization in the business of holding cash and other assets on behalf of others. Examples of financial institutions include commercial banks, savings associations, credit unions, insurance companies, pension funds, and investment companies. These financial institutions also act as fiduciaries of behalf of their depositors and investors. What makes these financial institutions distinctive is that they also act as financial intermediaries within the real estate markets.

**financial intermediaries** Financial institutions that act as a middleman between depositors and borrowers.

**fixed expenses (FE)** Those operating expenses that are usually unaffected by the level of occupancy and would continue even if the property were vacant. Traditional examples of fixed operating expenses include real estate (property) taxes and property insurance.

**intermediation** A process in which middlemen accumulate, combine, and consolidate a number of smaller, individual equity accounts for the purpose of either lending or investing in real estate properties. Due to their size and vast deposit base, intermediaries can provide financing or investment funds for larger, more complex, and more management- and capital-intensive real estate properties. However, if a state or federal charter regulates these institutions, they operate with significantly less risk tolerance and are more conservative than mortgage brokers, mortgage bankers, and correspondent lenders.

**internal rate of return (IRR)** Discounts the future benefits of an investment to a present value that is exactly equal to the initial investment. In this case, the net present value of the investment is zero. Stated differently, the IRR is the rate of return that makes the present value of the periodic cash flows and reversion equal to the initial investment.

**leverage** The effect that borrowed funds have on investment returns. Leverage may increase or decrease the investor's return that would otherwise be received on an all-cash basis. Usually, investors borrow money for purchases with the expectation that the investment's financial returns will increase.

**liabilities** Financial obligations, debts, and claims. Liabilities may be secured or collateralized debt such as mortgage notes payable or unsecured debt such as credit card balances. A liability is a debt owed to another person or entity that must be paid by a specified date.

**loan constant** The capitalization rate for debt. It is expressed as R*m*. Each year of the investment, the property generates income to the debt position. The relationship of the first year's debt service to the original loan amount is also known as the loan constant.

**loan-to-value ratio** A basic yet important ratio that expresses the relationship of borrowed funds as a percentage of the value of the property. The term is also known as the LTV. From a lender's perspective, the LTV is usually the lesser of the acquisition price or the appraised value of property. Accordingly, LTVs are an important risk measure for lenders, because the property is usually pledged as security for the loan.

**mezzanine equity** Also referred to as mezzanine financing, provides equity capital to fill the gap between the senior first mortgage loan and the owner's equity investment in a property. Because equity is not debt, the equity does not impact the loan-to-value ratio.

**mortgage** A pledge or conveyance of an interest in real property given as security for the payment of a debt. The mortgage creates a lien on the mortgaged property as security for the debt and is the document used to create a mortgage lien. The mortgage provides that the lender can count on possessing the property if the borrower defaults in paying the note.

**mortgage banker** May originate, close, and service a loan. Mortgage bankers can provide short-term, interim financing as well as long-term financing. Mortgage bankers use their own funds, or they may borrow funds from other commercial sources for the mortgage financing. Accordingly, mortgage bankers are not the ultimate lender in the transaction. Usually, a mortgage banker will sell the mortgage in the secondary mortgage market, a market in which existing mortgages and mortgage-backed securities are bought and sold. A mortgage broker may expand its services further by acting in the capacity of a mortgage banker.

**mortgage broker** Brings a borrower of funds and a lender of funds together for the purpose of providing financing. So mortgage brokers are intermediaries.

**mortgage note** A written acknowledgement of a debt and a promise to repay a debt, which is secured by a mortgage. The purpose of the mortgage note is to evidence a debt and create a personal liability for payment on the part of the borrower. The terms of repayment of the debt—including the loan amount, duration, interest rate, time, and method of payment—are stated.

**negative leverage** Occurs when the interest rate charged by a lender is greater than the rate of return that an investment is capable of generating on the borrowed funds. Accordingly, investors incur a loss on the borrowed funds. This loss is deducted from the investor's return, reducing the rate of return on the investor's cash portion of the investment. When leverage decreases the return to the investor, it is called negative leverage.

**net operating income (NOI)** The income that remains after all operating expenses are deducted from operating revenues, that is adjusted gross revenues before mortgage debt service and depreciation are deducted. NOI results from a property's operations. NOI does not consider the effects of mortgage debt service and depreciation. It can be calculated before or after deducting replacement reserves. It can be calculated on the basis of a property's actual or projected profit and loss statement. NOI is an important consideration for lenders and borrowers, as it represents the amount of money available to pay back debt service for the property. It is an important consideration for buyers and sellers, as the value of the property is determined by capitalizing the NOI. NOI is affected by the inclusion or exclusion of the degree of vacancy and collection loss as well as operating expenses. For example, lowering operating expense will result in an increase in NOI, which when capitalized, will result in a higher value.

**net present value (NPV)** The measured difference between the discounted present value of the investment, evaluated at a yield rate considered reasonable and appropriate for the investment, and the initial acquisition cost of the investment.

**net worth** The difference between total assets and total liabilities. Net worth represents the ownership claim on property and is also referred to as equity.

**origination fee** Charged by a lender for making a loan.

**overall rate** Also expressed as either OAR or Ro, is an income rate for a total real property interest. It reflects the relationship between a single year's expected net operating income and the total property sales price or value and can be used to convert one into the other. An OAR may be extracted from a property as an indicator of currently acceptable capitalization rates evidenced in the marketplace. An OAR extracted from one property may then be used to convert another property's income into an indicator of a its sales price or value.

**potential gross income** The total potential income that a real estate investment could generate, if the property was operating as follows: at full occupancy, before vacancy and collection losses are considered and deducted, and before operating expenses are considered and deducted. Potential gross income includes income attributable to all of the leaseable area, regardless if the space is actually leased, occupied, and generating rent.

**operating expenses (OE)** The periodic expenditures necessary to operate and maintain the real property and continue the production of effective gross income, assuming prudent and competent management.

**positive leverage** Occurs when the rate of return that an investment generates is greater than the interest rate charged by a lender for the funds borrowed to acquire that investment.

**pretax cash flow (PTCF)** The portion of net operating income that remains after total mortgage debt service (financing) is paid but before ordinary income tax on operations is deducted.

**profit and loss statement** Also known as a P&L or an operating statement, summarizes the revenues, expenses, and net operating income or loss of an investment during a defined period of time. There are different types of operating statements.

**pro forma operating statement** Also known as a pro forma P&L, is used to forecast a property's future revenues, expenses, and net operating income during a defined period based on specific assumptions and projections. Pro formas provide an estimate of an investment's anticipated future financial benefits.

**projection period** The expected period of property ownership. Projection periods are important to establish, because they represent the period of time over which the current and future year's revenues, expenses and operating income will be forecast. Usually, real estate ownership periods are for a number of years. Some consider the long-term nature of investment in real estate a disadvantage.

**rate of return on capital** Equivalent to the interest rate earned on the investment. For real estate investments, this interest rate is known as a yield rate. A yield rate is the overall rate of return actually earned, or forecasted to be earned, on the capital invested in a real estate endeavor.

**real estate** The physical land and all structures and other improvements attached to the land. However, real estate does not consider any of the rights associated with ownership.

**real property rights** The intangible rights associated with the ownership of the physical real estate. Real property rights are referred to as the bundle of rights.

**return of capital** The recovery of invested capital, usually through a property's income and reversion. The income component of the return of capital consists of the income stream generated by the investment. The reversion component of the return of capital is a lump-sum amount that an investor receives or anticipates receiving from the proceeds of sale at the end of the holding period.

**reconstructed operating statement** Prepared by an appraiser, investor, accountant, etc. and represents an opinion of a real estate investment's prior or current year's revenues, expenses, and income. In preparing these reconstructed operating statements, accountant's, auditor's, or seller's financial statements (source documentation) are usually referenced as the basis for the reconstruction of the P&L statement. Reconstructed P&Ls estimate the historical or current financial benefits of an investment.

**replacement reserves (RR)** Based on a combination of the estimated useful lives of various building components and the recognition that certain building components wear out faster than others. Land does not depreciate or wear out; accordingly, its allocated costs are excluded from a replacement reserve. Replacement reserves are also known as replacement allowances, reserves for replacements, and reserves. Replacement reserves consist of the annual average cost of replacing various building components and are reflected in the operating statement on an accrual basis. However, replacement reserves are not considered capital expenses, because allocating the cost over the life of the asset has the effect of an equivalent cash outflow for those expense items that are normally considered part of the current period's operations. Although not necessarily a cash expense in the year of recognition, it is the recognition of the inevitable expense, allocated annually, over the life of the asset. Prudent property owners should not only account for the replacement reserve, they should fund the replacement reserve from available income to ensure that the funds to replace the item will actually be available when needed.

**return on capital** An additional amount received as compensation for the use of an investor's capital until it is returned. The actual or anticipated return on capital plus the return of capital equal the investor's rate of return on invested capital.

**reversionary cap rate** Used to convert projected future stabilized income into an actual or expected price or value of a property at the conclusion of an investment's holding period. Reversionary rates are used to estimate the resale price or value of a property. Reversionary cap rates are also referred to as exit, terminal, disposition, or going-out capitalization rates.

**risk** The probability that anticipated events will not occur. Stated differently, risk is the probability that what we expect to happen during a real estate investment wil not in fact happen. Investors demand that, as an investment's risk increases, so should its return. Different conditions cause risk to enter into a real estate investment.

**scheduled base income** The portion of potential gross income that is based upon the existing leases in place. Scheduled base income is also known as scheduled base rent, base income, base rent, contract rent, and existing rent. The scheduled base rent may consist of flat rents and, if applicable, income from leases with rent escalation.

**secondary mortgage market** A market in which existing mortgages and mortgage-backed securities are bought and sold.

**servicing a loan** Includes the collection of payments, including interest, principal, insurance, and taxes, on a note from a borrower in accordance with the terms of the note. Servicing also includes accounting, bookkeeping, and preparation of insurance and tax records; loan payment follow-up; and delinquency follow-up and loan analysis. A servicing agreement is usually written and includes the obligations of both parties. Some lenders place a cap on annual serving income they receive from any one mortgage.

**stabilized cap rate** Used to convert stabilized income into an actual or expected price or value of a property that is operating at stabilized operating conditions, including occupancy, revenues, and expenses.

**time value of money** An economic principal that states that the value of a dollar received today is worth more than a dollar received in the future. A dollar received today can be invested and earn interest (a rate of return), thereby growing into a larger future amount than the same noninvested dollar received in the future. The concept of time value of money provides the foundation for all discounted cash-flow analysis. Discounted cash-flow analysis is also known as yield capitalization. Time value of money concepts include the future value of a dollar, the present value of a dollar, the future value of an annuity, and the present value of an annuity.

**total operating expenses** The sum of all fixed and variable operating expenses and replacement allowances. Deducting total operating expenses from effective gross income produces the property's net operating income. Expenses related to financing a property acquisition, such as interest expenses and loan principal amortization, are considered part of the property's debt service. Debt service is not considered an operating expense, because it is not "a periodic expenditure necessary to operate and maintain the real property and continue the production of the effective gross income." Debt service is a periodic expenditure necessary to repay a loan used to acquire a property, not operate a property.

**uncertainty** The probability that unforeseen events will occur. Stated differently, uncertainty is the probability that what we do not expect to happen during a real estate investment does in fact happen.

**vacancy and collection loss** An allowance for reductions in potential gross income attributable to unit vacancies, tenant turnover, and nonpayment of rents. The allowance amount represents the typical V&C loss for the property's type within the property's market area. For a proposed property, or when a market valuation is sought, V&C is based upon stabilized market conditions. For existing properties, the actual historical and current vacancy and collection loss is the most accurate indicator of the property's potential. Vacancy and collection loss may be stated as a fixed percent of PGI. It may be further segregated into the vacancy component and the collection component.

**variable expenses (VE)** Those operating expenses that usually vary in direct relation to the level of occupancy and would decline or possibly discontinue if the property were vacant. Traditional examples of variable expenses include management fees, administrative charges, payroll, advertising and promotion, telephone, utilities (including water, sewer, and electric), trash removal, repairs and maintenance, general supplies, pool maintenance, landscape maintenance, and pest control, among others.

**yield capitalization** The method used to convert future benefits into a present value by discounting each future benefit at an appropriate yield rate that explicitly reflects the investment's income patterns, value change, and rate of return. The value today represents a discounted value of the sum total of all the anticipated future income streams associated with the investment during the anticipated investment period. Because yield cap involves discounting cash flows, it is also referred to as discounted cash-flow analysis.

**yield rate** The overall rate of return actually earned, or forecasted to be earned, on the capital invested in a real estate endeavor.

**zero-coupon bonds** Bonds that do not pay any interest during the investment period. An investor can buy a zero-coupon bond today at a discount on its face value. Face value is the amount the bond will be worth when it matures or comes due. When the zero-coupon bond matures, the investor receives a lump sum equal to the initial investment plus accrued interest.

# INDEX

**R**



**S**



**T**



**U**



**V–W**



**Y–Z**